"In this readable collection of essays, Mark Boone brings together a remarkably diverse cast of thinkers, including Alvin Plantinga, St. Augustine, William James, Søren Kierkegaard, Immanuel Kant, Jean-Luc Marion, and Allama Iqbal, to mention only some of the major players. One might think these thinkers have little in common, and they are certainly different, but Boone succeeds in his goal of creating a kind of dialogue between them. In the course of doing so, he provides important insights about the nature of Christian faith and its relation to reason."

—C. STEPHEN EVANS
Emeritus university professor of philosophy, Baylor University

"Rejecting the modernist war of faith versus reason, Mark Boone argues in this fine collection of essays that faith transcends reason by exploring the personal element of trust built on the empirical foundation on which reason rests. With Kant, Augustine, Kierkegaard, William James, Alvin Plantinga, and Islamic philosopher Allama Iqbal as his interlocutors, Boone helps rescue the traditional Christian worldview from the artificial facts/values split propagated by the Enlightenment."

—LOUIS MARKOS
Professor of English, Houston Baptist University

"Drawing on an interesting variety of sources, Mark Boone develops a readable account of religious epistemology. He covers the usual suspects—Alvin Plantinga, Augustine, and William James—but also draws insights from Søren Kierkegaard, Jean-Luc Marion, and Islamic philosopher Allama Iqbal. The reader will benefit from the juxtaposition of these disparate voices. Also important is Boone's attention to questions beyond assessing knowledge claims: How do these claims apply to the reliability of Scripture and what does it look like to act on knowledge claims? The net result is a degree of cohesion and narrative unity that is rare among collections of essays. A valuable resource!"

—JAMES K. BEILBY
Professor of biblical and theological studies, Bethel University

"Religious epistemology is a notoriously thorny topic. However, Mark Boone masterfully helps us navigate the topic, drawing in important voices such as James, Kierkegaard, Kant, Augustine, Plantinga, and others. Perhaps the most important feature of this book is that it shatters the myth that religious knowledge must either be grounded in faith or reason. Instead, Boone offers a lucid vision of how both play a vital role in a robust understanding of religious truth."

—STEVEN WILKENS
Professor of philosophy and ethics, Azusa Pacific University

Faith, Reason,
and Beyond Reason

Faith, Reason, *and* Beyond Reason

Essays on Epistemology and Theology

By MARK J. BOONE

◠PICKWICK *Publications* • Eugene, Oregon

FAITH, REASON, AND BEYOND REASON
Essays on Epistemology and Theology

Copyright © 2024 Mark J. Boone. All rights reserved. Except for brief quotations in critical publications or reviews, no part of this book may be reproduced in any manner without prior written permission from the publisher. Write: Permissions, Wipf and Stock Publishers, 199 W. 8th Ave., Suite 3, Eugene, OR 97401.

Pickwick Publications
An Imprint of Wipf and Stock Publishers
199 W. 8th Ave., Suite 3
Eugene, OR 97401

www.wipfandstock.com

PAPERBACK ISBN: 978-1-6667-8829-7
HARDCOVER ISBN: 978-1-6667-8830-3
EBOOK ISBN: 978-1-6667-8831-0

Cataloguing-in-Publication data:

Names: Boone, Mark J. [author].

Title: Faith, reason, and beyond reason : essays on epistemology and theology / Mark J. Boone.

Description: Eugene, OR: Pickwick Publications, 2024 | Includes bibliographical references and index.

Identifiers: ISBN 978-1-6667-8829-7 (paperback) | ISBN 978-1-6667-8830-3 (hardcover) | ISBN 978-1-6667-8831-0 (ebook)

Subjects: LCSH: Faith and reason—Christianity. | Knowledge, Theory of. | Belief and doubt. | Christianity—Philosophy. | Bible—Evidences, authority, etc.

Classification: BT50 B66 2024 (paperback) | BT50 (ebook)

VERSION NUMBER 071124

"Alvin Plantinga's Reidian Particularism: An Overview of an Epistemological Project" copyright © 2021 by Criswell College. Used by permission.

"Proper Function and the Conditions for Warrant: What Plantinga's Notion of Warrant Shows about Different Kinds of Knowledge" copyright © 2012 by the Evangelical Philosophical Society. www.epsociety.org. Used by permission.

"Can Faith Be Empirical?" copyright © 2020 by Christians in Science—an international network of those concerned with the relationship between science and Christian faith. Used by permission.

"Augustine and William James on the Rationality of Faith" copyright © 2018 by Trustees for Roman Catholic Purposes Registered. Used by permission.

"William James and Allama Iqbal on Empirical Faith" copyright © 2019 by Trustees for Roman Catholic Purposes Registered. Used by permission.

"Blessed Are Those Who Have Not Seen and Yet Have Known By Faith: Knowledge, Faith, and Sight in the New Testament" copyright © 2020 by Brill. Used by permission.

"Inerrancy Is Not a Strong or Classical Foundationalism" copyright © 2019 by The Gospel Coalition. Used by permission.

"Ancient-Future Hermeneutics: Postmodernism, Biblical Inerrancy, and the Rule of Faith" copyright © 2016 by Criswell College. Used by permission.

"From Evidence to Total Commitment: Two Ways Faith Goes beyond Reason" copyright © 2021 Wipf and Stock Publishers. www.wipfandstock.com. Used by permission.

To Shonda, of course.

Contents

Introduction | xi

1. Alvin Plantinga's Reidian Particularism: An Overview of an Epistemological Project | 1
2. Proper Function and the Conditions for Warrant: What Plantinga's Notion of Warrant Shows about Different Kinds of Knowledge | 25
3. Augustine and William James on the Rationality of Faith | 45
4. William James and Allama Iqbal on Empirical Faith | 64
5. Can Faith Be Empirical? | 84
6. Trust: Biblical and Otherwise | 108
7. Blessed Are Those Who Have Not Seen and yet Have Known by Faith: Knowledge, Faith, and Sight in the New Testament | 121
8. Inerrancy Is Not a Strong or Classical Foundationalism | 139
9. Ancient-Future Hermeneutics: Postmodernism, Biblical Inerrancy, and the Rule of Faith | 165
10. Two Ways Faith Goes beyond Reason | 186
11. Dialogue on Faith and Reason | 208

Index | 253

Introduction

IT WAS THE YEAR 2012, and I was teaching my first epistemology class at Forman Christian College in Lahore, Pakistan. I had recently secured a home—*Philosophia Christi*, the journal of the Evangelical Philosophical Association—for my paper on Alvin Plantinga's epistemology. I thought I had this topic pretty well figured out when a student in my class unexpectedly taught me something. She mentioned in her research paper Linda Zagzebski's article "The Inescapability of Gettier Problems," and reading her paper was enough to show me that something big was missing in my understanding of epistemology. How had I earned a PhD in philosophy, taught for two years, cared about epistemology a lot, and even taught most of an epistemology course—and still managed to miss *this*? "The Inescapability of Gettier Problems" turned out to be a truly brilliant piece of philosophy, and it showed where I had made a mistake. There was no getting out of it; Zagzebski's logic was flawless. I knew then that I would have to revisit my first epistemology publication when I could—*inshallah, inshallah*, as they say in Pakistan: if God wills.

I am thankful to God—apparently it was willed. I have, in the pages below, corrected the egregious error to which my student's paper pointed me. As it happens, I have also written over the years eight other published articles on religious epistemology or on faith and reason. In this book I have made various corrections, extended the bibliographies, clarified the wording, and otherwise fixed up all nine articles, which I now present here in this new-and-improved form. The amended publications are chapters 1–5 and 7–10; consult the first footnote in each chapter for a summary of any major changes. Chapters 6 and 11 are printed here for the first time.

One special feature of my research is the particular source of the ideas I am working with. Mainly these are the religious epistemologies of Augustine, William James, and Alvin Plantinga. Other characters who make important contributions include Immanuel Kant, Søren Kierkegaard,

Jean-Luc Marion, and an Islamic philosopher of the Indian Subcontinent, Allama Iqbal. Another distinctive characteristic of my research is how it includes different ideas not often considered together. One of these is that belief in God and in Christian theology specifically may be knowledge even without evidence—an idea associated with Plantinga. Another is that the same beliefs are also supported by some good evidence—whether or not they *need* it. A third is that faith transcends reason—even if we have knowledge of some articles of faith, faith is a total commitment beyond what the evidence alone can guarantee, and some articles of faith are beyond human comprehension, even if we *do* have evidence that they are true.

THIS BOOK IN A BIT MORE DETAIL

Chapters 1 and 2 consider Plantinga's epistemology, which includes an important argument from epistemic parity with deep roots in the commonsense epistemology of Thomas Reid. Beliefs derived from sensory experience, memory beliefs, belief that other minds exist, and so on—these are commonsense beliefs whose warrant is beyond reasonable doubt. They do not, however, meet certain epistemic standards touted by some philosophers. That's good: it shows that those standards are the wrong ones, or at least that they do not describe necessary conditions for knowledge. The similarity of Christian belief to commonsense beliefs speaks in favor of its rationality. And *that*'s just the beginning of Plantinga's project; in the finished product, Plantinga explains that commonsense beliefs suggest a criterion for warrant which Christian belief likely meets. This criterion is a *necessary* condition for warrant, not a *sufficient* condition for warrant *in all cases*, and a belief's meeting this criterion does not rule out its also having evidence in its favor; Chapter 2 clarifies.

In Chapter 3 I consider the religious epistemologies of Augustine and William James—explaining, comparing, contrasting, and pointing towards some possible synthesis. Both defend the rationality of faith without knowledge, and both point towards the possibility of adding knowledge later— one by means of Platonic contemplation, one by means of pure empiricism. There is also a gap between Augustine's dogmatic orthodox Christianity and James' religious heresy. These differences do not mean their epistemologies are entirely incompatible. In Chapter 4 I give a fuller picture by looking at James in relation to Iqbal—a clarification of the fact that *faith can be empirical*. Chapter 5 refutes more directly the common theory that faith and empiricism are incompatible ways of believing. Significant twentieth-century philosophers representing Buddhism, Hinduism, Islam, Judaism, and Christianity claim that their religions have an empirical origin or a thoroughly empirical core. I explain this and clarify how Christian faith in particular is consistent with three major characteristics of empirical belief.

Secondhand knowledge, knowledge by trust, is a familiar and everyday occurrence, as Augustine and James explain, which I consider in Chapter 6. This prepares us for Chapter 7, in which I consider the nature of faith and reason in the New Testament. The New Testament treats faith in Jesus the Messiah as a form of knowledge. It makes a well-known distinction between faith and sight which is no separation of faith and knowledge, nor of faith and reason. Sight means firsthand knowledge, and faith means trust. That knowledge is by the testimony of reliable authority, including God, his Son, and his prophets and apostles.

The central authority is Jesus, and his authority establishes that of the Bible. This, at least, is a significant account of the authority of the Bible which I trace to the Chicago Statement on Biblical Inerrancy and some of its signers in Chapter 8. This and some other aspects of their accounts show that the doctrine of inerrancy does not use that theory in epistemology known as *strong foundationalism*; inerrancy fits the theories of *weak foundationalism* and *foundherentism* better than most versions of strong foundationalism.

In Chapter 9 I consider the limitations of human reason when it comes to faith and, particularly, the Bible. I consider the tradition of postmodern philosophy of religion, drawing especially from Jean-Luc Marion, and biblical inerrancy, showing that there is an unexpected degree of compatibility between the two. Or perhaps not so unexpected—it was all in Augustine long ago!

In Chapter 10 I consider the fact that the things of God are beyond our ability fully to comprehend, and I also consider the difference between recognizing the solid evidence for Christianity and *acting* on it. It is reasonable to say that faith goes beyond reason because faith requires a commitment and a life-change that the evidence, even if very good, cannot fully guarantee to be correct. For the evidence for Christianity is inevitably probabilistic; yet life, decisions, and action are not. All the same, I suggest that it is reasonable for us to go beyond reason; as James would say, it's just part of life; moreover, if the evidence for Christianity is as good as it appears to be, then the evidence itself says we should. Augustine, Kant, James, and Kierkegaard are all illuminating on these matters.

I have begun work to provide a more orderly and thorough account of all this and more—including some other writings of Zagzebski! But that will be in another book, hopefully to be in print in the year 2025 or early in 2026. In the meantime, Chapter 11 of this book will have to do. It's a dialogue featuring Phil and Sophy talking through this topic. It was originally a YouTube playlist—"Dialogue on Faith and Reason" on my channel, TeacherOfPhilosophy.

USES OF THIS BOOK

Why and how exactly is this book useful? To begin with, it may be used as a primer in Christian epistemology. It may also serve as an introduction to the epistemologies of Augustine, James, and Plantinga.

Any number of points in this book might be found elsewhere—the idea that faith is rational, the idea that Christian belief can be knowledge, the idea that it has evidence yet can be warranted independently of the evidence, the idea that faith in some important ways transcends reason, and so on. But they are not often found all in the same place.

Below is an overview of various other insights appearing here which are not so likely to be found elsewhere.

First, there is an insight articulated by both James and Augustine. Even though an unbeliever may avoid the risk of holding a religious belief in error, there is another risk to which he commits himself: the risk of not believing the *truth* about God, if there is a God.

Second, there are the close links between empiricism and traditional religion; modern culture accustoms us to ignore these connections, and even to doubt the very possibility of their existence! Yet the Dalai Lama (representing Buddhism), Sarvepalli Radhakrishnan (Hinduism), Allama Iqbal (Islam), and Eliezer Berkovits (Judaism) along with C. S. Lewis trace the core doctrines of their religions to empirical origins. And that does not even cover James' integration of religion with empiricism, or any number of other thinkers who did the same or who have developed an empirical natural theology. Moreover, there are central traits of empirical thinking which may easily be taken up by Christian thinking. Contrary to popular belief, key points of Christian theology are even verifiable or falsifiable!

Third, an insight about the verifiability of religious belief was discovered independently by James and Lewis. Not every belief can be tested by experiments that are under the experimenter's control; a belief about *a person* is difficult to test through experiment without some cooperation or assistance from the person. James develops this insight while making an argument for the rationality of faith, Lewis by explaining how we know the Trinity through the holy life of the church.

Fourth, the crucial distinction in the New Testament between "faith" and "sight" is not a distinction between faith and knowledge, nor between faith and reason. It is a distinction between knowledge *that comes by trust* and *firsthand* knowledge.

Fifth, beliefs are warranted in different ways—foundationally, inferentially, and coherentially—a topic I consider in an article published in 2014 in *Logos & Episteme*: "Inferential, Coherential, and Foundational Warrant: An Eclectic Account of the Sources of Warrant." All these ways matter, and Christian belief has all varieties of warrant according to the accounts we will consider. Plantinga's emphasis is on foundational warrant, but his epistemology is compatible with a recognition of the importance of inferential and coherential warrant, and even teaches this to some extent.

Sixth, the doctrine of biblical inerrancy measures up well by some philosophical standards. From the likes of Heidegger and Marion and the best of postmodern philosophy, we are reminded of epistemic humility. From analytic epistemologists trying to understand the structure of knowledge, we learn that knowledge needs a solid foundation, but that any evidence *for* such a foundation is still relevant. Measured by these epistemological standards, inerrancy does well.

Finally, and once again, the relationship between faith and reason must be understood to be multifaceted. Faith transcends reason in that it is more than reason alone can contain or fully guarantee. Yet it is neither unreasonable nor something to which reason is irrelevant—and reason says some pretty fine things about it!

FINAL WORDS FROM THE AUTHOR

I still have much to learn, and I am grateful for the chance to get at least this much corrected to at least this extent and combined in one volume. In addition to the obvious four people (God and my wife), I am grateful to the journal editors and others with whose permission this book was completed. The original published versions of all the previously published chapters are as follows.

"Alvin Plantinga's Reidian Particularism: An Overview of an Epistemological Project." *Criswell Theological Review* 19.1 (2021) 147–167.

"Proper Function and the Conditions for Warrant: What Plantinga's Notion of Warrant Shows about Different Kinds of Knowledge." *Philosophia Christi* 14.2 (2012) 373–86. More information about *Philosophia Christi* can be found at www.EPSociety.org.

"William James and Allama Iqbal on Empirical Faith." *The Heythrop Journal* 61.5 (2020) 775–87.

"Augustine and William James on the Rationality of Faith." *The Heythrop Journal* 61.4 (2020) 648–59.

"Can Faith Be Empirical?" *Science and Christian Belief* 32.1 (2020) 63–82.

"Blessed Are Those Who Have Not Seen and Yet Have Known By Faith: Knowledge, Faith, and Sight in the New Testament." *Evangelical Quarterly* 91.2. (2020) 133–46.

"Inerrancy Is Not a Strong or Classical Foundationalism." *Themelios* 44.3 (2019) 530–47.

"Ancient-Future Hermeneutics: Postmodernism, Biblical Inerrancy, and the Rule of Faith." *Criswell Theological Review* 14.1 (2016) 35–52.

"From Evidence to Total Commitment: Two Ways Faith Goes beyond Reason." *The Good, the True, the Beautiful: A Multidisciplinary Tribute to Dr. David K. Naugle*, co-edited with Rose M. Cothren, Kevin C. Neece, and Jaclyn S. Parrish, 172–92. Eugene, OR: Pickwick, 2021.

1

Alvin Plantinga's Reidian Particularism
An Overview of an Epistemological Project

PHILOSOPHY, THE LOVE OF wisdom, is about seeing things clearly.[1] Much good philosophy consists of explaining the obvious—which may lead to a non-obvious conclusion. Alvin Plantinga's epistemology is an explanation of the obvious fact that we know commonsense beliefs to be true, an explanation that uncovers something less obvious—that belief in God without evidence can be knowledge.

Plantinga is perhaps the single biggest contributor to religious epistemology in a generation, a source of unexpected philosophical insight important to our understanding of religious belief. His most significant accomplishment is fostering a sense of the intellectual respectability of theism in general and Christianity in particular. At the heart of this feat is his explicitly epistemological project, throughout which his goal has been to show that Christian beliefs are epistemically on a par with commonsense beliefs which we all recognize as cases of knowledge.[2] A massive project occupying the middle ground between theology and philosophy, spanning more than three decades and well over a thousand pages, Plantinga's epistemology may nevertheless be succinctly summarized: An investigation of commonsense beliefs which we rightly take to be knowledge suggests that there is no criterion for epistemic respectability that theistic belief fails to

---

1. The biggest change to this chapter since its initial publication in *Criswell Theological Review* is the addition of two paragraphs in the conclusion on how Christian apologists might be able to use this information.

2. On this aspect of the project, see Beilby, *Epistemology as Theology*, 28.

satisfy. Furthermore, Plantinga also suggests a criterion for warrant that it is plausible that theistic belief satisfies. The demonstration of epistemic parity begins (in the 1967 *God and Other Minds*) with the observation that belief does not require arguments in order to be rational; it continues in the articulation of Reformed epistemology; and it culminates in the articulation (in the Warrant Trilogy) of a criterion for warrant that Plantinga suggests theistic belief satisfies.[3]

Plantinga's epistemological project thus follows Thomas Reid in taking commonsense beliefs as clear cases of knowledge. It also follows the well-known particularist approach outlined by Roderick Chisholm in "The Problem of the Criterion," for Plantinga begins with these clear cases of knowledge and inspects them to determine a criterion for knowledge that can disambiguate less clear cases. The full extent of Plantinga's Reidian particularism has rarely been understood; and more rarely, if at all, have all the elements been tied together. Attention to the whole can help us correct some misunderstandings of the parts. For example, scholars may not notice that Plantinga's particularism is designed to confront the fact that belief in God is more controversial than commonsense belief; that particularism leads naturally to articulating a new criterion for proper basicality and not just refuting an old one; that the data set for particularism is no more controversial than Reidian commonsense beliefs; or that *Warranted Christian Belief* includes a real-world application of Plantinga's epistemic criterion as the final stage in a particularist methodology.

The structure of Plantinga's project is not easy to understand, especially for those who have not studied the entire project along with its sources in Chisholm and Reid. In short, we could do with a comprehensive overview attentive to Plantinga's epistemological sources.[4] I will provide that here, clearing up some errors in interpretation along the way. Hopefully, in future scholars will be able to spend less time interpreting Plantinga and more critiquing or building on him. Understanding particularism is especially helpful in one area where Plantinga's epistemology is, as is often observed, in need of improvement: His relative lack of interest in evidence for the truth of Christian belief. As I shall explain, the roots of Plantinga's strategy in Reid and Chisholm suggest the propriety of such evidence.

---

3. The major sources are Plantinga, *God and Other Minds*; Plantinga, "Reason and Belief in God;" Plantinga, *Warrant: The Current Debate* and *Warrant and Proper Function*; and Plantinga, *Warranted Christian Belief*.

4. A fine overview, less attentive to the influence of Chisholm and Reid, is Beilby, *Epistemology as Theology*.

I shall plot the development of Plantinga's Reidian particularism over three phases.[5] Each of the latter two phases goes deeper in its defense of theistic belief than the one preceding. *God and Other Minds*, the *first* phase, considers objections against the existence of God. Plantinga's contribution to Reformed epistemology, the name of a recent tradition in epistemology drawing from Reformation theology, is the *second* phase. Here Plantinga objects to *evidentialism*. Evidentialism, which grounds typical objections against God, is the theory that a rational belief must be based on evidence—with a handful of exceptions for some beliefs to serve *as* evidence for others. Plantinga's Warrant Trilogy is the *third* phase, in which Plantinga objects to *internalism*, the theory that grounds evidentialism. Internalism, aptly defined in another classic article by Chisholm (one less influential on Plantinga),[6] is the theory that we must have mental access to the conditions for warrant; when we know something, we can also say something about why we know it: "The internalist assumes that, merely by reflecting upon his own conscious state, he can formulate a set of epistemic principles that will enable him to find out, with respect to any possible belief he has, whether he is justified in having that belief. . . . In a word, one need only consider one's own state of mind."[7] Internalism's antonym is epistemic *externalism*, the theory that the conditions for warrant may be mentally inaccessible.

In what follows I shall first briefly look over the connections already noted by scholars and explain why we need a clearer and more comprehensive account. Then I shall review the relevant epistemological insights from Chisholm and Reid. Then I shall overview Plantinga's epistemological project in these three phases.[8] I shall next show how attention to Plantinga's Reidian particularism can help correct some misunderstandings. Finally, I shall summarize these matters and point to one lesson from them: Plantinga's Reidian particularism lends itself naturally to an appreciation of the evidence for properly basic beliefs.

THE SCHOLARSHIP ON PLANTINGA

As Christian puts it, "Plantinga's epistemological programme is . . . multidimensional; insofar as it is, it poses difficulties to those who would

---

5. My "phases" correspond to the "stages" of Beilby, *Epistemology as Theology*, 33-34.
6. Chisholm, "The Indispensability of Internal Justification," 285-96.
7. Chisholm, "The Indispensability of Internal Justification," 285-86.
8. I pass over the transition from the second to the third phases, a period overviewed in Beilby, *Epistemology as Theology*, 13-14, 66-67, and 69-71.

comprehend it, as well as to those who would adopt it."[9] In one article Helm notes the connections between Reid, Reformed epistemology, and the Warrant Trilogy and mentions a connection to particularism.[10] However, Helm gives few details and goes on to consider whether Reid thinks belief in God need not be warranted by evidence. In his review of *Warranted Christian Belief* Helm notes briefly that it includes concepts from Reformed epistemology[11] and suggests that someone else might want "to plot the development of his epistemology from *God and Other Minds* (1967) onwards"[12]—a suggestion I take up here.

The norm is to not even get this far. Steuer notes a connection of Reformed epistemology to *God and Other Minds*, but does not get into Reid or particularism.[13] Hatcher nicely describes the link between Chisholm and Reformed epistemology, but does not go into Reid or *God and Other Minds*.[14] Appleby is strong on Plantinga's approach as an argument from epistemic parity and notes the connection between *God and Other Minds* and Reformed epistemology, but neglects Reid and Chisholm.[15] Bolus and Scott note the connection to Reid, the roots of Reformed epistemology in *God and Other Minds*, and Plantinga's emphasis on epistemic parity. However, they do not explain the connection to Chisholm or link the definition of warrant in *Warrant and Proper Function* to commonsense beliefs.[16] In a separate article Scott observes the connections of Reformed epistemology to *Warranted Christian Belief*, but no other connections.[17] Clark and Barrett are attentive to Reid, leaving out Chisholm's particularism.[18] Hasker, on the other hand, is very clear on the connection between particularism and Reformed epistemology, but does not note *God and Other Minds* or Reid.[19] Baker helpfully links Reformed epistemology and the Warrant Trilogy, but barely mentions Reid and mentions Chisholm not at all.[20] Sudduth consid-

---

9. Christian, "Plantinga, Epistemic Permissiveness, and Metaphysical Pluralism," 556.

10. Helm, "Reid and 'Reformed' Epistemology," 103–22.

11. Helm, "Review of *Warranted Christian Belief*," 1110.

12. Helm, "Review of *Warranted Christian Belief*," 1111.

13. Steuer, "The Epistemic Status of Theistic Beliefs," 249. An article predating the Warrant Trilogy, of course, will not note connections to it.

14. Hatcher, "Some Problems with Reformed Epistemology," 21–31.

15. Appleby, "Reformed Epistemology," 129–41.

16. Bolus and Scott, "Reformed Epistemology."

17. Scott, "Return of the Great Pumpkin," 297–308.

18. Clark and Barrett, "Reidian Religious Epistemology," 1–37.

19. Hasker, "The Foundations of Theism," 52–54.

20. Baker, "Plantinga's Reformed Epistemology," 77–103.

ers the whole project from *God and Other Minds* to the Warrant Trilogy, but leaves out Reid *and* Chisholm.[21] Fales notes that the Warrant Trilogy is "a trilogy on Reformed Epistemology," but does not connect them to *God and Other Minds*, Reid, or Chisholm.[22]

We need not multiply examples endlessly. All the dimensions are noted by somebody, but hardly anybody notices all. I will not say that in this chapter I am teaching an aspect of Plantingian epistemology no scholar had ever previously *understood*. It had merely not yet, apparently, been *explained*; and, as a result, *some* have not understood it or have *mis*understood it. Moreover, Plantinga is not important to scholars alone; given the many laypeople (perhaps hundreds of thousands) interested in Plantinga, there is a great need for a clear explanation of the whole picture.

CHISHOLM'S PARTICULARISM AND REID'S COMMON SENSE

The first step to seeing the whole picture is to understand Chisholm and Reid.

In "The Problem of the Criterion," originally the 1973 Aquinas Lecture at Marquette University, Chisholm outlines a puzzle involving knowledge. Like Plato's Meno Paradox (*Meno* 80d–80e), the problem of the criterion can be interpreted as a skeptical argument demonstrating the impossibility of knowledge. In order to gain knowledge we need to have a criterion for recognizing it. In order to discover a criterion for knowledge we need to know whether it successfully identifies knowledge. In order to know whether it successfully identifies knowledge it is necessary to have some knowledge with which to test it. So we need a criterion if we want to get knowledge, but we need knowledge if we want to find a criterion![23]

Like the Meno Paradox, the problem of the criterion fails as a proof of skepticism. It relies on the absence of both knowledge *and* a criterion. There are two ways out. If we do have some knowledge, then we can learn from it what the criterion is. Alternatively, if we have a criterion for knowledge, then we do not need to discover it, and we can use it to find some knowledge. The first approach Chisholm labels *particularism*, for it relies on particular cases of knowledge already being available. The second approach is *methodism* because it relies on the criterion already being available, a criterion often taken to involve the right method of believing. Chisholm is a

---

21. Sudduth, "Reformed Epistemology and Christian Apologetics," 299–321.
22. Fales, Review, 353.
23. Chisholm, "The Problem of the Criterion," 64.

particularist and voices his support for the commonsense tradition which takes commonsense beliefs as cases of knowledge.[24] (Of course, in keeping with his commitment to internalism, Chisholm thinks we can have mental access to epistemic principles which show that those commonsense beliefs are justified.)

Chisholm's strategy invites us to study those commonsense beliefs inductively to determine a criterion for knowledge, and apply it to other cases. Plantinga accepts Chisholm's invitation—with a view toward applying the criterion for knowledge to religious belief. Let us look more closely at the commonsense tradition, focusing on Reid's philosophy, which Plantinga explicitly emulates.

"Common sense" is by now something of a technical term and must not be taken to mean what most people think at any particular time, as if theism, atheism, and geocentrism were all common sense in their own times and places. Commonsense beliefs are what *everyone* believes save only those whose minds are at least a little bit off—and those led into doubt by bad philosophy! Nor does Reid focus on just any belief that might possibly have this near-universal acceptance, but on the foundational principles from which our other beliefs derive, the "first principles." Geocentrism was never a commonsense belief, but the existence of the world outside one's own mind has always been. Note that the grounds for the truth of commonsense belief are not based in majority opinion. But what actually *are* these grounds? Reid tells us what commonsense beliefs are, but leaves it largely implicit how we know them; Plantinga, however, aims to give a thorough and explicit explanation.

Reid's work is largely a response to Hume. Hume had left philosophy with a skeptical problem, observing in Parts IV and V of *Enquiry Concerning Human Understanding* that our beliefs about the world outside the mind rest on a foundation of a very few principles, the principles by which we learn from experience—causality, the uniformity of nature, and the reliability of inductive reasoning. Also, according to Hume, these principles cannot be known.[25] So nothing that depends on these principles is known either. This would preclude the possibility of our having any knowledge of

---

24. Chisholm, "The Problem of the Criterion," 69.

25. Hume thinks all knowledge of the world outside the mind derives from experience. This prevents us from knowing any principle *by which* we learn *from* experience. Descartes famously argues for such principles, and so have others; for example, Loke argues for causality in Loke, *God and Ultimate Origins*, chapter 5; and McGrew argues that the world outside the mind is real in McGrew, *The Foundations of Knowledge*, chapter 7.

the world at all. Thus Reid took Hume's philosophy to lead to the unacceptable result of skepticism.[26]

Reid, however, thinks that a belief need not be justified by other beliefs to be known. We can know some truths without evidence. Everyone knows induction is reliable, just as everyone knows that the five senses connect him to the world outside the mind. We know without proof; we can even know without evidence. It's common sense! As Reid says in chapter 1, section 3 of *An Inquiry into the Human Mind on the Principles of Common Sense*:

> [P]hilosophers, pitying the credulity of the vulgar, resolve not to trust anything that isn't founded on reason. These philosophers ask philosophy to supply them with reasons for believing things that all mankind have believed without being able to give any reasons for doing so.

Commonsense beliefs are the foundation of all our other knowledge. To understand Plantinga's Reidian particularism we must know what exactly these commonsense beliefs are. In chapter 5 of the sixth Essay in *Essays on the Intellectual Powers of Man*, Reid offers a convenient list of twelve commonsense principles, which we may paraphrase as follows:

1. My perceptions really are my perceptions, and what I think I really do think.
2. I exist.
3. My memories are reliable.
4. My own past really did happen.
5. The world outside my mind which my five senses perceive really exists.
6. I have free will.
7. Reason is reliable.
8. Other minds exist in the beings wherein it appears to me that they exist; I am not the only conscious being in existence.
9. Physical and linguistic signs convey knowledge of the mental states of those other minds.
10. Testimony is a source of knowledge.
11. There is a degree of uniformity in the behavior of sane humans.

---

26. Additional helpful commentary on Reid may be found in Clark and Barrett, "Reidian Religious Epistemology," 5–10.

12. The past resembles the present. (I.e., there is a uniformity to events in nature.)

Note that most of these beliefs point to conditions for or sources of knowledge. Although we should keep in mind that these are fallible sources (memory having let us down in the past, and so on) commonsense principles are unavoidable sources for our beliefs. Even a Descartes who tries to construct a system of knowledge without relying on commonsense ends up relying on the first two commonsense beliefs. The alternative to accepting at least some common sense as knowledge is skepticism—denying that we have any knowledge at all.

THE OBJECTION TO ANTI-THEISM

In the initial phase of his project Plantinga defends theism from anti-theism, the philosophical stance of arguing against theism. Plantinga considers some arguments for and against the existence of God, finding that this thesis does not measure up very well to the standards of the anti-theist. But neither does the thesis that other minds exist, and so much the worse for those standards.[27] So these beliefs are in the same boat. Yet belief in other minds is rational; so, Plantinga concludes, is belief in God.

For the existence of God, Plantinga considers natural theology, the project of those who, like Aquinas, argue that God exists based on evidence observed in nature and elsewhere. Plantinga analyzes natural theology "by considering in turn the cosmological, ontological, and teleological arguments for the existence of God," concluding that the arguments, along with "natural theology generally," "must finally be judged unsuccessful."[28] Thus chapters one through four. *Against* the existence of God, Plantinga considers the problem of evil and the free will defense in chapters five and six, concluding ultimately that an argument against God's existence based on evil is "inconclusive."[29] In chapter seven he considers "a miscellany of atheological arguments," all of which are deemed unsuccessful.[30]

---

27. Of course, these standards are those of evidentialism, but Plantinga's attack on evidentialism here is still largely implicit.

28. Plantinga, *God and Other Minds*, xv. For a fuller picture of Plantinga on natural theology, consider his remarks that natural theology also aims to show that belief in God is rational, and that its arguments sometimes succeed; see Plantinga, *God, Freedom, and Evil*, 3 and 112.

29. Plantinga, *God and Other Minds*, 155.

30. Plantinga, *God and Other Minds*, 156–83.

How do we know that other minds exist? Plantinga examines the argument from my knowledge of my own mental state and the similarity of my outward behavior to that of other bodies. The argument is pretty good[31] but, ultimately, deficient.[32] The final conclusion of *God and Other Minds* is as significant as it is brief:

> Of course there may be other reasons for supposing that although rational belief in other minds does not require an answer to the epistemological question, rational belief in the existence of God does. But it is certainly hard to see what these reasons might be. Hence my tentative conclusion: if my belief in other minds is rational, so is my belief in God. But obviously the former is rational; so, therefore, is the latter.[33]

In other words, epistemic parity matters: These beliefs are the same with respect to evidence, so they are probably the same with respect to rationality.[34]

This is a rudimentary Reidian particularism (and actually pre-dating Chisholm's Aquinas Lecture). Plantinga reasons from the epistemic characteristics of belief in other minds to those of belief in God, including an apparent absence of both provability and *dis*provability. Since both beliefs have these characteristics and since we know that belief in other minds is rational, belief in God is probably rational too. This use of particularism begins with only one case of knowledge, and there is no clear acknowledgement that there is any need to identify a criterion for rationality. Yet a glimmer of light is shone on the matter: Rationality does *not* require evidence. But what actually *is* a good criterion for rationality, or any other epistemic quality for that matter? And what do *other* cases of knowledge suggest?[35]

THE OBJECTION TO EVIDENTIALISM

In his Reformed epistemology phase Plantinga digs deeper, looking past the question of rationality to the question of *justification*. He takes on a subtler foe—not the anti-theist, but the *evidentialist*, for it was evidentialism that inspired arguments against theism in the first place. Plantinga also expands

31. Plantinga, *God and Other Minds*, chapters 8–9.
32. Plantinga, *God and Other Minds*, chapter 10.
33. Plantinga, *God and Other Minds*, 271.
34. Quinn aptly summarizes the epistemic parity argument here in Quinn, "Epistemic Parity and Religious Argument," 335. Also Sudduth, "Reformed Epistemology and Christian Apologetics," 307.
35. On the good start and the need for going deeper, see Plantinga, *Warranted Christian Belief*, 69–71 and 81–82.

his list of commonsense beliefs: Memory, sensory evidence, and more join the commonsense belief in other minds. He also expands his list of salient epistemic characteristics of belief by considering the phenomenology of properly basic beliefs—the way things are when we find ourselves having them. This supports Plantinga's opinion that belief in God is, like commonsense beliefs, properly basic.[36] This, in short, is a development of Plantinga's Reidian particularism.

Plantinga's contribution to Reformed epistemology consists of a series of closely related articles in the late 1970s and the 1980s along with his chapter in the 1983 volume *Faith and Rationality*, co-edited with Nicholas Wolterstorff (a reminder that Plantinga's project is not strictly *his*, but is central in a *tradition* in epistemology). I will mainly follow Plantinga's article titled by his central question, "Is Belief in God Properly Basic?"[37] Plantinga considers "the *evidentialist* objection"—the theory that belief in God is only rational if justified by good evidence.[38] He notes that natural theology tends to agree with the evidentialist critic; although they disagree over whether the belief "God exists" is justified, they are both committed to evidentialism.[39] Evidentialists tend to be *classical foundationalists*. *Foundationalism* posits that the normal way for a belief to be warranted is by evidence from other beliefs. The exceptions are those beliefs at the foundation of the support structure—the basic beliefs—which are warranted or justified independently of other beliefs. So *most* beliefs have as the criterion for their being warranted having logical support derived from basic beliefs. There must be another criterion for the warrant of *basic beliefs*. What defines *classical* foundationalism is its account of the criterion for proper basicality: that a basic belief be either incorrigible, self-evident, or evident to the senses.[40]

Plantinga suggests that belief in God might actually be properly basic,[41] something we may properly believe without evidence. In any case,

---

36. Plantinga sometimes uses the word "justified" in the sense of noetic propriety; the narrower sense, being based on evidence, is a different matter, although Plantinga never wholly abandons the broader sense. See Plantinga, "Reason and Belief in God," 79 and *Warranted Christian Belief*, 100.

37. Plantinga, "Is Belief in God Properly Basic?," 41–51.

38. Plantinga, "Is Belief in God Properly Basic?," 41.

39. Plantinga, "Is Belief in God Properly Basic?," 41. See also Plantinga, "The Reformed Objection to Natural Theology," 187–98.

40. "Is Belief in God Properly Basic?," 44. Roughly, an *incorrigible* belief is one that cannot be corrected, such as my beliefs about what I am currently thinking. For Plantinga's efforts to explain what these three terms mean, see "Reason and Belief in God," 55–59.

41. Plantinga, "Is Belief in God Properly Basic?," 42. Plantinga notes that, technically, it may not be that "God exists" is properly basic but rather propositions entailing it such as "God made these beautiful stars I am looking at tonight."

classical foundationalism is mistaken, as Plantinga mentions with an allusion to some of his earlier work.[42] One crippling objection is that we cannot consistently accept classical foundationalism, for it is not self-evident, incorrigible, or evident to the senses; nor, so far as Plantinga can tell, has anyone yet explained how it might be justified by beliefs that are.[43] A different, particularist objection is somewhat more to our interest here.[44] There are properly basic beliefs that plainly do not satisfy classical foundationalism's criterion for proper basicality; Plantinga borrows from Reid, using the example of memory beliefs.[45]

Treating belief in God as properly basic does not make it "groundless, or gratuitous, or arbitrary."[46] There are *requirements* for proper basicality. Again Plantinga makes his Reidian particularist move: "Suppose we consider" perception, memory, and beliefs about other minds."[47] These are properly basic beliefs, and "there is a circumstance that serves as the *ground of justification*."[48] This is a clue to a better criterion for proper basicality. There is "some further condition—a condition hard to state in detail—" for proper basicality; "a belief is properly basic only in certain conditions . . . ."[49] A modest accomplishment of Reidian particularism is to show that Christian belief shares with these commonsense beliefs the characteristic of arising automatically in the right circumstances. As far as we can tell from the salient traits of the beliefs considered, Christian theology is on a par with commonsense beliefs.[50] Since *they* are properly basic, it is reasonable to suppose that Christian belief also is.

---

42. Plantinga, "Is Belief in God Properly Basic?," 44. The earlier work is Plantinga, "Is Belief in God Rational?," 7–27.

43. On this see Plantinga, "Reason and Belief in God," 60–63.

44. For an overview of the two objections, I suggest Beilby, *Epistemology as Theology*, 46–47.

45. Plantinga, "Reason and Belief in God," 60. Helm notes the connection to Chisholm's particularism and notes the "precedent in Reid" for taking memory as an example of a properly basic belief. Helm, "Reid and 'Reformed' Epistemology," 104–5.

46. Plantinga, "Is Belief in God Properly Basic?," 44.

47. Plantinga, "Is Belief in God Properly Basic?," 44.

48. Plantinga, "Is Belief in God Properly Basic?," 45.

49. Plantinga, "Is Belief in God Properly Basic?," 45–46.

50. Quinn does not see an epistemic parity argument here; Quinn, "Epistemic Parity and Religious Argument," 335–36. Penelhum sees one from the rationality of the classical foundationalist's recognized properly basic beliefs to the rationality of additional properly basic beliefs; Penelhum, *God and Skepticism*, 147–48; Penelhum considered by Quinn in Quinn, 337–39. However, Plantinga is arguing *to* the rationality of belief in God *from* the rationality of a range of properly basic beliefs, including commonsense beliefs which do *not* meet the classical foundationalist's standards. Appleby concurs; Appleby, "Reformed Epistemology, Rationality, and Belief in God," 137–38.

This is provisional. It would be good to know what the criterion for proper basicality actually *is*. Although Plantinga's point is merely *that* there is one, he admits there is more than he is yet prepared to articulate. The criterion is "hard to state in detail." It is something about which it would do to learn more, and we would have to begin by studying various properly basic beliefs. For now, it is enough for Plantinga to show that classical foundationalism's criterion is flawed; eventually, perhaps, it would be good to study some properly basic beliefs to identify the real criterion for proper basicality.

Consider Plantinga's response to the infamous Great Pumpkin objection: "If belief in God is properly basic, why can't *just any* belief be properly basic?"[51] Why may not Linus claim that his unevidenced belief in the Great Pumpkin is proper? Are we "throwing wide the gates to irrationalism and superstition?"[52] No. We can make some epistemic judgments without stating a criterion. Abandoning a lousy epistemic criterion is not equivalent to abandoning *all* epistemic criteria any more than abandoning logical positivism's verifiabiliy criterion for meaning means we should abandon *all* criteria for meaning and pretend that nonsense phrases from Lewis Carrol's "Jabberwocky" mean something.[53]

Moreover, we can always articulate another criterion. How we go about trying to find an epistemic criterion is "an important question—one Roderick Chisholm has taught us to ask."[54] We need not have a criterion ready-made before making epistemic judgments.[55] We can begin by listing the solid epistemic judgments we do have and examine our properly basic beliefs to learn what criterion they satisfy. Plantinga lucidly presents the particularist approach:

> [T]he proper way to arrive at such a criterion is, broadly speaking, *inductive*. We must assemble examples of beliefs and conditions such that the former are obviously properly basic in the latter, and examples of beliefs and conditions such that the former are obviously *not* properly basic in the latter. We must then frame hypotheses as to the necessary and sufficient conditions of proper basicality and test these hypotheses by reference to those examples.[56]

51. Plantinga, "Is Belief in God Properly Basic?," 48.
52. Plantinga, "Is Belief in God Properly Basic?," 48.
53. Plantinga, "Is Belief in God Properly Basic?," 48.
54. Plantinga, "Is Belief in God Properly Basic?," 48.
55. Plantinga, "Is Belief in God Properly Basic?," 48.
56. Plantinga, "Is Belief in God Properly Basic?," 50.

We should not presume that everyone will agree on what examples are properly basic.[57] Christians need not feel pressured to stick to atheist-approved examples. However, Plantinga's own examples are remarkably uncontroversial; other than a few beliefs about God, which he mentions when considering the phenomenology of religious experience, his examples are invariably Reidian.

To inductively derive a criterion for proper basicality from a good list of examples is Reformed epistemology's unfinished business.[58] Plantinga notes that "there are plenty of candidates" for a difference between belief in God and belief in the Great Pumpkin,[59] i.e., for a criterion. He makes no promise to do this work; to answer the objection it was enough to point out that the work *can* be done. All the same, he *did* do it later in the Warrant Trilogy.

Should Plantinga perhaps have been a little more explicit that this is Chisholm's strategy for finding an epistemological criterion, paused to exegete Chisholm, and cited him every time he made a particularist move?[60] A fair question, one perhaps best answered by an epistemologist from an earlier generation than mine: "When I was a graduate student in the 1960s, the pantheon of American philosophy enshrined just four *theoi*: in alphabetical order, Roderick Chisholm, Nelson Goodman, W. V. Quine, and Wilfred Sellars."[61] Plantinga was talking to epistemologists familiar with Chisholm's strategy. For them, it was enough to overview the particularist strategy and attribute it to Chisholm.

In sum, we have a larger sample set to draw from including belief in other minds, memory beliefs, and perceptual beliefs. The account has improved, and puts Plantinga in a much better position to argue that belief in God can be reasonable without evidence. There is a recognition of the need for a criterion in any *complete* account. Besides the insight that rationality does not require inferential support, we are given a further hint concerning what makes a belief epistemically appropriate: Belief in God arises automatically when we are in the right circumstances, much like my belief that there is a desk before me right now.

---

57. Plantinga, "Is Belief in God Properly Basic?," 50.

58. Hasker, along with Philip Quinn, was quite right that Reformed epistemology would do well to articulate the criterion; Hasker, "The Foundations of Theism," 52–54.

59. Plantinga, "Is Belief in God Properly Basic?," 50.

60. Plantinga does cite "The Problem of the Criterion" in "Reason and Belief in God," 75–77.

61. Lycan, "Plantinga and Coherentisms," 3. See also Beilby, *Epistemology as Theology*, 7.

THE OBJECTION TO INTERNALISM

The third phase of Plantinga's project presents an epistemic criterion, contrasting it with some alternative accounts. Plantinga digs deeper still, looking beneath the questions of rationality and evidence and directly at *warrant*.[62] He takes on a subtler foe—neither the anti-theist nor the evidentialist, but the *internalist*. Internalism justifies evidentialism. If we need mental access to the grounds of our beliefs, then very few beliefs can be properly basic—only those whose truth is directly evident to the conscious mind, such as $2 + 2 = 4$. (In allowing sensory beliefs to count as properly basic, the classical foundationalist has already lowered his internalist standards a bit, and a self-respecting internalist isn't about to let God be another exception.)[63] Plantinga also expands his list of commonsense beliefs, now approximately mirroring Reid's. And, finally, he gives a very detailed account of the characteristics of both these commonsense beliefs and belief in God, accompanied by the proposal that these commonsense beliefs are *warranted* and *known*, and the claim that belief in God may reasonably be said to be so as well.

In the early stages of a particularist analysis one may want to refute flawed accounts of an epistemic criterion, perhaps in the process finding clues concerning a better criterion. (Thus in earlier phases Plantinga refutes criteria for rationality and proper basicality, and finds a clue to a better criterion in the conditions in which properly basic beliefs arise.) In the Warrant Trilogy, Plantinga looks at several criteria for warrant, especially internalism's.[64] He finds that various accounts of warrant founder when it comes to the proper functioning of our epistemic faculties. Internalist theories of justification may fail to describe necessary conditions for warrant, since properly functioning faculties may give us warranted beliefs without justification; or they may fail to describe sufficient conditions for warrant, since the beliefs of a person with cognitive malfunction might be justified yet lack warrant. This is also a clue to a better criterion; this is the role of *Warrant: The Current Debate* in Plantinga's particularism.[65]

The Warrant Trilogy also aims to finish Reformed epistemology's unfinished business by articulating a better criterion for proper basicality. *Warrant and Proper Function*'s criterion for warrant, that which makes the

---

62. See also Beilby, *Epistemology as Theology*, 23.
63. See also Beilby, *Epistemology as Theology*, 56.
64. He also identifies some imperfections in externalist theories.
65. I go over this in more detail in the next chapter of this book.

difference between knowledge and mere true belief,⁶⁶ is also a criterion for proper basicality. The criterion:

> [A] belief has warrant for me only if (1) it has been produced in me by cognitive faculties that are working properly (functioning as they ought to, subject to no cognitive dysfunction) in a cognitive environment that is appropriate for my kinds of cognitive faculties, (2) the segment of the design plan governing the production of that belief is aimed at the production of true beliefs, and (3) there is a high statistical probability that a belief produced under those conditions will be true.⁶⁷

We might refer to these conditions for warrant collectively as *the proper functionalist criterion*. It is an externalist rather than an internalist condition. Although we presumably are not in the Matrix, we do not have mental access to this fact. Note also that it pertains to basic beliefs: A belief satisfying this criterion may be warranted independently of other beliefs. Note also that it is presented as a necessary condition for warrant—not necessarily a sufficient one. It describes the minimum requirements for warrant, not necessarily the maximum; however, Plantinga clearly thinks it is sufficient for the warrant of properly basic beliefs. This leaves some more work to do articulating the necessary *and* sufficient conditions for warrant for different kinds of belief.⁶⁸

Warrant and Proper Function is a Reidian particularism. The proper functionalist criterion replaces the flawed criteria suggested by internalists, and Plantinga spends most of the book arguing that consideration of plainly warranted commonsense beliefs supports his criterion. These beliefs, though ordered differently, correspond remarkably well to Reid's list of twelve. There is knowledge of oneself, of the past, and of other minds; the legitimacy of their testimony; sense perception; non-empirical reasoning; and knowledge of the uniformity of nature.⁶⁹ The appeal to Reid is explicit⁷⁰ and oft-repeated in the Warrant Trilogy.⁷¹ The circumstances of the warranting of these properly basic beliefs suggest the proper functionalist criterion as the sole criterion for their warrant. In short, this is a continuation of the Reidian particularist strategy begun in earlier phases.

---

66. A definition of warrant from Plantinga, *Warrant and Proper Function*, v.
67. Plantinga, *Warrant and Proper Function*, 46–47.
68. On these matters, see the next chapter of this book.
69. Plantinga, *Warrant and Proper Function*, chapters 3–7.
70. Such as in the Preface; Plantinga, *Warrant and Proper Function*, x.
71. Also in Plantinga, "Respondeo," 333.

Plantinga's strategy is inductively to derive his criterion from common-sense instances of knowledge, and note that each instance fits that criterion. So particularism has coherence built in. Whatever criterion is eventually reached, it will, if properly inducted from particular cases of knowledge, inevitably be a criterion which those cases satisfy.

Warranted Christian Belief, a late entry in the Reformed epistemology literature, is also a very advanced stage of particularism. The point of finding an epistemic criterion is not only to replace lousy accounts of criteria and to defend our beliefs from criticisms based on them. We would also like to apply the newly discovered criterion to particular beliefs. *Warrant and Proper Function* articulates the criterion for proper basicality, and *Warranted Christian Belief* looks at Christian belief to see if it satisfies that criterion. It is not possible to give a direct and simple answer. Rather, there is an account of how Christian belief might be warranted by a faculty satisfying that criterion—a faculty given by God. Accordingly, Christian belief is likely warranted *if* it is true.

Whereas in the Reformed epistemology era Plantinga made only brief allusions to the *sensus divinitatis* of which Calvin spoke, now he develops a more detailed model, dubbed the Aquinas/Calvin model and drawn from their theology.[72] Plantinga also explains why some apparently do not have this faculty in good working order, looking at "sin and its cognitive consequences."[73] His account has limitations: The very idea of this faculty is deeply Christian and theological. So his account can only be accurate if God exists and if Christianity is largely correct. So we cannot demonstrate that belief in God is warranted by this faculty; we can only show that it is probably warranted and known *if Christian theology is correct*. Moreover, there is an alternative account of the way some us believe in God: that, as certain critics such as Freud and Marx have alleged, it is by some other process—by cognitive *mal*function or by some mechanism not aimed at truth. Plantinga accordingly considers their accounts of theistic belief, which he finds to be poor,[74] poorer than the Aquinas/Calvin model.[75]

---

72. Plantinga, *Warranted Christian Belief*, chapter 6. A helpful commentary is Baker, "Plantinga's Reformed Epistemology," 78–79. Also Beilby, *Epistemology as Theology*, 89–99.

73. Plantinga, *Warranted Christian Belief*, chapter 7.

74. Plantinga, *Warranted Christian Belief*, chapter 5. Sudduth is helpful in explaining Plantinga on this point; Sudduth, "Reformed Epistemology and Christian Apologetics," 303–4.

75. Plantinga considers other objections in *Warranted Christian Belief*; for a helpful overview I recommend Sudduth, "Reformed Epistemology and Christian Apologetics," 79–87.

This is a significant accomplishment of a Reidian particularism on behalf of Christianity. Christian belief shares with a rather large number of commonsense beliefs the characteristic of being apparently produced by properly functioning cognitive faculties; so, since those other beliefs are warranted and known, Christian belief probably is also warranted and known (if true). And, as far as we can tell, Christian theology is on a par with commonsense beliefs.

MISTAKEN INTERPRETATIONS

Understanding Plantinga's project as a Reidian particularism can help correct a number of misunderstandings. One mistake is to think that Plantinga's strategy is to avoid rather than confront the epistemic challenge posed by the fact that religious belief is not universally shared. Another is to take Plantinga's references to Calvinism or the phenomenology of Christian belief as an articulation of a criterion for proper basicality. Another is to think Plantinga is not interested in an objective account of an epistemic criterion. Yet another is to think that Plantinga's strategy limits him to listing examples of beliefs he thinks are properly basic, not seeing that he can also articulate an epistemic criterion. Moreover, one may fail to see how particularism leads naturally from the critique of a lousy criterion in Reformed epistemology to the articulation of a better one in the Warrant Trilogy. Finally, one may not notice that Plantinga's analysis of Christianity *vis-à-vis* the views of Freud and Marx is an application of particularism to a real-world dispute about knowledge. This does not pave the way for any conceivable epistemic account to compete with the Aquinas/Calvin model.

Let us consider some examples of these misunderstandings.

Perhaps the most serious I have come across is exemplified in Christian's remark: "Whereas perceptual belief, memory belief, and belief about other minds all meet with wide approval, belief about God lies at the heart of controversy. Plantinga, of course, recognizes this difference in adopting particularism, a doctrine designed to discount its importance."[76] In fact, Plantinga uses Reidian commonsense cases as a sample set for particularism in order to address this very difference. Particularism allows us to learn from a non-controversial set of beliefs in order to have a more informed consideration of more controversial ones, and this is what Plantinga is doing.

Christian takes "particularism" as the name Plantinga gives to his inductive strategy of searching for a criterion for proper basicality, missing

---

76. Christian, "Plantinga, Epistemic Permissiveness, and Metaphysical Pluralism," 564.

the connection to Chisholm.⁷⁷ Not noticing that particularism needs a good sample set before it can get started and that Plantinga's samples are borrowed from Reid, she presumes that his analysis of Calvin and of the phenomenology of Christian belief is meant to elucidate the criterion for proper basicality.⁷⁸ Not quite. At this stage, Plantinga's analysis is provisional, showing only that there is a phenomenology common to common sense and Christian belief. This is a clue to the criterion,⁷⁹ naming which would take more work and would have to wait for the Warrant Trilogy. Along similar lines, Hatcher thinks that at this stage Plantinga is merely adding the option of a belief's being "based on strong immediate experience" to classical foundationalism's account of proper basicality.⁸⁰ In fact, Plantinga had not yet begun to articulate his criterion; the talk about experience was just a preliminary observation about where to look.

Similarly, Bolus and Scott do not notice that Plantinga's approach leads naturally to articulating a criterion based on Reidian examples of warranted belief. They note that Plantinga's response to the Great Pumpkin objection relies on the availability of criteria for proper basicality and that Plantinga claims that "the religious believer need not offer any criteria" in order to claim that her belief in God is properly basic.⁸¹ They aptly describe his Chisholmian particularism without naming it as such.⁸² Bolus and Scott present the definition of warrant in *Warrant and Proper Function* as an alternative account of warrant, as if it has no connection to the Great Pumpkin objection.⁸³ They seem to think that Plantinga is not at all interested in giving an objective list of properly basic beliefs or an objective account of a criterion: "Instead each community is responsible for determining its own starting points and reasoning on that basis."⁸⁴ This interpretation also suggests an objection made by Martin and others. If the criterion for proper basicality is to be determined from properly basic beliefs and if a community can come up with its own list of these beliefs, then *any* belief (for example, voodoo theology) can be called properly basic if some community can derive from

77. Christian, "Plantinga, Epistemic Permissiveness, and Metaphysical Pluralism," 553–73.

78. Christian, "Plantinga, Epistemic Permissiveness, and Metaphysical Pluralism," 563–72.

79. See Plantinga, "Is Belief in God Properly Basic?," 50–51.

80. Hatcher, "Some Problems with Reformed Epistemology," 29.

81. Bolus and Scott, "Reformed Epistemology," 7.a.

82. Bolus and Scott, "Reformed Epistemology," 5.a.

83. Bolus and Scott, "Reformed Epistemology," 6.c.

84. Bolus and Scott, "Reformed Epistemology," 7.a. Steuer's reading of Plantinga is similar; Steuer, "The Epistemic Status of Theistic Beliefs," 248.

whatever beliefs *they* think are properly basic a criterion which their beliefs satisfy.[85]

This largely misses the point. Plantinga's strategy is, ideally, to name the criterion for proper basicality after deriving it from Reidian common-sense beliefs. Rather than invite any random community to come up with its own list of properly basic beliefs, Plantinga merely observes that we may not agree on all examples and notes that Christians need not limit themselves to the atheist's examples.[86] Yet Plantinga limits himself to *Reid*'s examples, from which his criterion in the Warrant Trilogy is derivable.

Commenting on Reformed epistemology, Johnsen says, "Unfortunately, we are told almost nothing about the normative content of" Plantinga's theory on proper basicality, "and hence at a crucial juncture we are left to the consideration of examples and analogies."[87] This was, strictly speaking, correct at this time when Plantinga's business was to refute a bad criterion for proper basicality and to point out that there are other options. Ideally, however, articulating a better criterion was always part of the long-term plan. Further, Johnsen is mistaken that "the logic of his own position prevents Plantinga from mounting any defense of the proper basicality of belief in God beyond" listing circumstances he takes to involve properly basic belief in God.[88] Particularism entails that Plantinga could *also* articulate a better criterion.

The link between Reformed epistemology and the Warrant Trilogy can also be misunderstood from the other direction. Hasker observes that in the Warrant Trilogy "Plantinga does address the task of formulating epistemic criteria," but he says that Plantinga's shift towards externalism renders it "unclear how this new material is to be related" to Reformed epistemology.[89] That Plantinga formulates a criterion at last is itself sufficient to relate the two phases. Moreover, a shift towards externalism is unsurprising. It is natural that Plantinga's understanding of the epistemic criterion would develop as he finally articulates it. (In any case, there was a strong hint of externalism

---

85. Martin, *Atheism*, 270–73. Similarly, Beilby suggests that "Criteria for properly basic belief, therefore, are community-relative," although he notes that they are still subject to refutation. Beilby, *Epistemology as Theology*, 50–51. On the voodoo objection (or the "Son of the Great Pumpkin" objection, as Plantinga calls it), see Bolus and Scott, 7a. Also Christian's analysis with comparisons to such belief systems as voodoo, Hinduism, and astrology in Christian, "Plantinga, Epistemic Permissiveness, and Metaphysical Pluralism," 561–69.

86. Plantinga, "Reason and Belief in God," 77.

87. Johnsen, "Basic Theistic Belief," 457.

88. Johnsen, "Basic Theistic Belief," 463.

89. Hasker, "The Foundations of Theism," n7, 65.

in the Reformed epistemology talk of beliefs arising automatically in the right circumstances.)

Finally, let's reconsider just what Plantinga is up to in his comparison of the Aquinas/Calvin model to its secular competitors. In his article "Return of the Great Pumpkin," Scott suggests a revised Great Pumpkin objection. It would not show that on Plantinga's terms Linus's belief in the Great Pumpkin can be properly basic, but rather that people who believe in neither Christianity nor the Great Pumpkin have no reason to think the former is warranted but not the latter. Following Duncan Pritchard, Scott argues that the best way to handle this objection is to look to evidence for Christianity, and to people who have looked at the evidence. For my part, I have argued for a similar adjustment to Plantingian epistemology (also drawing from Pritchard).[90] As it happens, this sort of approach to Plantinga is pretty common.[91] However, I think Scott is missing something. He says, "One can use Plantinga's method to defend a belief p if one can give a model in which the target belief is warranted, and this model must be logically and epistemically possible."[92] Similarly, in the *Philosophia Christi* Book Symposium on *Warranted Christian Belief*, Geivett and Jesson make an interesting suggestion.[93] Unless, they say, the details of classical theism (omnipotence, omniscience, and so on) are written into Plantinga's account of the design of our noetic faculties, it seems a convenient counterexample to his theory is possible: Suppose space aliens have designed us with a faculty for knowing them! In this scenario, belief in them is, if true, warranted. These are fair enough hypothetical suggestions from Scott, Geivett, and Jesson. However, that does not mean that "there is no reason why some other model could not be inserted in" place of the Aquinas/Calvin model.[94] Nor is it quite right that "A principled choice" between the Aquinas/Calvin model and the Geivett/

---

90. See, again, the next chapter of this book.

91. Sudduth's analysis of Reformed epistemology and apologetics is similar; Sudduth, "Reformed Epistemology and Christian Apologetics." Also Baker's; Baker, "Plantinga's Reformed Epistemology." Also Beilby, *Epistemology as Theology*, 135–40, 193–97, and 212–13. Fales also strongly emphasizes the usefulness of evidence to supplement the warrant (allegedly) provided by the *sensus divinitatis*; Fales, Review, 353–70. Similarly, in the *Philosophia Christi* Book Symposium on *Warranted Christian Belief*, Richard Fumerton (who is very clear on Plantinga's approach of arguing by way of epistemic parity from commonsense belief) argues for the usefulness of evidence for Christian belief and for the importance of evidence against. Fumerton, "Plantinga, Warrant, and Christian Belief," 341–51.

92. Scott, "Return of the Great Pumpkin," 300.

93. Geivett and Jesson, "Plantinga's Externalism and the Terminus," 336–40.

94. Scott, "Return of the Great Pumpkin," 300.

Jesson space alien model "cannot be made if there is no place where the models significantly differ."[95] There is a little more going on at this stage.

To explain: On particularism, a criterion is not merely an end in itself; it ought to be *useful*; the idea is to be able to apply an epistemic criterion, once found, to a real-world question about beliefs whose epistemic status is in dispute. When we encounter the Aquinas/Calvin model we are, as a final particularist move, applying an epistemic criterion to real-world epistemological questions. There are many apparently sane people who apparently believe in God by some sort of instinct, and many apparently sane people who don't. Probably, either a faculty satisfying this criterion produces this belief in God, or some other mechanism produces it. Which is it? The likeliest candidates are the *sensus divinitatis* as described by the Aquinas/Calvin model, a faculty satisfying the criterion, and a mechanism like those described by Freud's and Marx's inferior models. So not just *any* model can substitute. We can have a principled preference for a model that successfully describes our real-world epistemic situation. At this late stage in the particularist strategy, any putative model ought to concern beliefs which some people actually have, and it also ought to be at least as good as the Aquinas/Calvin model.

CONCLUSION

We have seen that the epistemic propriety of belief in God is determined with reference to an expanding set of Reidian commonsense beliefs and based on, initially, their parity with respect to arguments for and against (*God and Other Minds*); later, their parity with respect to their automatically arising in the right circumstances (Reformed epistemology); and, ultimately, their parity with respect to their being apparently produced by properly functioning cognitive faculties (the Warrant Trilogy). This is an application of particularism remarkable for its brilliance, detail, and scope. The strategy is Chisholm's; it begins with a set of beliefs easily recognized as satisfying the desired epistemic criterion, reasons inductively from them to the criterion, and then uses that criterion as needed. As it happens, we needed to see if the existence of God is a solid belief, epistemically speaking. And it is, according to Plantinga's epistemological project from *God and Other Minds* until the Warrant Trilogy.

Not that everyone will agree with him, but the first thing is to know what we're disagreeing with. In fact, I have some concerns myself, such as one that has already come up: If it should happen that a belief is warranted

---

95. Geivett and Jesson, "Plantinga's Externalism and the Terminus," 337.

independently of evidence, there is no harm in giving evidence for it, and this evidence might be quite useful. Although various people have noted this, it is rarely if ever noticed that Reidian particularism itself suggests as much. The structure of a particularist strategy is to study beliefs whose epistemic status is well-known, inductively derive an epistemic criterion from them, and apply that to a belief whose epistemic status is less well known. Nothing at all prevents us from also giving evidence for the truth of a belief that satisfies that criterion. This is an observation which we may make of Reidian commonsense beliefs, as Fales notes (without mentioning Reid).[96] Indeed, Reid himself apparently understood this, and was willing to offer arguments for trusting commonsense beliefs.[97] We may also argue for the importance of evidence with respect to belief in God.[98] If this or some other enhancement of Plantinga's epistemology is correct, we shall be better able to pursue it after better understanding Plantinga's Reidian particularism.

Still, this philosophy remains brilliant and insightful. Allow me to close with a reminder of the strength of Plantinga's philosophy and one of its practical applications for Christian apologetics. I already suggested that a Reidian particularism arguing that a belief is, or can be, rational, properly basic, or warranted without evidence need not lead us to conclude that evidence is not available or useful. This clears the way for the apologist to continue appealing to the evidence for his beliefs. Plantinga, however, reminds us of the apologetic force of simply paying attention to the epistemic criteria we already accept, which speak quite well of Christian belief. A Christian might ask a critic what are the epistemic criteria on the grounds of which they make their objections to Christian faith. Is it that beliefs should be verifiable, or falsifiable, or based on evidence, or something like that? But no one who objects to Christianity on *those* grounds applies those criteria consistently—not counting, perhaps, the occasional oddball skeptic who won't admit that the past, other people, and a world outside his mind are real. Reid's twelve are all accepted without those criteria. If Christian faith cannot be rational, properly basic, or warranted simply due to its (supposed) failure to meet such criteria, then oddball skepticism really is the best philosophy—no other worldview is consistent with such a criterion for

---

96. Fales, Review, 361.

97. Four arguments for trusting our faculties of perception may be found in chapter 6, section 20 of the *Inquiry into the Human Mind*. (These arguments do not work if *no* commonsense beliefs are warranted; Reid is arguing to those who are prepared to accept *some* commonsense beliefs.) The sort of arguments mentioned above in note 24 may also be employed at this point. Also the evidence from Fales, Review, 361.

98. Plantinga himself suggests that there are good arguments; see Plantinga, Appendix, 461. Also see Beilby, *Epistemology as Theology*, 24.

rationality, warrant, or proper basicality. The same insight can be run in reverse, putting a more optimistic spin on things. An unbeliever already holds, without insisting on prior proof, to such proper and salutary beliefs as that the past, other people, and a world outside the mind exist. And, if this be right, precisely why—against such serious philosophy indicating that Christian faith, even prior to considering the evidence for it, is just as proper and salutary—should the unbeliever remain an unbeliever?

What, in any case, has he to lose by belief, or to gain by *un*belief? But that is a topic on which we shall have to consult Augustine and William James—after another quick look in the next chapter at why Plantinga's epistemology is consistent with giving evidence for the truth of Christianity.

WORKS CITED

Appleby, Peter C. "Reformed Epistemology, Rationality, and Belief in God." *Philosophy of Religion* 24 (1988) 129–41.

Baker, Deane-Peter. "Plantinga's Reformed Epistemology: What's the Question?" *International Journal for Philosophy of Religion* 57 (2005) 77–103.

Beilby, James. *Epistemology as Theology: An Evaluation of Alvin Plantinga's Religious Epistemology*. London: Routledge, 2006.

Bolos, Anthony, and Kyle Scott. "Reformed Epistemology." *Internet Encyclopedia of Philosophy*. http://www.iep.utm.edu/ref-epis/. Accessed 19 April, 2018.

Chisholm, Roderick. "The Indispensability of Internal Justification." *Synthese* 74.3 (1988) 285–96.

———. "The Problem of the Criterion." In *The Foundations of Knowing*, 61–75. Minneapolis: University of Minnesota Press, 1982.

Christian, Rose Ann. "Plantinga, Epistemic Permissiveness, and Metaphysical Pluralism." *Religious Studies* 28 (1992) 553–73.

Clark, Kelly James, and Justin L. Barrett. "Reidian Religious Epistemology and the Cognitive Science of Religion." *Journal of the American Academy of Religion* 79.3 (2011) 1–37.

Fales, Evan. Review of Alvin Plantinga, *Warranted Christian Belief*. *Noûs* 37.2 (2003) 353–70.

Fumerton, Richard. "Plantinga, Warrant, and Christian Belief." *Philosophia Christi* 3.2 (2001) 341–51.

Geivett, R. Douglas, and Greg Jesson. "Plantinga's Externalism and the Terminus of Warrant-Based Epistemology." *Philosophia Christi* 3.2 (2001) 329–40.

Hasker, William. "The Foundations of Theism: Scoring the Quinn-Plantinga Debate." *Faith and Philosophy* 15.1 (1998) 52–67.

Hatcher, Donald. "Some Problems with Reformed Epistemology." *American Journal of Theology and Philosophy* 10.1 (1989) 21–31.

Helm, Paul. "Reid and 'Reformed' Epistemology." In *Thomas Reid: Context, Influence, Significance*, edited by Joseph Houston, 103–22. Edinburgh: Dunedin Academic, 2004.

———. "Review of *Warranted Christian Belief*" by Alvin Plantinga. *Mind* 110.440 (2011) 1110–15.

Johnsen, Bredo C. "Basic Theistic Belief." *Canadian Journal of Philosophy* 16.3 (1986) 455–64.

Loke, Andrew Ter Ern. *God and Ultimate Origins: A Novel Cosmological Argument*. Cham, Switzerland: Palgrave Macmillan, 2017.

Lycan, William G. "Plantinga and Coherentisms." In *Warrant in Contemporary Epistemology*, edited by Jonathan L. Kvanvig, 3–23. Lanham, MD: Rowman & Littlefield, 1996.

McGrew, Timothy. *The Foundations of Knowledge*. Lanham, MD: Rowman & Littlefield, 1995.

Martin, Michael. *Atheism: A Philosophical Justification*. Philadelphia: Temple University Press, 1992.

Penelhum, Terence. *God and Skepticism*. Dordrecht, Holland: D. Reidel, 1983.

Plantinga, Alvin. Appendix: Plantinga's Original "Two Dozen (or so) Theistic Arguments." In *Two Dozen (or so) Arguments for God: The Plantinga Project*, edited by Jerry Walls and Trent Dougherty, 461–79. New York: Oxford University Press, 2018.

———. "Is Belief in God Properly Basic?" *Noûs* 15.1 (1981) 41–51.

———. "Is Belief in God Rational?" In *Rationality and Religious Belief*, edited by C. Delaney, 7–27. Notre Dame, IN: University of Notre Dame Press, 1979.

———. *God, Freedom, and Evil*. Grand Rapids: Eerdmans, 1977.

———. *God and Other Minds: A Study of the Rational Justification of Belief in God*. New York: Cornell University Press, 1967.

———. "Reason and Belief in God." In *Faith and Rationality: Reason and Belief in God*, edited by Alvin Plantinga and Nicholas Wolterstorff, 16–93. Notre Dame, IN: University of Notre Dame Press, 1991.

———. "The Reformed Objection to Natural Theology." *Christian Scholars Review* 11 (1982) 187–98.

———. "Respondeo." In *Warrant in Contemporary Epistemology*, edited by Jonathan Kvanvig, 307–78. Lanham, MD: Rowman & Littlefied, 1996.

———. *Warranted Christian Belief*. New York: Oxford University Press, 2000.

———. *Warrant: the Current Debate*. New York: Oxford University Press, 1993.

———. *Warrant and Proper Function*. New York: Oxford University Press, 1993.

Plato. *Meno*.

Quinn, Philip L. "Epistemic Parity and Religious Argument." *Philosophical Perspectives* 5 (1991) 317–41.

Reid, Thomas. *Essays on the Intellectual Powers of Man*.

Scott, Kyle. "Return of the Great Pumpkin." *Religious Studies* 50 (2014) 297–308.

Steuer, Axel D. "The Epistemic Status of Theistic Beliefs." *Journal of the American Academy of Religion* 55.2 (1987) 235–56.

Sudduth, Michael. "Reformed Epistemology and Christian Apologetics." *Religious Studies* 39 (2003) 299–321.

2

Proper Function and the Conditions for Warrant

What Plantinga's Notion of Warrant Shows about Different Kinds of Knowledge

WHAT IS THE TASK of analytic epistemology?[1] There are two possible responses to this question. One response assumes that justification through reason is the major (or only) ingredient that makes the difference between mere true belief and knowledge, and that the task of epistemology is to lay out rules for how a knower can achieve this justification. Descartes, Locke, Roderick Chisholm, and Laurence BonJour are just a few of the adherents to this view. The other response challenges the claim that justification is the main thing that stands between mere true belief and knowledge, and suggests that the primary task of epistemology is simply to give an account of the quality that does. Alvin Plantinga has in recent decades been the foremost representative of this view. These rival conceptions of epistemology inform rival perspectives on religious epistemology. Two religious epistemologies are particularly noteworthy for their relationship to these views on the task of epistemology. The natural theology tradition, informed by the former view, seeks to discover some knowledge of God independently of help from special revelation and, accordingly, relies on reasoning, and especially on arguments for the existence of God which provide justification for belief in

---

1. The major change to this chapter since its initial publication in *Philosophia Christi* is the inclusion of some insights from Linda Zagzebski on what is known in philosophy as the Gettier Problem.

God. Reformed epistemology, informed by the latter view, considers such arguments unnecessary.

My concern in this chapter is: Does Plantinga describe conditions necessary and sufficient for the difference between mere true belief and knowledge? I think he does, but not for all instances of knowledge. There are different kinds of knowledge, and the things we know are warranted in different ways. Some beliefs require only the conditions Plantinga describes, but others require justification. Accordingly, both responses regarding the task of epistemology have a place, and, thus, so do both natural theology and Reformed epistemology.

Actually, we must be just a little bit more precise than this, for, as Linda Zagzebski shows, there is a complication arising from what philosophers call the "Gettier Problem." As long as warrant, however we define it, is something that helps us believe the truth without fully *guaranteeing* that we will believe it, there is a possibility that warrant will fail to achieve true belief but that a warranted belief will be true anyway by sheer good luck. This means only that a definition of warrant cannot be complete unless the definition either states that warrant provides a 100% guarantee of true belief or else says *something* about luck. Accordingly, even for beliefs *not* requiring justification, the conditions Plantinga describes are not *quite* sufficient to make the difference between knowledge and mere true belief; it is also necessary that those conditions, and not luck, are what lead a person to true belief; his true belief must not be an accident.

I will first look at three notable, and distinct, definitions of the word warrant from *Warrant and Proper Function*; following that, I will describe Plantinga's arguments concerning warrant in *Warrant: The Current Debate*.[2] Next, I will describe BonJour's arguments against the sufficiency of Plantinga's idea of warrant in his article "Plantinga on Knowledge and Proper Function." Then I will suggest a modification of Plantinga's notion of warrant that allows for a fuller description of the necessary and sufficient conditions for warrant, a definition which accounts for different kinds of knowledge. I will explain two advantages of this expanded definition of warrant: that it successfully counters BonJour's arguments and that it explains several seemingly contradictory remarks of Plantinga. Next, a pause will be necessary in order to respond to Zagzebski and give a more complete definition of warrant. Finally, I will apply this expanded definition of warrant to the dispute between natural theology and Reformed epistemology. I will show that my expanded definition of warrant satisfies some of the concerns of, or is anticipated by, some of Plantinga's other critics, including

---

2. Hereafter abbreviated in notes as *WCD* and *WPF*.

John Greco, Duncan Pritchard, Michael Czapkay Suddoth, and John Zeis. And I will suggest that, based on Plantinga's own definitions of warrant, natural theology has an important role within the contours of a Plantinginian epistemology.

DEFINITIONS OF WARRANT IN *WARRANT AND PROPER FUNCTION*

Let us consider three definitions of warrant offered by Plantinga. The most general of the three comes in the Preface to *Warrant and Proper Function*, where warrant is described as that "quality or quantity enough of which, together with truth and belief, is sufficient for knowledge."[3]

Throughout *Warrant and Proper Function* Plantinga describes warrant in terms of the proper functioning of our cognitive faculties. The first chapter of the volume, appropriately entitled "Warrant: A First Approximation," describes warrant in these terms:

> [W]e may say that a belief B has warrant for S if and only if the relevant segments [of the design plan] (the segments involved in the production of B) are functioning property in a cognitive environment sufficiently similar to that for which S's faculties are designed; and the modules of the design plan governing the production of B are (1) aimed at truth, and (2) such that there is a high objective probability that a belief formed in accordance with those modules (in that sort of cognitive environment) is true; and the more firmly S believes B the more warrant B has for S.[4]

Here we are told that these conditions describing the proper functioning of our cognitive faculties are necessary and sufficient for warrant. After several "Objections and Refinements" in the second chapter of *Warrant and Proper Function*, we are given this description of warrant:

---

3. Plantinga, *WPF*, v. *WCD* defines warrant as "that, whatever precisely it is, which together with truth makes the difference between knowledge and mere true belief," *WCD*, 3. The definitions are subtly different. "Warrant" may, as in *WPF*, be defined as that *enough of which* makes the difference between knowledge and mere true belief. Or, as in *WCD*, "warrant" may denote the same quality *when there is enough* of it to make the difference. The former definition is the more general sense of warrant, the latter the more specific. "Warrant" in the first sense comes in degrees; when the degree is high enough to make the difference between knowledge and mere true belief, "warrant" in the second sense is present.

4. Plantinga, *WPF*, 19.

[A] belief has warrant for me only if (1) it has been produced in me by cognitive faculties that are working properly (functioning as they ought to, subject to no cognitive dysfunction) in a cognitive environment that is appropriate for my kinds of cognitive faculties, (2) the segment of the design plan governing the production of that belief is aimed at the production of true beliefs, and (3) there is a high statistical probability that a belief produced under those conditions will be true.[5]

Three conditions, then, are necessary for warrant. There is the condition that my cognitive faculties be functioning properly in the right environment, the condition that they be aimed at producing true beliefs,[6] and the condition that beliefs formed by said faculties in said environment are usually true. For simplicity's sake I will refer to these three conditions taken together simply as *proper function*, and to the failure to obtain of just one of these conditions as *improper function*.

Since it is the refined one, the third definition of warrant supersedes the second.[7] While the "first approximation" describes several conditions of warrant in terms of necessity and sufficiency ("if and only if"), the refined definition simply describes several conditions in terms of necessity ("only if"). Since warrant is described the final time in terms of necessity but not in terms of sufficiency, we infer that the description of warrant does not give necessary and sufficient conditions for warrant in *all* cases of knowledge. There may be cases in which these conditions are necessary but not sufficient for the difference between knowledge and mere true belief. This suggests that justification may also be necessary for warrant in some cases.

---

5. Plantinga, WPF, 46–47.

6. As opposed to the faculty that provides the "optimistic overrider," for a discussion of which see Plantinga, WPF, 42.

7. In this I disagree with Richard Feldman, Peter J. Markie, and Michael Czapkay Suddoth, who take the definition of warrant given on page 19 of WPF as primary. Feldman, "Plantinga, Gettier, and Warrant," 209; Markie, "Degrees of Warrant," 222; Suddoth, "The Internalist Character and Evidentialist Implications," 167. In addition to pages 19 and 46–47 of WPF, Markie references page ix of the Preface, in which Plantinga speaks of "the conditions necessary and sufficient for the central paradigmatic core of our conception of warrant." Markie also notes that the language of "the central core of our concept of warrant" appears again on page 47 of WPF. Suddoth does not reference page 19 but presumably has it in mind in saying that, according to Plantinga, "a belief has warrant, roughly, just if" it is produced by proper function. The titles of the first two chapters of WPF are my main reason for disagreeing with Markie, Feldman, and Suddoth, but not my only, as I will explain in the next section. I will return to the issue of "the central core" of the concept of warrant in Section IV.

PROPER FUNCTION DESCRIBED AS ALWAYS NECESSARY AND SOMETIMES SUFFICIENT IN *WARRANT: THE CURRENT DEBATE*

This is corroborated by a careful reading of *Warrant: The Current Debate*, in which Plantinga invariably describes other notions of warrant as *insufficient* for the difference between knowledge and mere true belief; each time he does so, an example of improper function is provided to demonstrate the insufficiency of the other alleged conditions for warrant. Furthermore, it is said of several of the other epistemological views that they do not even describe conditions *necessary* for warrant; in these situations, an example reminiscent of Thomas Reid's principles of commonsense is typically used as an example.[8] The effect of Plantinga's arguments here is to support the thesis that proper function is always necessary for warrant, and sufficient in at least some cases.

- Classical Chisholmian internalism (chapter 2) is *insufficient* for warrant because of the possibility of improper function.[9] From this we are meant to infer that proper function is at least *necessary* for warrant; and the same is true of every other instance in which Plantinga describes another epistemological view as describing conditions insufficient for warrant. Furthermore, Plantinga believes that classical Chisholmian internalism is not even *necessary* for warrant because we can imagine a situation in which a person by obsessing over justification comes to doubt his self-presenting beliefs.[10] Without justification there would have been warrant, so justification is not necessary for warrant. From this we infer that proper function is *sufficient* for warrant in at least some cases. The cases given as examples are sensory beliefs, one of Reid's genres of naturally trustworthy commonsense belief.

- Post-classical Chisholmian internalism (*Warrant: The Current Debate*, chapter 3) is insufficient for warrant because of the possibility of improper function.[11] There is no objection that it is not necessary for warrant.

---

8. For a list of twelve such types of beliefs, see Reid, "Essays on the Intellectual Powers of Man," Essay 6, chapter 5, pages 151–63.
9. Plantinga, *WCD*, 42–43.
10. Plantinga, *WCD*, 45.
11. Plantinga, *WCD*, 63–65.

- Coherentism (chapter 4) is insufficient for warrant because of the possibility of improper function.[12] Given such beliefs as memory beliefs (another Reidian case), coherence is unnecessary for at least some degree of warrant in at least some cases.[13]
- BonJourian coherentism (chapter 5) is insufficient for warrant because of the possibility of improper function.[14] It is not even necessary for some degree of warrant in several cases, including sensory and memory beliefs.[15]
- Bayesian coherentism (chapter 6) is insufficient for warrant because of the possibility of improper function.[16] It is not necessary for some degree of warrant in cases such as the truths of reason and my belief about my spatial location (at least one of which, the truths of reason, is certainly a Reidian counterexample).[17]
- Pollockian quasi-internalism (chapter 8) is insufficient for warrant because of the possibility of improper function.[18] I find no charge that it is not even necessary for warrant.
- Alstonian justification (chapter 9, section I) is insufficient for warrant because of the possibility of improper function.[19] Alston himself never claims that it is necessary.[20]
- Dretskian reliabilism (chapter 9, section II) is insufficient for warrant because of the possibility of improper function.[21] Plantinga does not say that it is not so much as necessary for warrant (which might be expected, as we are dealing with a form of externalism, and so are a little bit closer to Plantinga's own view).
- The old Goldman's reliabilism (chapter 9, section III.A) is insufficient for warrant because of the possibility of improper function.[22] The new Goldman's reliabilism (chapter 9, section III.B) is insufficient for

---

12. Plantinga, *WCD*, 80–82.
13. Plantinga, *WCD*, 82–83.
14. Plantinga, *WCD*, 110–12.
15. Plantinga, *WCD*, 112.
16. Plantinga, *WCD*, 128–29.
17. Plantinga, *WCD*, 126.
18. Plantinga, *WCD*, 167–68.
19. Plantinga, *WCD*, 190–92.
20. Plantinga, *WCD*, 190.
21. Plantinga, *WCD*, 197.
22. Plantinga, *WCD*, 199.

warrant for the same reason.[23] Plantinga does not say that either the new or the old Goldman's reliabilism is not so much as necessary for warrant (again, this might be expected from his encounter with a form of externalism).

Here, then, is the final tally: Ten out of ten views are charged with *insufficiency* because of the possibility of improper function; from this we infer that proper function is at least *necessary* for warrant. Four times Plantinga argues that the notions of warrant in question are *not even necessary* for warrant; the cases given as evidence are reminiscent of Reid's principles of commonsense. From this we infer that proper function is *sufficient* for warrant in at least some cases.

With this in mind, we may take Plantinga as being confident that proper function is always necessary for warrant as well as sufficient for at least a degree of warrant in at least some cases.

BONJOUR *CONTRA* PLANTINGA

I now turn to BonJour's contribution. BonJour's main concern in "Plantinga on Knowledge and Proper Function"[24] is whether proper function is sufficient for warrant. First, BonJour argues that, although it is plausible that the conditions in Plantinga's proper functionalist account are necessary for knowledge, they may not be sufficient.[25] Second, he argues that Plantinga's account leads to skepticism.

---

23. Plantinga, *WCD*, 205–8.

24. BonJour, "Plantinga on Knowledge and Proper Function," 47–71.

25. BonJour also describes situations that suggest proper function is not always necessary for what we intuitively think of as knowledge. A mutant who is the first of his kind to possess a mutation conferring on the species a reliable faculty for the production of true beliefs cannot be said to have proper function in the full Plantingian sense, since prior to the activity of natural selection there is no "design" and hence no "design plan." See BonJour, "Plantinga on Knowledge and Proper Function," 61–62. Counterexamples of this sort do not call for justification; as a rigorous role for justification is the main thrust of BonJour's argument, I have consigned this issue to a footnote. But I provide below two possible responses to BonJour's intriguing counterexample.

One response is to disassociate the notion of a design plan from raw natural selection; in the later chapters of *WPF* Plantinga does in fact argue that the notion of a design plan works best when associated with theism. An alternative response is to disassociate the notion of proper function from the notion of a design plan; this approach could take inspiration from the second of Ernest Sosa's contributions to *Warrant in Contemporary Epistemology*, "Proper Function and Virtue Epistemology," in which Sosa argues that the notion of proper function makes sense without teleological implications (253–70).

The better part of BonJour's article is spent in objecting to Plantinga's contention that warrant is sufficient for knowledge. His attack is two-pronged, dealing first with Plantinga's relation to Edmund Gettier and second with the sort of knowledge that is uniquely human. To begin with, BonJour notes that epistemologists have long known of four necessary conditions for knowledge. There are belief, truth, and a third *something* that is often described as "justification;" what Gettier showed is that the third condition is not always sufficient.[26] (I will return to Gettier myself in due time, but let's stick with BonJour for now!) So a fourth condition is needed, one "intended to exclude" Gettier cases; BonJour adapts from Peter Unger a description of the fourth condition, "that it not be an *accident* in relation to whatever satisfies the third condition that the belief is true."[27] BonJour notes Plantinga's recurrent attempts to use examples of improper function to show that the various internalist views are insufficient for warrant.[28] While this may show that the conditions pointed to by internalists are insufficient, it does not show that they are not at least necessary; it is possible that proper function describes that annoying little fourth condition Gettier showed we were missing; it is possible that Plantinga's typical improper function counterexample "is just a Gettier case."[29] Thus proper function may be necessary but, by itself, insufficient for warrant.

BonJour's strategy of examining proper function in light of Gettier is appropriate. Plantinga believes that externalist epistemologies escape the Gettier problems that plague internalism.[30] After convincing an internalist that proper function is at least necessary for knowledge, an externalist might ask why, if we have proper function, we should even need anything else to satisfy the gap between mere true belief and knowledge. In BonJour's words, "this in turn might seem to make the internalist third condition merely idle, with the fourth condition, which is after all fundamentally externalist in character, doing all the real work."[31] Yet this does not show that there is no condition for knowledge such as the internalists point to:

> [E]ven if some such argument succeeds in the end in showing that the third condition of knowledge must itself have an externalist ingredient of some sort, it still does not show . . . that a *purely* externalist third condition, one according to which the

26. BonJour, "Plantinga on Knowledge and Proper Function," 49.
27. BonJour, "Plantinga on Knowledge and Proper Function," 49–50.
28. BonJour, "Plantinga on Knowledge and Proper Function," 50.
29. BonJour, "Plantinga on Knowledge and Proper Function," 51.
30. Plantinga, *WPF*, 31–37, esp. 36–7.
31. BonJour, "Plantinga on Knowledge and Proper Function," 53.

possessor of a "warranted" belief need not have even a subjective reason for thinking it to be true, is acceptable.[32]

Even if externalist factors are necessary, this would not entail that they are sufficient; accordingly, BonJour believes that a significant role remains for internalist justification.

Moving on to the second prong of the same theme, BonJour believes that we cannot be confident that proper function is "clear and unequivocal enough to be very strongly relied on," for there may be more than one sort of knowledge.[33] Merely animal knowledge could be gained by proper function of the sort described by Plantinga, but the rational knowledge that is uniquely human may require some sort of justification.[34] Uniquely human knowledge seems to require more than just proper function; therefore, proper function is not sufficient for specifically human knowledge.

On to BonJour's contention that Plantinga's epistemology leads to skepticism.[35] To quote BonJour, "do we, on Plantinga's view, have any good (non-question-begging) reasons of any sort for thinking either (1) that most or even any of our beliefs in the area in question are true, or (2) that Plantinga's conditions for warrant are satisfied for most or even any of those beliefs?"[36] How would we know a belief formed by proper function from a belief formed by improper function? What other than some form of internalist justification can answer this probing question? More than an appeal to proper function is required if we are to have confidence in our beliefs.

REFINING PLANTINGA'S NOTION OF WARRANT

In this section I will briefly respond to his objection that proper function is not sufficient for warrant. Then I will offer an expanded definition of warrant that accounts for different sorts of knowledge. Next, I will comment on some implications of the expanded definition, including how it can handle BonJour's charge that Plantinga's epistemology implies skepticism and how it explains several puzzling remarks of Plantinga. After a necessary return to Gettier, in the final section of this article I will show how this expanded definition of warrant serves to mediate the conflict between Reformed

32. BonJour, "Plantinga on Knowledge and Proper Function," 55.
33. BonJour, "Plantinga on Knowledge and Proper Function," 59.
34. BonJour, "Plantinga on Knowledge and Proper Function," 59–60.
35. I think that veterans of the Plantingianly epistemological will notice here a resemblance of BonJour's charge to the famous Great Pumpkin objection leveled against Reformed epistemology back in the 1980s.
36. BonJour, "Plantinga on Knowledge and Proper Function," 63.

epistemology and natural theology, and will show that it satisfies the concerns of others among his critics, or is anticipated by their arguments.

BonJour is compelling when he says that the mere necessity of proper function would not demonstrate its sufficiency for warrant; so I agree with the first prong of his attack. Furthermore, since we humans have a capacity for reason beyond that of animals, it would seem good to describe a necessary role for reason to play in lending warrant to at least some of our beliefs; thus I lend my support to the second prong.

But we have different kinds of knowledge, and the beliefs involved receive warrant in different ways. In light of the foregoing considerations I offer this expanded definition of warrant, that enough of which makes the difference between knowledge and mere true belief:

> A belief has warrant for me if and only if:
>
> (1) The cognitive faculties involved in producing the belief are (a) working properly (functioning as they ought to, subject to no cognitive dysfunction) in a cognitive environment that is appropriate for my kinds of cognitive faculties, (b) the segment of the design plan governing the production of that belief is aimed at the production of true beliefs, and (c) there is a high statistical probability that a belief produced under those conditions will be true,
>
> AND
>
> (2) the belief is either (d) efficiently produced by these faculties, OR (e) justified.

Condition 1 recaps Plantinga's three conditions for the proper functioning of our cognitive faculties. All faculties involved in the production of a belief have to be aimed at the truth and functioning properly in the right environment in order for that belief to have warrant. If the faculties are sufficient to produce that belief (2d), then that belief is warranted. If the faculties are insufficient to produce that belief, then some form of justification will be necessary (2e) for providing warrant. Even in these latter cases, note that proper function (1) is still necessary because cognitive faculties are involved in the production of all our beliefs. For reason itself is a faculty that must be functioning properly in an appropriate environment in order for a person to believe something on the basis of justification.

This definition describes the conditions for warrant as they apply to different kinds of knowledge. First, there are beliefs for which proper function alone is insufficient to confer any degree of warrant, and for which justification is therefore necessary for warrant. Such beliefs include anything I can only properly believe solely on the basis of evidence. We need more than proper function for some beliefs to be warranted. (Again, proper function is still necessary for the warrant of these beliefs, since reason is a faculty.)[37] Second, there are beliefs for which justification is not necessary for at least a degree of warrant. Readily available examples are Reidian beliefs such as sensory beliefs and memory beliefs. Proper function is all we need for such beliefs to be warranted.

This latter category can be further broken down into two subcategories. There are those beliefs for which proper function provides a degree of warrant sufficient to make the difference between knowledge and mere true belief, and those for which proper function provides a degree of warrant insufficient for this.[38] Beliefs in the latter subcategory require justification for a person to really *know* them. Beliefs in the former subcategory are properly basic, such that they can be responsibly believed without supporting evidence; they can be *known* without justification.

So some beliefs which possess a degree of warrant via proper function alone require a higher degree of warrant via justification before they can really be *known*. Furthermore, nothing prevents justification from providing even properly basic beliefs with a higher degree of warrant than proper function alone can provide. There are beliefs for which we can get a good measure of warrant by proper function, but for which additional warrant through justification doesn't hurt—and frequently helps.

In short, the "OR" in my expanded definition of warrant is inclusive. Some beliefs are described by both 2d and 2e. Although there are some beliefs warranted through justification which cannot also be warranted by proper function alone, there is a large region of overlap. A belief can be warranted by proper function alone, yet be *more* warranted through justification. Indeed, most, if not all, beliefs warranted by proper function alone could receive a higher degree of warrant through justification. This is sometimes helpful for knowers of beliefs in the first subcategory described by 2d. It is *essential* that beliefs only in the second subcategory be warranted through justification if they are to be known at all.

In this way my expanded definition of warrant answers BonJour's charge that skepticism follows from an appeal to proper function. Plantinga

---

37. According to Michael Bergmann, Plantinga's account needs an additional condition for warrant—a warranted belief cannot be one which the evidence shows is false. I disagree: Since reason is a faculty and since believing what is shown to be false is believing without a proper use of reason, believing against defeaters is not consistent with proper function. See Bergmann, *Justification without Awareness*, chapter 5.

38. Or, those beliefs which are warranted according to Plantinga, *WCD*, 3, and those which are only warranted according to *WPF*, v. See above, footnote 3.

answers that charge by pointing out that "there is nothing in my account of warrant to suggest" that there is no room for fact-checking of beliefs.[39] He is right, but we can take this further. The warrant of beliefs by proper function need not preclude additional warrant for those same beliefs through justification. Indeed, Plantinga acknowledges that justification may be a necessary condition for some kinds of knowledge,[40] and that natural theology "might increase the degree of warrant," perhaps quite significantly, for the belief in God.[41]

This distinction between categories of knowledge helps to explain some other, more puzzling remarks of Plantinga. On the one hand, he says he intends "to give necessary and sufficient conditions for warrant."[42] But, on the other hand, he concedes the possibility of knowledge that requires a degree of justification, saying "perhaps there is also an important variety of knowledge for which explanatory coherence is crucial."[43] Again, he says that "at least certain kinds of knowledge demand the sort of coherence of which he [Keith Lehrer] speaks."[44] How can justification via coherence be necessary if proper function, by itself, is necessary and sufficient for knowledge? The answer is that Plantinga thinks proper function is necessary and sufficient for warrant for beliefs that are part of "the central paradigmatic core of knowledge,"[45] a core which he thinks consists of beliefs like those described by my condition 2d. But outside the core are other cases of knowledge for which proper function is not sufficient and for which justification is necessary, those described by condition 2e. When it comes to these beliefs, the conception of the task of epistemology as providing rules for a knower to follow in order to achieve justification is surely correct. Accordingly, as I shall soon explain, natural theology, which applies this conventional epistemological view to religious epistemology, is also correct when it comes

---

39. Plantinga, "Respondeo," 340–41.

40. Plantinga says, "I don't think (epistemic) justification construed deontologically is either necessary or sufficient for *warrant*; a person can fulfill all relevant intellectual duties but fail to know, and a person can know (so I am inclined to think, anyway) even when flouting intellectual duties." But then he adds, "there may be certain *kinds* of knowledge such that satisfaction of intellectual duty is a necessary condition of possessing knowledge of *those* kinds, even if it is neither necessary nor sufficient for knowledge in general." See Plantinga, "Reliabilism, Analyses and Defeaters," 447.

41. Plantinga, "Prospects for Natural Theology," 311–12.

42. Footnote 43 to Plantinga, "Respondeo" in *Warrant in Contemporary Epistemology*, 377.

43. Plantinga, "Respondeo," 332.

44. Plantinga, "Respondeo," 333.

45. Plantinga, *WPF*, ix.

to religious beliefs described by 2e only, as well as to at least some beliefs described by 2d.

WHAT ABOUT LUCK? REFINING OUR DEFINITION OF WARRANT

Unfortunately, this definition of warrant is still incomplete, and to understand why we must consider the Gettier Problem.

Epistemologists have known for millennia that knowledge needs three things. First, there is belief—I don't know what I don't even believe. Second, there is truth—I don't know what is *false*. (Speaking loosely, we sometimes refer to things people "know" that aren't true; it would be more precise to refer to things people *think* they know or are very *confident* that they know which, unfortunately, are not true and not actually known either.) Third, there is a third thing mentioned by Socrates in Plato's *Meno*—a third thing which ties belief to truth. This third thing would make true belief more than a happy accident or something that just happens from time to time. It would help our beliefs be, with some degree of consistency, true ones. It would lead us, with regularity, to the truth. Presumably, this third thing is, or at least has something to do with, having reason, evidence, justification, or warrant for our beliefs.

Thus it was that, for quite some time, epistemologists tended to describe knowledge as if it were just those three things; knowledge was justified true belief, or something rather similar. In 1963, however, Edmund Gettier demolished this—as it now seems in retrospect—careless simplicity in his article "Is Justified True Belief Knowledge?"[46] In a remarkably short article—less than three full pages!—Gettier transformed epistemology. All he had to do was give a couple of thought experiments in which a person has justified true belief but does not have knowledge. Briefly, to use his first example, suppose that Smith and Jones are competing for the same job, that Smith has good evidence that Jones will get the job, that Smith also has good evidence that Jones has ten coins in his pocket, that Smith has absentmindedly forgotten that he *also* has ten coins in his pocket, and that *Smith* rather than Jones is going to get the job. So Smith has good evidence that the man who will get the job has ten coins in his pocket, and believes it. Yet, although the belief is true, it is not *knowledge*.

And there Gettier leaves us. Zagzebski later came along with "The Inescapability of Gettier Problems" in 1994 to finish the job.[47] Zagzebski

---

46. Gettier, "Is Justified True Belief Knowledge?," 121–23.
47. Zagzebski, "The Inescapability of Gettier Problems," 65–73.

explains with perfect clarity just what is going on with the Gettier Problem. We understand that that third thing rarely if ever can *guarantee* truth. Reason, evidence, justification, warrant, or however else we may care to describe it—it just gives us good probability that what we believe is true. (The skeptical thought experiments of the philosophers help to confirm this—it is notoriously difficult to give a proof establishing with 100% certainty that I am not in the Matrix, or a brain in a vat, or deceived by the powerful demon Descartes described.) It's no problem for the definition of knowledge that this third thing fails to give a perfect, 100% guarantee of truth; reasoned, justified, evidenced, or warranted *false* belief is not knowledge, and no one was saying it was. Sometimes, through bad luck, reason, justification, evidence, or warrant fail to give us the truth. No problem. But what Gettier showed is that epistemologists had failed to account for the rare possibility that that third thing might fail to lead us to the truth while the belief to which it leads us is *still* true—by sheer good luck!

And, as Zagzebski explains, there is no avoiding this possibility just as long as we recognize that the third thing does not *guarantee* truth. Nor is there any escape by adding to our definitions of knowledge some clever account of a fourth thing, or a fifth thing. As long as we recognize that knowledge is true belief plus *some* thing or things to connect belief to truth—some thing or things which can sometimes fail to make that connection—there is always a possible Gettier case that shows the incompleteness of our definition of knowledge. The third thing, or set of things, can fail through bad luck, but along comes a bit of *good* luck and gives us true belief anyway! Towards the end of her article, Zagzebski thus politely informs us of the unavoidable truth: We only have two conceivable strategies for giving a complete definition of knowledge.[48] *One* strategy would be to say that knowledge requires something which *guarantees* truth. And then we are left with precious little we can say we *know* beyond Descartes's "I think, therefore I am." Then I do not know that the earth orbits the sun, that Socrates was a philosopher, or even that two and two make four, for all this knowledge depends on fallible ways of knowing. The *other* strategy is the better one: Include luck in our definition of knowledge.

This doesn't have to be as weird as it may sound. It doesn't mean knowledge is simply a matter of luck. It means that my belief's being true should not be a matter of luck rather than a matter of my having *that third thing*. A belief to which my reason, justification, evidence, or warrant leads me should not just *happen* to be true. My reason, justification, evidence or warrant should have done their job. We could simply state that knowledge

---

48. Zagzebski, "The Inescapability of Gettier Problems," 72.

equals true belief plus that third thing *plus some good luck*. Alternatively, we could just say that knowledge equals true belief plus that third thing plus the additional condition that *bad* luck did not screw things up—knowledge equals true belief plus that third thing *plus an absence of bad luck*. Or we might just say that knowledge is true belief plus that third thing plus the additional condition that the third thing happened to *work* this time.

Now, despite Plantinga's optimism, Zagzebski's article explains that his account cannot avoid vulnerability to Gettier cases.[49] The vulnerability is built right into his epistemology, for his conditions for warrant are not taken to be a 100% guarantee of truth.

Neither can my modified Plantingian epistemology avoid this weakness, unless I take Zagzebski's advice. I therefore do so now. Here is what I take to be a better expanded definition of warrant, that enough of which makes the difference between knowledge and mere true belief:

> A belief has warrant for me if and only if:
>
> (1) The cognitive faculties involved in producing the belief are (a) working properly (functioning as they ought to, subject to no cognitive dysfunction) in a cognitive environment that is appropriate for my kinds of cognitive faculties, (b) the segment of the design plan governing the production of that belief is aimed at the production of true beliefs, and (c) there is a high statistical probability that a belief produced under those conditions will be true,
>
> AND
>
> (2) the belief is either (d) efficiently produced by these faculties, OR (e) justified,
>
> AND
>
> (3) whatever faculties have produced this belief in me did not, in this case, fail to lead me to the truth.

This adjustment is necessary for crafting a complete definition of warrant. However, I regard it as the smallest piece of the definition of warrant, and in the next section of this chapter we can assume that this condition is already in place when I refer to the other conditions for warrant.

---

49. Zagzebski, "The Inescapability of Gettier Problems," 66–69. For another look at why Plantingian epistemology is vulnerable to Gettier cases, see Evan Fales, Review, 355–58.

AN APPLICATION TO RELIGIOUS EPISTEMOLOGY

I now turn to religious epistemology. Laying out this description of the necessary and sufficient conditions for warrant has important implications for mediating a significant dispute over the status of religious beliefs. Plantinga believes that, for some religious beliefs to have warrant, proper function is sufficient.[50] Natural theology seeks to justify religious beliefs, but the Reformed epistemologist thinks natural theology and the justification it seeks for religious belief are unnecessary. Perhaps the debate between Reformed epistemology and natural theology is partly the result of confusion as to whether religious beliefs are the sort of beliefs which properly functioning faculties are able to efficiently produce.

This expanded account of the necessary and sufficient conditions for warrant makes it possible to mediate the dispute, as long as it is possible for at least some religious beliefs to receive a degree of warrant through properly functioning faculties and for some (perhaps the same) religious beliefs to receive a degree of warrant through justification. That is, if some religious beliefs fall into the category described by 2d, then the Reformed epistemologists are right that justification is not necessary for their being conferred some degree of warrant. But natural theology is right to seek justification for religious beliefs described by 2e, for such beliefs are warranted in virtue of being justified.

Moreover, since 2d and 2e are not mutually exclusive, justification can also confer warrant on religious beliefs described by 2d. For example, if the *sensus divinitatis* is a cognitive faculty able to provide warrant for the belief that God exists, then the belief that God exists is described by 2d for those in whom it is functioning properly. But the definition of warrant is indexical to a believer; a belief has warrant "for me" under the right conditions. Thus, for anyone in whom the *sensus divinitatis* is *not* functioning properly, the belief that God exists will not be warranted by the *sensus divinitatis*; but justification can confer warrant on that belief. For such a person, the belief that God exists is described by 2e. For that matter, for a person who is aware of objections to existence of God or of the fact that others do not have the same belief but in whom the *sensus divinitatis* is functioning properly, justification may provide an additional, and welcome, degree of warrant for the belief that God exists; it can help assure this believer that religious pluralism and the various objections waged against the existence of God do not constitute defeaters for religious belief.

---

50. See Plantinga, *God and Other Minds*, 271; Part IV of Plantinga, "Reason and Belief in God," 16–93; and Plantinga, *Warranted Christian Belief*.

The development in Plantingian epistemology I propose accommodates some of the concerns of Plantinga's critics. I will cite four examples. To begin with, John Greco[51] argues that praiseworthiness in believing is a necessary condition for knowledge, and that coherence among one's beliefs, experiences, and cognitive faculties is a source of praiseworthiness. Moreover, this coherence is a necessary condition for religious knowledge for a theist in "epistemically hostile conditions," and most theists in modern society these days are in such conditions due to the challenge to religious belief posed by evil as well as widespread disbelief in and disagreement with one's own religious beliefs. Though these may trouble a religious believer, natural theology can help by justifying religious belief. This is rather like my analysis of warrant in that, even for the believer whose *sensus divinitatis* is functioning properly, natural theology's project of justifying religious belief can confer a higher degree of warrant than proper function alone.

Duncan Pritchard[52] adopts Keith DeRose's "foundherentist" proposal (itself inspired by Susan Haack): that there are different sorts of beliefs, some of which are properly basic and others of which are only warranted by their coherence with other beliefs. Pritchard develops this model using virtue epistemology, saying that a necessary condition for non-properly basic beliefs to possess "positive epistemic status" is that they be held as a result of the operation of reflective virtues. Thus: "certain sorts of knowledge" only require proper function, "whereas other sorts of knowledge . . . might solely depend upon the reflective virtues. In between one will find the vast majority of knowledge that requires a mixture" of proper function and reflection.[53] This parallels nicely my description of different kinds of knowledge, some of which require only proper function in addition to true belief, and others of which require a mixture of proper function and some degree of justification. Pritchard's category of beliefs knowing which requires only proper function parallels my first subcategory of beliefs described by 2d, and his category of beliefs knowing which requires a mixture of proper function and reflection parallels my second subcategory. The difference is that my model, treating reason as a faculty which must function properly in order for reflective virtue to take place, treats proper function as always necessary; so Pritchard's category of beliefs whose warrant requires *only* reflection parallels those beliefs which on my model are described by 2e but not by 2d.

Michael Czapkay Suddoth argues that Plantinga's inclusion of a defeater system in his description of the cognitive design plan entails that there

---

51. Greco, "Is Natural Theology Necessary for Theistic Knowledge?," 168–98.
52. Pritchard, "Reforming Reformed Epistemology," 43–66.
53. Pritchard, "Reforming Reformed Epistemology," 63–64.

are, at least sometimes, internalist requirements for warrant.[54] Specifically, when a believer has a defeater for a belief, evidence constituting a defeater for that defeater is necessary for warrant to be present. Suddoth emphasizes the problem of evil as a defeater for theistic belief, and evidence provided by natural theology as defeating that defeater. This is remarkably similar to my development of Plantingian epistemology in that, without downplaying the importance of proper function, it describes the necessity of reason and evidence for some beliefs to be warranted, and concludes that natural theology has a place in Plantingian epistemology.

Finally, John Zeis argues that Plantinga's is not "a complete epistemological theory" because it fails to provide an adequate criterion for distinguishing warranted from non-warranted belief.[55] There ought to be a way of "establishing or defending warrant claims."[56] The only way to know whether a belief is warranted via proper function is to examine the evidence for it. In other words, *justification* of a belief is the best way of knowing whether it has warrant. As usual, the really interesting cases are religious beliefs. According to Zeis, even if a religious belief is warranted by proper function, natural theology is (along with Scripture, the church, and the fruits of the Spirit) one of the things that provides evidence *that* it is warranted. Moreover, justification might provide a higher degree of warrant for the belief than proper function alone can provide, or might be necessary for some sorts of knowledge; as Zeis notes, Plantinga himself says as much.[57] This is consistent with my proposal, in that a religious belief warranted by proper function alone can receive a higher degree of warrant through the justification provided by natural theology.

In sum, even if some religious beliefs are warranted through proper function alone, this does not preclude that other religious beliefs require justification for their warrant. Religious beliefs that *can* be warranted through proper function may not *in actuality* be warranted in this way for every believer, but even so nothing prevents them from receiving warrant through justification. Finally, even when these beliefs possess a degree of warrant through proper function alone, they can receive an additional degree of

---

54. Suddoth, "The Internalist Character and Evidentialist Implications."

55. Zeis, "Plantinga's Theory of Warrant," 23–38. See also Zeis, "A Foundherentist Conception," 133–60.

56. Zeis, "Plantinga's Theory of Warrant," 32

57. Zeis, "Plantinga's Theory of Warrant," 36–37. The Plantinga remarks to which he refers are found in "Reliabilism, Analyses and Defeaters" and "Prospects for Natural Theology." See above for my citation of these articles. In Zeis's earlier responses to Plantinga's earlier work, he was already developing the same insights; see Zeis, "Natural Theology: Reformed?," 48–78.

warrant through justification. These considerations suggest that Plantinga's arguments for the importance of proper function for warrant do not preclude that reasoned justification is sometimes necessary and often helpful even when it is not necessary. Plantinga's critics suggest as much. But, if my analysis is correct, so do Plantinga's own definitions of warrant and arguments for the importance of proper function. Accordingly, the project of natural theology has an important role within a Plantingian epistemology.

So, more generally, do other ways of giving evidence for faith. Alongside a quick look at the idea of believing without evidence, chapters 3–6 will consider some views on how that might be done.

WORKS CITED

Bergmann, Michael. *Justification without Awareness: A Defense of Epistemic Externalism.* Oxford: Oxford University Press, 2006.

Bonjour, Laurence. "Plantinga on Knowledge and Proper Function." In *Warrant in Contemporary Epistemology*, edited by Jonathan L. Kvanvig, 47–71. Lanham, MD: Rowman & Littlefield, 1996.

Fales, Evan. Review of Alvin Plantinga, *Warranted Christian Belief. Noûs* 37.2 (2003) 353–70.

Feldman, Richard. "Plantinga, Gettier, and Warrant." In *Warrant in Contemporary Epistemology*, edited by Jonathan Kvanvig, 199–220. Lanham, MD: Rowman & Littlefield, 1996.

Gettier, Edmund. "Is Justified True Belief Knowledge?" *Analysis* 23.6 (1963) 121–23.

Greco, John. "Is Natural Theology Necessary for Theistic Knowledge?" In *Rational Faith: Catholic Responses to Reformed Epistemology*, edited by Linda Zagzebski, 168–98. Notre Dame, IN: University of Notre Dame Press, 1993.

Markie, Peter J. "Degrees of Warrant." In *Warrant in Contemporary Epistemology*, edited by Jonathan Kvanvig, 221–38. Lanham, MD: Rowman & Littlefield, 1996.

Plantinga, Alvin. *God and Other Minds.* Ithaca, NY: Cornell University Press, 1967.

———. "Reason and Belief in God." In *Faith and Rationality*, edited by Alvin Plantinga and Nicholas Wolterstorff, 16–93. Notre Dame, IN: University of Notre Dame Press, 1983.

———. "Reliabilism, Analyses and Defeaters." *Philosophy and Phenomenological Research* 55.2 (1995) 427–64.

———. "Respondeo." In *Warrant in Contemporary Epistemology*, edited by Jonathan L. Kvanvig, 307–78. Lanham, MD: Rowman & Littlefield, 1996.

———. "Prospects for Natural Theology." In *Philosophical Perspectives 5: Philosophy of Religion, 1991*, edited by James E. Tomberlin, 287–315. Atascadero: Ridgeview, 1991.

———. *Warrant: The Current Debate.* New York: Oxford University Press, 1993.

———. *Warrant and Proper Function.* New York: Oxford University Press, 1993.

———. *Warranted Christian Belief.* New York: Oxford University Press, 2000.

Pritchard, Duncan. "Reforming Reformed Epistemology." *International Philosophical Quarterly* 43.1 (2003) 43–66.

Reid, Thomas. "Essays on the Intellectual Powers of Man." In *Epistemology: The Classic Readings*, edited by David E. Cooper. Oxford: Blackwell, 1999.

Sosa, Ernest. "Proper Function and Virtue Epistemology." In *Warrant in Contemporary Epistemology*, edited by Jonathan Kvanvig, 253–70. Lanham, MD: Rowman & Littlefield, 1996.

Suddoth, Michael Czapkay. "The Internalist Character and Evidentialist Implications of Plantingian Defeaters." *International Journal for Philosophy of Religion* 45 (1999) 167–87.

Zagzebski, Linda. "The Inescapability of Gettier Problems." *The Philosophical Quarterly* 44.174 (1994) 65–73.

Zeis, John. "A Foundherentist Conception of the Justification of Religious Belief." *International Journal for Philosophy of Religion* 58.3 (2005) 133–60.

———. "Natural Theology: Reformed?" In *Rational Faith: Catholic Responses to Reformed Epistemology*; edited by Linda Zagzebski, 48–78. Notre Dame, IN: University of Notre Dame Press, 1993.

———. "Plantinga's Theory of Warrant." *American Catholic Philosophical Quarterly* 72.1 (1998) 23–39.

3

Augustine and William James on the Rationality of Faith

AUGUSTINE AND WILLIAM JAMES are among the greatest defenders of religious faith in the history of thought. Their arguments on behalf of faith mark important connections between theology and philosophy, with further links to psychology, history, and social and political thought. Augustine argues that religious faith is trust and that trust is a normal and necessary way of believing, foundational to family and social life. It is also the proper way for us to get to the truth when we lack knowledge. Beginning with faith, we then work towards knowledge by means of philosophical contemplation. James, in "The Will to Believe," makes two pragmatic arguments for the rationality of faith. We do not know (yet) whether God exists, but faith meets a well-established criterion for rational decision-making. It is, at least for many of us, a highly consequential choice we must make between multiple possibilities that are open to us; it is a choice between the risk of believing something false and the risk of not believing something true, and in the absence of very clear evidence we may decide for ourselves which risk we prefer. James further explains that we may be able to experience God in the future and thereby gain knowledge, yet even this may be contingent on our willingness to believe.

I am not aiming to break any new ground on Augustine or James or to directly confront any scholarly debates on their texts; rather, I aim to compare and contrast their religious epistemologies, with a brief look towards future possible synthesis. This will help us to understand both thinkers better, and promises to enrich contemporary discussions of faith and reason through a better awareness of the past dialogue on the subject.

In both thinkers, faith is understood to be rational, to be practical, and to precede knowledge. Yet there are key differences. The object of faith in Augustine is Christian testimony from Christ, Scripture, and the church. James, however, is defending the rationality of whatever religious commitment may be of interest to us. Moreover, the eventual acquisition of knowledge, according to Augustine, relies mainly on philosophical contemplation whereas, according to James, it relies on experience. In other words, Augustine's analysis of faith and rationality is distinguished from James's in that the former is a Christian somewhat under the influence of Neoplatonist rationalism. James, however, is an empiricist and a pragmatist. These differences, however, may be less significant than they first appear, as I will show. After explaining Augustine and then James I will draw out the major points of comparison and contrast and suggest a few reasons their insights might be at least partially synthesized.

AUGUSTINE

Faith is trust—in one of Augustine's customary Latin terms, *fides*. Augustine consistently defends *fides* in Christ, the Bible, and the church as rational. This faith is epistemically on a par with faith in other areas of human life such as family relations, geography, and history—where trust reveals itself as both rational and practically necessary. Although it falls short of knowledge, which requires a full understanding of the truth, it is an appropriate and necessary way of getting to religious truth for most of us, and indeed a propaedeutic for knowledge of that truth. This knowledge will come after faith and by means of contemplation of the sort modeled by the Platonist philosophers.[1]

Let us consider some of the major texts.

In his earliest surviving writing, *Contra Academicos* or *Against the Academics*, Augustine offers an interesting analogy for faith (*c. Acad.* 3.15.34). Suppose two people are walking to Alexandria and come to a fork in the road. They do not know which way to go, but a local shepherd who happens to be present points down one way, saying that it is the way to Alexandria.

---

1. Much has been written on faith and reason in Augustine. The interested reader might consult Rist, "Faith and Reason," 26–39; Gilson, *The Christian Philosophy of Saint Augustine*, Part One, chapter 1; Van Fleteren, "Authority and Reason, Faith and Understanding," 33–71; MacDonald, "The Epistemology of Faith," 167–96; Matthews, *Augustine*, chapter 10; TeSelle, *Augustine*, chapter 2; King and Ballantyne, "Augustine on Testimony," 195–214; or Boone, *Reason, Authority, and the Healing of Desire*, chapter 1.

The first traveler, ready to believe whatever he is told, immediately takes the road indicated. His companion, unwilling to assent without proof and doubting the reliability of this scruffy fellow's testimony, waits at the fork for more evidence to come along. Later it does—in the testimony of a more sophisticated person who also happens to be a prankster who deceives him and sends him down the wrong path! Although he protests that he does not *believe* that this new testimony is true, only that it seems likely, he errs all the same. Sometime later, the first traveler is resting in Alexandria while the other is lost in the wilderness.

The immediate epistemological point is that trust in testimony is a viable means of pursuing the truth, and sometimes a necessary one. When we know not the truth, we may trust those who do. Even if we are not sure a testimony is from one who knows, trust is a responsible course of action. It may be the best way for us to get to the truth. Moreover, we risk error by *dis*believing no less than by believing since we will *not* know the truth if we make no judgments.[2] It is likely that the shepherd has a more specific meaning in theology and in specifically religious epistemology. Some suggest that the shepherd stands for Christ or the apostles, the church, or some combination of these.[3] Thus the trust involved in becoming a Christian is justified by the possibility that trust is the way to find the truth about God.

Elsewhere Augustine addresses these matters a bit more systematically and without relying on illustration. Let us take a brief survey. Also in *c. Acad.*:

> But there is no doubt that we are urged on to learn by a twin weight of authority (*auctoritas*) and reason (*ratio*). Therefore, I am certain not to depart ever, in any way, from the authority of Christ, for I find nothing more powerful. But what should be accomplished by a most subtle reason (*sublitissima ratio*)—for I have already been so affected that I impatiently long to learn what is true not only through believing (from *credo*) but also through understanding (from *intelligo*)—I trust in the meantime I shall find among the Platonists, insofar as it is not incompatible with our sacred [teachings].[4]

Again, in *Ord.*, written at the same time, Augustine says:

2. For additional commentary on this passage, see Kenyon, *Augustine and the Dialogue*, 51–54.

3. See Curley, *Augustine's Critique of Skepticism*, 122; McWilliam, "The Cassiciacum Autobiography," 28; and Boone, *Conversion and Therapy of Desire*, 63.

4. *Against the Academics*, 3.20.43. Translator Michael Foley notes here Augustine later "expresses regret for exaggerating the compatibility of Christianity and Platonic philosophy, filled as it is with 'grievous errors.'"

> Twofold is the path we follow when we are moved by the obscurity of things: either reason (*ratio*), or at least authority (*auctoritas*). Philosophy promises reason but it barely frees a very few. Nevertheless, it drives them not only *not* to disdain those mysteries, but to understand them alone, as they should be understood.[5]

He further explains that philosophy teaches the existence of God, and authority the doctrines of the Trinity and the incarnation. The authority of Christ (conveyed via Scripture and church) is necessary for teaching some religious truths, yet others may be able to understand by the power of the mind exercised in advanced reflection in imitation of the Platonists.

Later, in the *Confessions*, Augustine explains how, in Milan under the influence of Bishop Ambrose and with his mind beginning to clear, he had come to appreciate the position of orthodox Christianity. It commended faith in what was beyond understanding, whereas the Manichean heretics reviled faith and promised certainty, yet ended up asking for blind faith in silly doctrines.[6] Augustine, meanwhile,

> began to consider the countless things I believed which I had not seen, or which had happened with me not there—so many things in the history of nations, so many facts about places and cities which I had never seen, so many things told me by friends, by doctors, by this man, by that man: and unless we accepted (*credo*) these things, we should do nothing at all in this life. Most strongly of all it struck me how firmly and unshakeably I believed that I was born of a particular father and mother, which I could not possibly know (*scio*) unless I believed (*credo*) it upon the word of others.

Moreover, "since men had not the strength to discover the truth by pure reason (*ratio*)," "we needed the authority of Holy Writ."[7] We needed "the medicine of faith (*fides*)."[8] This faith or trust in the Bible is the same sort of trust as that which we exercise in many cases where we lack firsthand knowledge. Entire fields of study—history and geography—are mentioned, and especially the truths foundational to familial and social life—who our parents are. Augustine even goes so far as to suggest that some *knowledge* comes by this *faith* in reliable testimony.

---

5. *On Order*, 2.5.16.
6. Augustine, *Confessions*, 6.5.7.
7. Augustine, *Confessions*, 6.5.8.
8. Augustine, *Confessions*, 6.4.6.

In *The Advantage of Believing*, written to help his friend Honoratus escape the Manichean heresy, Augustine employs the same argument for the permissibility of trust based on its necessity for knowing who our parents are and elaborates eloquently on the immorality and the devastating social consequences that would follow if we should refuse to trust.[9] He also applies the same argument to friendship, which requires belief in one's friend's good intentions.[10] (In *Faith in the Unseen* there is an extended passage on this same theme and on the devastating social consequences that would follow from a refusal to trust in the minds of our friends.)[11] Augustine includes in *Advantage of Believing* a neat little argument building on the importance of trust in a fellow human's good will.[12] If we are coming to someone who might have the truth and might be willing to share it with us, we expect that person to believe in our sincerity as truth-seekers. So we should return the favor and believe *their* sincerity in dispensing the truth. To believe by trust alone, even rational trust, is not the same thing as *intellegere*, to understand, or *discere*, to know.[13] Yet further proofs of the truth, such that we could *know* it apart from faith, may be simply impossible at this stage, since we might not even be able to understand it.[14]

Yet "faith (*fides*) prepares the ground for understanding (*ratio*)."[15] Suppose we cannot understand the truth and its evidence (that sort of truth with which Platonic philosophy might be able to help). Here is Augustine's advice:

> when you do not have the ability to appreciate the arguments, it is very healthy to believe (*credo*) without knowing the reasons (*ratio*) and by that belief (*fides*) to cultivate the mind and allow the seeds of truth to be sown. Moreover, for minds that are ill this is absolutely essential, if they are to be restored to health.[16]

In this way, we shall seek the truth, first by faith and later by reason, and in seeking we *shall* find.[17]

---

9. Augustine, *Advantage of Believing*, 12.26.

10. Augustine, *Advantage of Believing*, 10.23. Helpful commentary on the importance of faith in friends may be found in King and Ballantyne, "Augustine on Testimony," 208–11.

11. Augustine, *Faith in the Unseen*, 1.2–3.4.

12. Augustine, *Advantage of Believing*, 10.23.

13. Augustine, *Advantage of Believing*, 11.25.

14. Augustine, *Advantage of Believing*, 10.24.

15. Augustine, *Advantage of Believing*, 17.35.

16. Augustine, *Advantage of Believing*, 14.31.

17. Augustine, *Advantage of Believing*, 14.30.

And where shall we seek? In orthodox Christianity—in the institution of the orthodox church. Honoratus should "follow the path of the Catholic teaching, which has flowed down to us from Christ himself through his apostles and will continue to flow down to our descendants."[18]

Let's review. We may summarize this survey of Augustine's religious epistemology in seven points.

First, *fides*, or trust, is the placing of epistemic credit in the testimony of a person, text, or institution. It is the acceptance of that testifier as reliable and of that testimony as true.

Second, this trust is justified and rational. It is justified by its practicality. Trust is the thread out of which social life is woven and, moreover, a normal and necessary practice for getting truth when we lack the knowledge borne of firsthand experience or understanding. It underlies geography and history no less than religion. Faith is also justified as a *reliable* way of getting to the truth—it is epistemically as well as practically justified, we might say[19]—insofar as it commonly relies on *reliable* testimony.

Third, religious *fides* is best placed in orthodox Christianity. Christ, his apostles, the Bible, and the institution of the orthodox church as conveyor of doctrine and interpreter of Scripture are all necessary objects of trust.

Fourth, in the case of Christian *fides*, when we believe (*credo*) we (most of us at least) do not *know* (*disco, intelligo*); we do not believe by reason (*ratio*) as such, for this involves a full comprehension or some direct experience of a fact; it means belief borne of our own capacity for accessing the truth, not the capacities of others. (We should note that Augustine later reconsidered his language here, recognizing belief without complete understanding yet based on reliable authority as a loose but satisfactory everyday understanding of *knowing*.)[20] While the apostles witnessed the resurrection of the Messiah, we did not; we trust their reliable testimony. While some philosophically trained theologians may have some contemplative wisdom concerning God and the soul, most of us do not.

Fifth, however, we aim for it. We must seek to add understanding to faith. And, sixth, faith prepares us for this understanding. Seventh, and finally, achieving this understanding relies largely on philosophically informed contemplation.

---

18. Augustine, *Advantage of Believing*, 8.20.

19. In other words, there is some logical support of premises for their conclusion. We should beware of positing a *dichotomy*, however, between epistemic and practical justifications of belief; the relevance of practical concerns to those concerns we think of as epistemic is an aspect of Augustine's analysis, as well as James'.

20. Augustine, *Retractiones* (*Retractions* or *Reconsiderations*), I.xiv, 285. Noted by Fiedrowicz in note 48 to *Advantage of Believing*, 11.25.

JAMES

For purposes of brevity we may focus on James's most famous analysis of religious belief, "The Will to Believe," which is "an essay in justification *of* faith, a defense of our right to adopt a believing attitude in religious matters, in spite of the fact that our merely logical intellect may not have been coerced."[21] James gives two arguments for this conclusion. The first is based on the propriety of religious belief *sans* proof in situations in which whether to believe is a decision between options which are *live, forced*, and *momentous*. In these situations life forces a decision on us, and it is permissible simply to decide. The second argument is based on the idea of a personal God. If God is like human persons, James explains, God cannot be expected to provide compelling proof before we are willing to believe. We may be required to meet him halfway by having at least some faith, hoping to verify his existence and good intentions later.[22]

The first argument relies on the idea of a *live, forced*, and *momentous* decision between two choices. A decision is *live* if we could really go either way. I once had a live decision between pursuing a PhD in philosophy from a research university or a theology degree from a seminary. I also might have chosen an alternative career course; I honestly think I could have been happy as a dentist.[23] Philosophy, seminary, dentistry—these were live options for me. They were not *forced*, however, because I could have gone some other way—computer programming, perhaps. The decision whether to go to grad school or not *was* forced; it was either one or the other. In a forced decision between two options, I cannot avoid the decision; I must

21. William James, "The Will to Believe."

22. Much has been written on "The Will to Believe," and a few sources would provide ample opportunities for the interested reader to analyze the arguments in the text and begin to explore the scholarly debates on its interpretation. An honorable mention must go to O'Connell as a scholar of both Augustine *and* James; O'Connell, *William James on the Courage to Believe*; chapter 1 is an admirable commentary on the text. For a reconsideration of James *vis-a-vis* his nemesis here, W. K. Clifford, see Hollinger, "James, Clifford, and the Scientific Conscience," 69–83. Southworth is insightful on James's first argument (neglecting the second if I understand him rightly), and uncovers an interesting aspect of it—that it is not supporting wishful thinking, nor merely the *right* to believe, but also the *courage* to believe when belief is necessary for acting on our moral commitments; Southworth, "The Passional Nature," 62–78. Fuller explains that James's view that belief is rooted in passion rather than pure objective reason is rooted in his idea that the function of belief is practical; this, moreover, is a life-affirming view rooted in science rather than a nihilistic view rooted in relativism; Fuller, "'The Will to Believe': A Centennial Reflection," 633–50. Another helpful source is Slater, *William James on Ethics and Faith*, chapters 1–2.

23. At least I used to; in recent years, I've been wondering whether such noble work is far beyond my abilities.

choose one. In a *momentous* decision, there are significant and irreversible consequences, such as the enormous (and happy) consequences of my decision in 2006 to ask Miss Richardson to marry me.

Now when a decision is live, forced, *and* momentous it is necessary to decide; life leaves us no alternative. Moreover, if it should happen that there is no convincing evidence which way to go, this does not negate the necessity of the decision. In such cases we "not only lawfully may, but must, decide" not on purely rational, but on other, grounds—based, at least in part, on what we *want*.

And, as the circumstances of life would have it, some such decisions concern what we are going to believe—or not believe—about "life, the universe, and everything."[24] Religion, James grants, is not a live option for everyone; some of us, perhaps, would not be able to believe if we tried. Others, apparently, would have difficulty *not* believing. For *some* of us, however, there is a *live* decision between religion and no religion. That decision is *forced* for everyone. Whether to be a Reformation Christian or a Shiite Muslim is not forced; there are plenty of other options in Christianity, Islam, other religions, and irreligion. However, the decision whether or not to adopt the religious view of life is a forced decision; each of us either will or will not. Agnosticism, when it comes to this choice, is the same answer as atheism, no less a form of *un*belief than *dis*belief is. Finally, the religious question is *momentous* for all of us. It affects how we live, which is, perhaps, enough to establish its momentousness. There is also the possibility of the afterlife, which may also be enough. James, however, builds his case on the promised benefits of religion in *this* life. He explains that, while we use science to explain *what* things exist and morality to determine *how good* those things are, "religion says essentially two things": that "the best things are the more eternal things," and that "we are better off even now" if we believe this. It is here that James locates the potential benefits of religion, and for this reason religion is a momentous decision.

Now, since religion can be live, forced, and momentous, this decision—for those of us faced with it—need not rely on reason alone. If it should be the case that the evidence does *not* determine the question for us, we are forced by life itself to decide on other grounds. "The will to believe" is thus, even without proof, an acceptable grounds for deciding to be religious.

James strengthens his case with an analysis of the risks we face when we decide whether to believe. His primary target is a sort of skeptic—those who tout the overriding importance of avoiding error. To be precise, these folks—exemplified by W. K. Clifford—refuse to believe unless the evidence

---

24. Douglas Adams's fine phrase.

should prove thoroughly decisive, and their refusal is on the grounds that belief might be an error. Fair enough, James grants—it *might* be an error, and believing in error would be bad, and they have the right to avoid this outcome by not believing.

But this is not the whole story. Unbelief will protect us from errant belief, but it also prevents us from believing the *truth*. Believing the truth is also important, and carries its own benefits. There is not *one* risk here, but *two*: the risk of believing what is false, and the risk of *not* believing what is true. James figures that, when the evidence is unclear, we have the right to decide for ourselves which risk we prefer to take—whether we are more afraid of believing an error and so never believe yet risk missing out on the truth, or whether we are just as afraid of *not* believing any religious truths there may be and so believe yet risk being in error. Our live, forced, and momentous decision is not only between two ways of life, but between two equally legitimate practical epistemologies. "No one of us ought to issue vetoes to the other, nor should we bandy words of abuse" against those who prefer one risk to another.

Let us take a look at James's second argument. He introduces it thus:

> Now, to most of us religion comes in a still further way that makes a veto on our active faith even more illogical. The more perfect and more eternal aspect of the universe is represented in our religions as having personal form. The universe is no longer a mere It to us, but a Thou, if we are religious; and any relation that may be possible from person to person might be possible here.

The argument that follows is both interesting and important, although it is often overlooked in favor of the first argument of "Will to Believe." It is particularly important for our purposes because it points to the possibility of knowing God in the future. James has not been convinced by conventional philosophical arguments for the existence of God (ontological, cosmological, teleological, and so on); if he were he would not so emphasize the permissibility of belief in the *absence* of convincing evidence. However, this does not mean that James thinks confirmation of the existence of God (if such a being exists) is forever impossible. He is, in fact, very optimistic about the possibility of evidence that confirms God's existence, the only difference being that, as a good empiricist and pragmatist might well do, he looks to experience for this knowledge, and primarily to *future* experience.[25]

---

25. James's long and careful look at *past* experience, written some time later, is *The Varieties of Religious Experience*.

That is what this second argument is all about—that, and a likely restriction on the possibility of this evidence and the relevance of this restriction to what we do now. We may reconstruct the bulk of the argument as follows:

1. Experiencing a personal God by means of a relationship with God may be our best chance of confirming the existence of God.
2. God is personal.
3. Persons in our human experience tend not to take all of the initiative in relationships; instead, they contribute to the relationship on *their* end largely in response to the trust and initiative we put forward on *our* end.
4. So it is likely that God will not take all of the initiative in our relationship with him, but will contribute to the relationship largely in response to our willingness to trust him prior to proof (from 2 and 3).
5. So our best chance of confirming the existence of God may be that we show some willingness to trust him prior to proof (from 1 and 4).

The first premise here is James's own pragmatic application of empiricism to the idea of a personal God: Unconvinced by other purported proofs of God, he looks to future experience as a likelier way of knowing such a God. The second premise is taught by most of our major religions; for most of us who find ourselves able to believe in God, a personal God is the God we are able to believe in. The third premise is an observation from experience. James's own presentation of the analogy from human to divine persons is very nice:

> We feel, too, as if the appeal of religion to us were made to our own active good-will, as if evidence might be forever withheld from us unless we met the hypothesis half-way. To take a trivial illustration: just as a man who in a company of gentlemen made no advances, asked a warrant for every concession, and believed no one's word without proof, would cut himself off by such churlishness from all the social rewards that a more trusting spirit would earn,—so here, one who should shut himself up in snarling logicality and try to make the gods extort his recognition willy-nilly, or not get it at all, might cut himself off forever from his only opportunity of making the gods' acquaintance.

Now this does not mean that our beliefs create the God we believe in, that belief can create reality out of nothing, or any such fiddle-faddle. What it means is that divine reality might possibly be in that special category of things where our beliefs have some effect either on the reality itself or at least on our knowledge of it. One of the great contributions of the pragmatist tradition in philosophy is the insight that some things can be affected by our beliefs concerning them, and that some truths cannot be confirmed apart from our belief in them. We are not spectators on reality, watching it from elevated seating; we are active players on the field of reality, and our beliefs about it make a difference. Our beliefs effect our behavior, which effects the world; in some cases, this effect may be on the same region of reality with which our beliefs are concerned. (This is particularly true with social realities, those from which James's analogy is drawn.)[26]

Could God be such a reality? Certainly not, unless some very strong version of process theology is true.[27] But our *relationship* with God might easily be such. If that relationship is sufficiently like the personal relationships we know from experience—the human-to-human ones—then truths about it may be, in part, the result of our beliefs about God. More importantly, our *knowledge* of God will likely depend on our relationship with God, which is shaped in no small part by our beliefs about God. Using my favorite example, we will learn that God exists and is favorably disposed towards us much like Benedick and Beatrice in Shakespeare's *Much Ado About Nothing* learned of their mutual love—by *believing* in its existence.

We have not yet looked directly at the *final* conclusion of James's second argument. Some truths can only be known after a certain degree of trust has already been placed in them. The likelihood that belief in God will help to verify the truth about God—if there be any such truth—shows that a rule against believing in the absence of prior compelling proof is "a rule of thinking which would absolutely prevent me from acknowledging certain kinds of truth if those kinds of truth were really there . . . ." Such a rule, James says, "would be an irrational rule." Thus the final conclusion of James's second argument is the same as that of his first: Religious belief without prior proof can be rational.

In short, James with his two arguments is telling us that religious belief must be judged on practical grounds, not merely on the grounds of whether it is a conclusion deriving good logical support from its premises.[28] And,

26. On James's strategy of thinking about cosmic or divine reality by analogy from social relationships, see Lamberth, "Interpreting the Universe after a Social Analogy," 237–59.

27. And, in fact, James may subscribe to a process theology. But this is outside the scope of this text and not, so far as I can tell, what he is talking about in this particular argument.

28. Slater: In general, "for James, while the content of religious beliefs and experiences does not reduce to their practical value—for truth-value is not the same sort of value as utility, even if the latter serves as our best *indicator* of the former—we nonetheless have a practical reason to be persons of faith if, and only if, such beliefs and

on these practical grounds, there is no convincing case against religion. Religion is epistemically permissible. And belief in God may well lead to knowledge of God—as a result of that very belief.

Two final observations, just for the sake of clarity. First, James actually tells us in the Preface to *The Will to Believe and Other Essays* that in other contexts he might be arguing in the opposite direction—against religious beliefs that he takes as unreasonable or, more generally, against faith carelessly indulged in *sans* reason. However, in "The Will to Believe" and the other early writings associated with it, gathered together in *The Will to Believe and Other Essays*, he is primarily addressing those academics whose idea of reason has excluded faith. Second, while he here generally considers religion in pretty general terms, he recognizes the importance of selecting a more specific religious outlook towards the end of *The Varieties of Religious Experience*. He outlines his own philosophical religious outlook there and in his late book *A Pluralistic Universe*.

It might be helpful to overview some of the main points of James before relating him to Augustine. First, epistemic rules are partly a function of the practical requirements of belief for life.

Second, belief in God without proof can be rational, and rationality is in no small part a function of practicality. Proof is not a requirement for rationality. We can believe what we do not yet know without violating the requirements of reason.

Third, the widespread theological claim that the ultimate and divine reality is personal has its own special relevance for the rationality of religion; specifically, it counts in favor of it.

Fourth, knowledge of religious truth (if there is any) is a real possibility. However, and fifth, the truth about God might be such that we will not be able to learn it without first believing it. Knowledge comes after belief, not vice versa. Belief may lead to knowledge by the natural processes of personal relationship between the human and the divine.

FAITH AND KNOWLEDGE

There is between Augustine and James a significant general agreement on the rationality of faith without knowledge. They converge on a number of points including the danger of unbelief, the practicality of faith, its nonidentity (at least as things currently stand for most of us) with knowledge, and its role in leading us toward knowledge. No less significant, however,

---

experiences prove to be valuable for how we live." Slater, *William James on Ethics and Faith*, 13.

are the differences. One is that Augustine is devoted to Christian orthodoxy while James defends our right to choose what to believe. Another is that Augustine's efforts to add knowledge to faith are largely rationalistic whereas James's are largely empirical. Yet these differences should not lead us to think that James and Augustine represent fundamentally inconsistent epistemological perspectives, for there are several clues pointing to the possibility of a degree of synthesis of their insights.

Let us consider first the major points of comparison, then those of contrast, and finally the possibility of synthesis.

Major Points of Comparison

We must understand the close connection between Augustine's illustration for faith at *c. Acad.* 3.15.34 and James's first argument. Let us modify Augustine's illustration in a Jamesian direction. Say *three* friends are going to Alexandria: one who believes everything she's told, a hard skeptic who *dis*believes everything he's told, and a soft skeptic who withholds belief whenever proof is lacking. The shepherd testifies concerning the right way to Alexandria, which represents the (allegedly) true religion leading to its promises (whether these involve a happy afterlife, a good *next* life following reincarnation, a bodily resurrection when Christ returns, or merely earthly blessings). The credulous friend, representing the religious believer, believes and follows that way. The second friend, representing the disbeliever, thinks the shepherd is wrong and follows the other way. The soft skeptic, representing the doubter who opines only when he has proof, simply sits down at the fork to wait for more evidence. Sticking to James's perspective, we don't know what happens to any of them. Perhaps there is no Alexandria—no real God, no true religion. Perhaps the believer is in Alexandria and the disbeliever is eaten by wolves—perhaps one goes to heaven and one to hell. Perhaps they all make it to Alexandria somehow—perhaps an all-forgiving God welcomes all into heaven in the end. The first two friends have made their choice what to believe, taking the risk of being wrong. There are only two things of which we can be sure: that at least one of the first two is wrong about *something*, and that the *third* one will never be *right* as long as he persists in his indecision.

On this much Augustine and James agree: Withholding judgment on religion carries with it the certain consequence of not believing any religious truths which might be there to believe, and of missing out on any good consequences of believing these truths. Stubborn agnosticism avoids the risk of error in belief, but has a risk of its own. As James puts it:

Believe truth! Shun error!—these, we see, are two materially different laws; and by choosing between them we may end by coloring differently our whole intellectual life. We may regard the chase for truth as paramount, and the avoidance of error as secondary; or we may, on the other hand, treat the avoidance of error as more imperative, and let truth take its chance.

There are at least four additional major points of comparison.

First, faith in the absence of knowledge can be rational. Second, faith is practical, and this is no small part of what justifies its rationality. In "Will to Believe," faith (for those for whom it is live, forced, and momentous) is a practical decision made along life's course—less an academic epistemological situation and more like figuring out whether to marry, whom to marry, and whether to become a philosopher or a dentist. In Augustine, faith in religious testimony is, epistemically speaking, on a par with faith in historians, geographers, and parents. Not only is this sort of trust useful as a way of getting to know the truth when we lack knowledge, but it is also the foundation of familial and social life.

Third, religious faith is *not* knowledge. Yet, fourth, it *precedes* knowledge. This is true in a literal and temporal sense: Faith comes first, knowledge later. It is also true in causal terms: Faith *leads* to knowledge. Faith is a propaedeutic for knowledge. In Augustine, those who would eventually understand God by reason must begin by believing his message and, by thus believing, learn to *understand*. In James's second argument God, as a personal being, may well reward faith with experiential knowledge of himself, knowledge that would not be given to one churlish in the use of her capacity to trust.

Major Points of Contrast

There remain notable differences in what we have considered here. There is one notable difference in method and another in goals.

Let us consider first the very important difference in goals. Augustine is aiming at orthodox Christianity, and he will not have our faith go any other way. The object of this faith, if we *had* to choose just one, would be Jesus Christ. It is better, however, to list at least four related objects of faith. Christ is foremost. However, he established the apostles as authoritative teachers of his way. The apostles both wrote the New Testament as an authoritative repository of Christian doctrine and established the orthodox church. This church now teaches this doctrine and stands as our interpreter of the Bible.

James is different. He is defending the right of our "passional nature" to decide when convincing evidence is lacking; in other words, we may opt to believe without following any organized religion. We may "pray for the victory of the religious cause"[29] without praying "Our Father in Heaven." To be sure, there appear to be some empirical and pragmatic restrictions on religious belief. I think James would not approve of a faith inconsistent with the findings of science, for example. Religion must also help us make life better in the future; religious beliefs are tested by their fruits,[30] and religious belief ought to unleash the "strenuous mood,"[31] the vigorous struggle to make a better world. Still, this is nothing like Augustine's rigorous commitment to Christian orthodoxy; James is happy to be a heretic.[32]

As to the difference in method, Augustine aims to add knowledge to faith by means of contemplation which intentionally draws from the Platonic philosophers. That Augustine admired much in this tradition is well known, and this is hardly the place to overview, much less settle, any debates about the nature and extent of these borrowings. It suffices for our purpose to observe that, as he said in some of the texts we examined, Augustine hopes that Platonic reflection will give him some knowledge of God. The heart of Platonism is its insight into non-physical reality. God and the soul are not physical things, and the Platonic methods for reflecting on such realities, Augustine thinks, will prove useful in gaining an understanding of God. Platonism, of course, tends more toward rationalism than towards empiricism; in other words, its epistemology considers knowledge to be found in the mind rather than in worldly experience. In both Plato's *Meno* and Augustine's *De Magistro*, we find interesting accounts of the origins of knowledge in the mind rather than experience accumulated in this life.

Not so James, a devoted empiricist. Knowledge comes from experience and is tested in future experience. Knowledge comes "by systematically continuing to roll up experiences and think," and for it we look always to the end rather than to the beginning.[33] When, in James's second argument, he suggests that we might in the future be able to gain knowledge of God, he expects us to gain it in a different way than Augustine had aimed for it—in experience. (Not, by the way, in sensory experience as such, but in *experience*, which in James's thinking is a broader category than mere sensory

---

29. James, "The Moral Philosopher and the Moral Life."
30. James, *Varieties of Religious Experience*, Lecture I.
31. James, "The Moral Philosopher and the Moral Life."
32. Rosenbaum, Introduction, 3.
33. James, "Will to Believe."

experience. This is what distinguishes an American pragmatist's empiricism from the earlier British empiricists in the Enlightenment era.)

Synthesis

Are these difference irreconcilable? Do Augustine and James represent the incompatible religious epistemologies of a medieval Christian Neoplatonist and a modern empiricist? Things are not quite that simple. There are at least three reasons their epistemologies might be at least partially synthesized, although working out a detailed synthesis is outside the scope of this chapter (and even this book).

First, we may opt not to commit ourselves to an absolute dichotomy of empiricism and rationalism. Perhaps knowledge can come by philosophical reflection. Perhaps it can also come by experience. We do not have to say that *all* knowledge comes by *only* one of those routes. There may be different kinds of knowledge and, perhaps, sometimes different ways of gaining knowledge might converge on the same truth. As we will see below, Augustine's own epistemology suggests as much, and so does that of another more recent Christian thinker whose epistemology has notable points in common with James.

Second, other connections between Augustine and James present themselves when we look at a slightly bigger picture. Although we cannot look at them in detail in this close-up study, they suggest that the methodologies of Augustine and James are not so far apart as they might appear.

Note, for one thing, that James elsewhere makes a defense of the necessity of faith in everyday life and knowledge much like Augustine's.[34] We find this in his *Pragmatism: A New Name for Some Old Ways of Thinking*, in which he describes knowledge using an economic metaphor. Knowledge involves "a credit system" in which we accept the testimonies of others; nearly all knowledge comes by this trust, and the whole system relies on being able to cash in our notes of credit from time to time by confirming some bit of knowledge in experience.[35]

Note, also, that there is an empirical streak in Augustine's religious epistemology. Most importantly, there are the historical miracles that confirm the Messiahship of Jesus.[36] This is religious knowledge from experience.

---

34. And also applied to *truth*, although this suggests some further difference between Augustine and James—perhaps a difference in metaphysics, or perhaps just a difference concerning philosophy of language and meaning.

35. William James, *Pragmatism: A New Name*, Lecture VI.

36. For example, Augustine, *Advantage of Believing*, 14.32–15.33.

There is also the contemporary fulfillment of prophecies concerning the church.[37] (This aspect of Augustine's epistemology requires a slow, careful look; I have done my best in another article.)[38]

Third, there is one thinker in particular whose thought suggests the possibility of a significant degree of integration of the epistemologies of James and Augustine. C. S. Lewis, perhaps the most influential Augustinian in his century, is also an orthodox Christian, yet comes rather close to James on at least one occasion. He makes the same discovery concerning the verification of truth about God—that, since God is a person, we will not be able to test our beliefs about him through controlled testing as a geologist will test a theory about rocks. Lewis develops this insight at length and then does something James does not: He offers a specific account of how the verification of Christian theology comes about. Not only is belief needed; we must also be *good*. The right way of knowing God in experience, in Lewis's eventual conclusion, is also corporate; if we are to know God in experience, we must enter into the loving orthopraxy of the church.[39] Lewis thus comes alongside James in rejecting a spectator theory of knowledge, developing his own views in a more classical direction informed by his study of Christianity. We interact with the object of knowledge; we must be changed by what we know; we must become more like God in order to know him well.

We have seen that two of the greatest defenders of religion, one ancient and one modern, agree that faith can be rational in the absence of knowledge and yet itself may lead towards knowledge. One is a Christian with a Neoplatonic bent, and the other is an empiricist defending the right to choose a religion. These differences notwithstanding, there is a possibility of a greater integration not necessarily of Augustine's and James's own views, but at least of the ideas they touted. This is a promising theme for future research. "Of making many books there is no end"—nor of considering the rationality of faith. However, progress towards understanding of faith and rationality has been made in the past. Future progress will be spurred on by better understanding these two participants in the past conversation, as well as by a follower of James whom we will consider in the next chapter.

WORKS CITED

Augustine. *The Advantage of Believing*. Translated by Ray Kearney, notes by Michael Fiedrowicz. The Works of Saint Augustine: A Translation for the 21st Century, Part

---

37. A major emphasis in the later chapters of *Faith in the Unseen*.
38. Boone, "The Empirical Aspect," 45–87.
39. Lewis, *Mere Christianity*, 163–65.

I—Books, Vol. 8: *On Christian Belief*, edited by Boniface Ramsey. Introductions by Michael Fiedrowicz. Hyde Park, NY: New City, 2005.
———. *Against the Academics*. In *The Cassiciacum Dialogues of St. Augustine*. Translated by Michael P. Foley. New Haven, CT: Yale University Press, 2019.
———. *Confessions*. Translated by F. J. Sheed. Introduction by Peter Brown. 2d ed. edited and notes by Michael P. Foley. Indianapolis: Hackett, 2006.
———. *Faith in the Unseen*. Translated by Michael G. Campbell. The Works of Saint Augustine: A Translation for the 21st Century, Part I—Books, Vol. 8: *On Christian Belief*, edited by Boniface Ramsey, Introductions by Michael Fiedrowicz. Hyde Park, NY: New City, 2005.
———. *On Order*. In *The Cassiciacum Dialogues of St. Augustine*. Translated by Michael P. Foley. New Haven, CT: Yale University Press, 2020.
———. *The Retractiones of Saint Augustine*. Translated by Meredith Freeman Eller. Available at https://archive.org/details/retractationesof00elle/mode/2up.
Boone, Mark J. *The Conversion and Therapy of Desire: Augustine's Theology of Desire in the Cassiciacum Dialogues*. Eugene, OR: Pickwick, 2016.
———. "The Empirical Aspect of Augustine's Epistemology." *Augustiniana* 71.1 (2021) 45–87.
———. *Reason, Authority, and the Healing of Desire in the Writings of Augustine*. Lanham, MD: Lexington, 2020.
Curley, Augustine J. *Augustine's Critique of Skepticism: A Study of* Contra Academicos. New York: Peter Lang, 1996.
Fuller, Robert C. "'The Will to Believe': A Centennial Reflection." *Journal of the American Academy of Religion* 64.3 (1996) 633–50.
Gilson, Etienne. *The Christian Philosophy of Saint Augustine*, translated by L. E. M. Lynch. New York: Random House, 1960.
Hollinger, David A. "James, Clifford, and the Scientific Conscience." *The Cambridge Companion to William James*, edited by Ruth Anna Putnam, 69–83. Cambridge: Cambridge University Press, 2006.
Kenyon, Erik. *Augustine and the Dialogue*. Cambridge: Cambridge University Press, 2018.
James, William. "The Moral Philosopher and the Moral Life." In *The Will to Believe and Other Essays in Popular Philosophy*. Available at https://gutenberg.org/files/26659/26659-h/26659-h.htm.
———. *Pragmatism: A New Name for Some Old Ways of Thinking*. New York: Longmans, Green, and Co., 1907.
———. *The Varieties of Religious Experience: A Study in Human Nature*. New York: Longmans, Green, and Co., 1902.
———. "The Will to Believe." In *The Will to Believe and Other Essays in Popular Philosophy*. Available at https://gutenberg.org/files/26659/26659-h/26659-h.htm.
King, Peter, and Nathan Ballantyne. "Augustine on Testimony." *Canadian Journal of Philosophy* 39.2 (2009) 195–214.
Lamberth, David C. "Interpreting the Universe after a Social Analogy: Intimacy, Panpsychism, and a Finite God in a Pluralistic Universe." *The Cambridge Companion to William James*, edited by Ruth Anna Putnam, 237–59. Cambridge: Cambridge University Press, 2007.
Lewis, C. S. *Mere Christianity*. 1952. New ed. New York: HarperCollins, 2001.

MacDonald, Scott. "The Epistemology of Faith in Augustine and Aquinas." *Augustine and Philosophy*, edited by Phillip Cary, John Doody, and Kim Paffenroth, 167–96. Lanham, MD: Rowman & Littlefield, 2010.

Matthews, Gareth B. *Augustine*. Malden, MA: Blackwell, 2005.

McWilliam, Joanne. "The Cassiciacum Autobiography." Studia Patristica 18.4, edited by Elizabeth A. Livingston: 14–43. Louvain: Peeters, 1990.

O'Connell, Robert J. *William James on the Courage to Believe*. Bronx, NY: Fordham University Press, 1997.

Rist, John M. "Faith and Reason." In *The Cambridge Companion to Augustine*, edited by Eleonore Stump and Norman Krutzman, 26–39. Cambridge: Cambridge University Press, 2001.

Rosenbaum, Stuart. Introduction to *Pragmatism and Religion: Classical Sources and Original Essays*, edited by Stuart Rosenbaum, 1–12. Champaign, IL: University of Illinois Press, 2003.

Southworth, James. "The Passional Nature and the Will to Believe." *Transactions of the Charles S. Pierce Society* 52.1 (2016) 62–78.

Slater, Michael R. *William James on Ethics and Faith*. Cambridge: Cambridge University Press, 2009.

TeSelle, Eugene. *Augustine*. Nashville: Abingdon, 2006.

Van Fleteren, Frederick E. "Authority and Reason, Faith and Understanding in the Thought of St. Augustine." *Augustinian Studies* 4 (1973) 33–71.

4

William James and Allama Iqbal on Empirical Faith

ALLAMA IQBAL IS AN underappreciated character in the history of philosophy.[1] Although he is familiar to many scholars of Islamic philosophy, he is less well known to historians of Western philosophy, epistemologists, and philosophers of religion, despite his significance in these areas. His own citations and influences include Kant, Nietzsche, and William James as well as Al-Ghazali, Averroes, and Rumi. One of these connections is particularly salient to religious epistemology. James and Iqbal both believe that religious experiences are an important class of those experiences with which empiricism is concerned. In their way of thinking, the idea that we should look to experience for knowledge is compatible with religious faith and practice, and is also a ground for understanding, defending, and testing religious belief. James includes this as one important aspect of his pragmatism, intentionally a more thorough empiricism than the earlier British empiricism of the Enlightenment era. Iqbal in *The Reconstruction of Religious Thought in Islam* presents his religious empiricism as part of his strategy for renovating Islamic thought in the modern world by recovering the empirical aspect of religion. This requires that we learn to see science and religion as distinct but complementary spheres of empirical enquiry.

In what follows I will compare and contrast James's and Iqbal's religious epistemologies in order to understand both of them better and, hopefully,

1. I am grateful to many friends, colleagues, and former students at Forman Christian College, where for five years I taught philosophy and learned the rudiments of Iqbal.

enrich contemporary reflection on faith and reason through a better awareness of the past dialogue on the subject. James and Iqbal, despite the different cultures and traditions they represent, agree that religious as well as sensory experience counts as a source of empirical knowledge and that the results of religious belief are a legitimate means of testing them. This is no accident, for James influenced Iqbal on this very point. However, they diverge in some matters. James defends the right to diverse religious belief and eventually articulates his own account based on religious experience—an account that is intentionally philosophical and not reliant on any religious authority. Iqbal, however, is out to reconsider and defend Islam understood along largely traditional lines.

I shall first consider James first and then Iqbal, and then compare and contrast them.

JAMES'S RELIGIOUS EPISTEMOLOGY

James's religious epistemology is a massive field of study in itself. The central idea is what he calls *radical empiricism*. Others have analyzed radical empiricism,[2] and for our purposes it will suffice to overview its development in a few key texts.[3] First, I shall introduce James's empirical approach to religion in the Preface to *The Will to Believe and Other Essays in Popular Philosophy*. Then I shall review his famous talk "The Will to Believe" and explain its connection to radical empiricism. Then I shall consider James's constructive project in radical empiricism in *The Varieties of Religious Experience* and *A Pluralistic Universe*.

Religious Empiricism

The classical British empiricists—Francis Bacon, Thomas Hobbes, John Locke, George Berkeley, and David Hume—believed that knowledge comes

---

2. One early analysis and critique, from when James was still lecturing and writing, is Sabine, "Radical Empiricism as a Logical Method," 696–705. A recent, useful, and thorough overview of radical empiricism, although not much focused on its religious aspect, is Campbell, *Experiencing William James*, chapter 5; chapter 7, however, is a helpful study of James in religion. Similarly, David Lamberth nicely overviews radical empiricism but gives little attention to religion in *William James and the Metaphysics of Experience*, chapter 1; however, the following chapters look at religion as an application of radical empiricism. The interested reader might also consult Smith, "Radical Empiricism," 206–18.

3. For another overview, the interested reader might consult Proudfoot, "William James on an Unseen Order," 58–61.

from sensory experience alone.[4] James's philosophical project is, in part, an attempt to expand the scope of empirical thinking from sensory experience alone to a broader range of experience and to take experience as we find it, recognizing its pluriform nature but also the interrelatedness of its parts.

The Preface to *The Will to Believe and Other Essays in Popular Philosophy*, first published in 1897, presents the idea of what he calls radical empiricism:[5]

> Were I obliged to give a short name to the attitude in question, I should call it that of *radical empiricism* .... I say "empiricism," because it is contented to regard its most assured conclusions concerning matters of fact as hypotheses liable to modification in the course of future experience; and I say "radical," because it treats the doctrine of monism itself as an hypothesis, and, unlike so much of the half-way empiricism that is current under the name of positivism or agnosticism or scientific naturalism, it does not dogmatically affirm monism as something with which all experience has got to square.[6]

The idea is to take experience as we find it, not a single organized unity so much as a set of distinct facts. James is talking about epistemology and metaphysics, but he soon clarifies that this is also about religion:

> There is no possible point of view from which the world can appear an absolutely single fact. Real possibilities, real indeterminations, real beginnings, real ends, real evil, real crises, catastrophes, and escapes, a real God, and a real moral life, just as common-sense conceives these things, may remain in empiricism as conceptions which that philosophy gives up the attempt either to "overcome" or to reinterpret in monistic form.

---

4. On the need to improve on traditional empiricism, see Sabine, "Radical Empiricism as a Logical Method," 697 and Smith, "Radical Empiricism," 206–7. Campbell is helpful on the inadequacies of traditional empiricism and on the contrasts between it, radical empiricism, and Hegelian rationalism; Campbell. *Experiencing William James*, chapter 5. See also Lamberth, *William James and the Metaphysics of Experience*, chapter 1. Indeed, as oversimplifications go, I think that would not be a bad one which defines radical empiricism as that philosophy which takes from classic British empiricism the insight that reality as we experience it is a plurality rather than a unity, and which takes from the Hegelians the insight that we do not experience reality as a set of disconnected atoms or monads.

5. For an interesting introduction to the Preface and a commentary on the social dimensions of James's epistemology, see Algaier, "Reconstructing James's Early Radical Empiricism," 46–63.

6. William James, Preface; in *The Will to Believe and Other Essays in Popular Philosophy*.

The abstracting philosopher may try to force every fact into the box of one fact into which he presumes the world he experiences must fit. But not the empiricist. He must take the world as we find it. We experience what appear to be real possibilities, beginnings, endings, evil, redemption, and even God. We must take these into consideration. Religious belief, like all beliefs concerning the facts of human experience, must be handled empirically. In James's view, this means that each religious belief is to be treated as *a hypothesis* to be tested in experience by our believing it:[7]

> If religious hypotheses about the universe be in order at all, then the active faiths of individuals in them, freely expressing themselves in life, are the experimental tests by which they are verified, and the only means by which their truth or falsehood can be wrought out. The truest scientific hypothesis is that which, as we say, "works" best; and it can be no otherwise with religious hypotheses.

Radical empiricism is in no small part about finding the true home of responsible religious belief. An important remark in *A Pluralistic Universe*, written much later, gets right to the point: "Let empiricism once become associated with religion, as hitherto, through some strange misunderstanding, it has been associated with irreligion, and I believe that a new era of religion as well as of philosophy will be ready to begin."[8]

In short, radical empiricism shows us the true home of responsible religious belief and the direction empiricism should go in the future. Religion ought to be empirical, and empiricism ought to consider the nature and importance of religious experience.

"The Will to Believe"

James's most famous work is his talk in favor of our right to religious belief even in the absence of convincing evidence—"The Will to Believe," delivered "to the Philosophical Clubs of Yale and Brown Universities" and first published in 1896.[9] James gives two practical arguments for the rationality of such belief. Although these arguments have been explained before[10] and

---

7. On this topic see Proudfoot, "William James on an Unseen Order," 55.
8. James, *A Pluralistic Universe*, Lecture VIII.
9. James, "The Will to Believe."
10. The interested reader might consider the following as helpful commentaries on "Will to Believe" and paths into the scholarly discussion: O'Connell, *William James on the Courage to Believe*, chapter 1; Hollinger, "James, Clifford, and the Scientific Conscience," 69–83; Slater, *William James on Ethics and Faith*, chapters 1–2; and, of course,

are simple enough on their own terms, we must consider how they contribute to a radical empiricism.

First a short summary of the arguments would be in order. The first argument draws attention to the practical necessity of choice, a practicality not removed by any putative absence of convincing evidence. Sometimes a decision is *live*, *forced*, and *momentous*. These are James's technical terms introduced to describe a choice where we really could go either way, where we *must* go one way, and where the decision will have important and irreversible effects on our lives. In such cases, deciding is a practical necessity, with or without convincing evidence which way is right. The decision whether to be religious presents itself to many of us in just this way. We could go either way, we must be either religious or not, and this has important effects on our lives, including the alleged benefits of religious belief. Whichever way we decide, we take a risk. If we believe, we risk being in error. If we do not believe, we run the risk of not believing any religious truths there may be, and missing out on their benefits. We have the right to make this decision not solely on the basis of the evidence.

The second argument draws an analogy from the characteristics of ordinary human relationships to the likely characteristics of a relationship with God. Relationships as we know them are built partly upon a willingness to trust others. It is indeed that very trust which nourishes the relationship which in time provides the evidence of another's goodwill. Suppose that, as we have long been told, God is a person (or, on the Christian reading James does not mention, *three* Persons). We should not expect God to provide, prior to our decision whether to believe, all possible evidence and proof. It is likely that some amount of evidence will only be made available after we show ourselves willing to believe. So the rule, touted by religion's rational critics, that we should only believe that for which we have seen convincing evidence is, in fact, "an irrational rule." It would prevent us from ever knowing a certain kind of truth—truth concerning a personal God whom we know through relationship—if that truth were there to know.

Now this is the religious aspect of radical empiricism. With these arguments James is applying a thoroughgoing empiricism to the question of religion. The whole point of figuring out religion is to gain truth by empirical means. He remarks that "as empiricists we give up the doctrine of objective certitude" yet ceaselessly pursue truth "by systematically continuing to roll up experiences and think." It is with the goal of truth and the method of

---

the previous chapter of this book. One source is especially interesting for explaining the importance of evidence in James's approach, and explaining why James is not recommending non-rational fideism or wishful thinking: Brown, *William James on Radical Empiricism and Religion*.

learning it from experience in mind that he offers his arguments for the rationality of faith. These arguments apply to circumstances in which we have not (yet) accumulated sufficient evidence from experience to demonstrate a conclusion concerning religion. The belief defended by these arguments is a belief whose truth we would then seek to test in future experience. The defense of faith's rationality is not based on any *a priori* argument but on practicality—on the nature and significance of the experience of life. James's second argument envisions religious belief as an aspect of a relationship with God that itself becomes an experiment to test the religious hypothesis, leading (hopefully) to empirical religious knowledge.

The Varieties of Religious Experience and *A Pluralistic Universe*

In order to understand religion's role in radical empiricism and Iqbal's relation to James, we need to take a look at the course religious empiricism takes in the rest of James's work.[11] Let us consider two of his most important works, *The Varieties of Religious Experience* and *A Pluralistic Universe*.

The *Varieties* was based on James's Gifford Lectures at the University of Edinburgh, delivered in 1901 and 1902.[12] The *Varieties* is a study of religious experience with particular attention to its value and to the provisional conclusions that may be inductively derived from it. The first lecture argues for an empirical criterion for determining the value of religious experience.[13] We know its value by its fruits, by the ways it has added to or detracted from life. It is not good to judge religion by the theory that it is rooted in neurological problems.

Most of the *Varieties* is a lengthy study of the different kinds of religious experience with attention to their fruits.[14] In the final chapter,[15] James attempts to draw things to a conclusion. After summarizing some major beliefs and "psychological characteristics" of religion, he considers some

---

11. An aspect of James's writings nicely explained in Brown, *William James on Radical Empiricism and Religion*.

12. For an introduction to the *Varieties*, see Proudfoot, "William James on an Unseen Order," 56–8; Niebuhr, "William James on Religious Experience," 214–36; Campbell, *Experiencing William James*, chapter 7; or Lamberth, *William James and the Metaphysics of Experience*, chapter 3.

13. James, *The Varieties of Religious Experience*, Lecture I.

14. James, *Varieties of Religious Experience*, Lectures II–XIX.

15. James, *Varieties of Religious Experience*, Lecture XX.

pertinent questions. Is it lamentable that there is so much religious diversity? No. Should we "espouse the science of religions as our own religion?" No.

There are still some preliminary jobs to do on the way to his conclusion.[16] James explains that that which is conscious, mental, and subjective is a part of the world we experience, and that religion takes this aspect of reality as the most important. Our ultimate goal is to make a decision whether we should agree with religion on this point. Religion further posits "that there is *something wrong about us* as we naturally stand" and that "*we are saved from the wrongness* by making proper connection with the higher powers," by getting our own souls into the right link with the higher mind or minds. Should we agree?

James thinks so.[17] Philosophy, he explains, may posit a theory that takes religious belief as true in such a way as to be consistent with science.[18] This theory would be a "hypothesis," and James offers his own.[19] He suggests that there is a (usually) subconscious region of our human minds with which religious experience puts us in contact:

> Let me then propose, as an hypothesis, that whatever it may be on its *farther* side, the "more" with which in religious experience we feel ourselves connected is on its *hither* side the subconscious continuation of our conscious life.

It is the business of the particular religious perspectives to state whether our minds connect to the God of classical theism, the Hegelian Absolute, to Brahman, or whatever else. We may choose to follow a particular religion in this or philosophically to arrive at our own more detailed beliefs. James opts to develop his own philosophical account (on the details of which more later). When we choose, however, "we do so in the exercise of our individual freedom . . . ."[20] This choice is logically subsequent to the choice whether to accept the religious hypothesis, a choice made, as "Will to Believe" had

16. James, *Varieties of Religious Experience*, Lecture XX.
17. James, *Varieties of Religious Experience*, Lecture XX.
18. Lamberth: "Presuming that his view is a form of radical empiricism, we should expect that such a position cannot ignore the empirical findings of the individual special sciences. Rather, it should seek to bring them into a higher unity, resolving their disputes with one another through adjusting their shared or conflicting presuppositions;" *William James and the Metaphysics of Experience*, 137.
19. On earlier passages in *Varieties* which anticipated this hypothesis, see Niebuhr, "William James on Religious Experience," 227–29 and 233–34; also Lamberth, 131–34 and 136–38.
20. On this freedom, and its limitations, see Campbell, *Experiencing William James*, 275–76.

described, for the purposes of living: "the religious question is primarily a question of life, of living or not living in the higher union which opens itself to us as a gift...."

This belief, although we are free to choose to accept it or not, we are justified in taking as *"literally and objectively true as far as it goes."*[21] There is a good reason for that: The preceding empirical investigation (several hundred pages long) serves to establish "the fact that the conscious person is continuous with a wider self through which saving experiences come...."[22]

A Pluralistic Universe comes from James's Hibbert Lectures at Oxford's Manchester College from 1908, thus representing a late development in his radical empiricism. It also presents James's religious views in a highly developed form (building on the provisional philosophical interpretation of religious belief from the end of *Varieties*),[23] and I leave to others a careful and thorough analysis.[24] Here we need only make a few observations on James's method and his conclusions at this late stage.

First, James is still using the term "radical empiricism," an articulation and defense of which is largely the point of the lectures. James informs us that it is a fitting name for the philosophy which in these lectures he is developing in opposition to the followers of Hegel.[25]

Second, the term continues to have pluralistic metaphysical connotations. We take the universe as we find it, and it appears to be a pluralistic thing, not the monism sought by the Hegelians. Empiricism at its most fundamental means *"the habit of explaining wholes by parts, and rationalism means the habit of explaining parts by wholes."*[26] Radical empiricism begins its study of the universe by recognizing its apparent pluralistic aspect.

Third, there is a strong sense of the interconnectedness of things. Reality may be pluralistic, but it is not a collection of monads or severed atoms.[27] Traditional empiricism suggests that our ideas derive from "mental atoms,"

21. Italics here and in the next quote are in the original.

22. See, for further analysis, Campbell, *Experiencing William James*, 272 and Lamberth, *William James and the Metaphysics of Experience*, 142–43.

23. See Campbell, *Experiencing William James*, 266–67.

24. The interested reader might consider Lamberth, *William James and the Metaphysics of Experience*, chapter 5 as well as Campbell, *Experiencing William James*, 180–97. Since the initial publication of this chapter, I have gone through *A Pluralistic Universe* myself in some detail online; the interested reader can look it up in the William James playlist at TeacherOfPhilosophy on YouTube and Rumble.

25. James, *A Pluralistic Universe*, Lecture I. Campbell: "... it is clear from everything that he says that the central issue for him in contemporary philosophy was advancing the challenge to Idealism;" Campbell, *Experiencing William James*, 181.

26. James, *A Pluralistic Universe*, Lecture I.

27. James, *A Pluralistic Universe*, Lecture VII.

separated units of experience which are to be interpreted as referring to discrete units of reality. By contrast, radical empiricism recognizes that the things we experience are connected and effect one another.

Fourth, the term continues to have religious significance. Radical empiricism recognizes the importance (and indeed the unity) of the human and divine aspect of reality, but does not insist that only an absolute oneness can be divine.[28] Our own individual human minds may connect with one another and with a higher mind.[29] James suggests "the continuity of our consciousness with a wider spiritual environment," proposing a conception of the divine as "a wider self" and asking, "may not we ourselves form the margin of some more really central self in things . . . ?"

Fifth, religious hypotheses continue to have validity. As said long before in the Preface to *Will to Believe and Other Essays*, they are legitimate hypotheses to be tested. Moreover, as suggested in "The Will to Believe," our belief may be a part of what helps to make them come true. He closes his final lecture in this series with a reference to "The Will to Believe" and a proposal that the same theology he has been describing in these lectures be taken as a religious hypothesis.[30] He overviews what he calls the "faith-ladder," a series of steps in the testing of a religious hypothesis. The first step is merely to have that hypothesis; the second and third steps are to confirm its logical consistency and the possibility that it is true in this world; the fourth step is to recognize that it *should* be true; fifthly, "something persuasive in you" (no doubt the "passional nature" of "Will to Believe") insists on its truth; sixthly, one decides to *take* it as true. Finally, "your acting thus may in certain special cases be a means of making it securely true in the end."

IQBAL'S *RECONSTRUCTION*

We now turn to Iqbal's *Reconstruction*.[31] Like many writings of James, it was originally a series of lectures—"undertaken at the request of the Madras Muslim Association and delivered at Madras, Hyderabad, and Aligarh."[32] In this book Iqbal aims to reconstruct Islamic philosophical thinking along

---

28. James, *A Pluralistic Universe*, Lecture I.
29. James, *A Pluralistic Universe*, Lecture VII.
30. James, *A Pluralistic Universe*, Lecture VIII.
31. Who is Iqbal? A philosopher, a poet, a visionary—simultaneously an Indian, a British Knight, and the founder of the idea of Pakistan. For a more detailed introduction one might consult Diagne, *Open to Reason*, 86–88. Also Diagne, *Islam and Open Society*, 1–3.
32. Iqbal, *Reconstruction*, v.

empirical lines. He does so by integrating the empirical aspects of two traditions. One of these is modern science with its emphasis on knowledge via sensory experience. The other is religious mysticism—especially of the Islamic Sufi variety—with its emphasis on religious experience. Iqbal argues that knowledge derives from experience plus interpretation, and that religious experience is no less a legitimate place to start than sensory experience. Indeed, the ultimate interpretation of sensory experience would itself require the insight into the ultimate non-physical nature of reality which religion teaches.

We will consider these matters with, first, a brief look at the Preface to the *Reconstruction* and, second, a study of Iqbal's account of knowledge.

The Preface

A brief look at the book's short Preface helps to clarify Iqbal's sources, methodology, and plans. Iqbal is drawing from two traditions, modern science and religious mysticism, particularly its sub-tradition of Islamic Sufism. On the science side of things, Iqbal claims that "religious faith ultimately rests" on a certain "type of inner experience," experiences psychological and spiritual and physical.[33] However, "the modern man" has learned "habits of concrete thought" ill-suited to replicating such experiences, and modern man is moreover skeptical of non-public experience as a source of knowledge. These modern mental habits are not bad, however, and "Islam itself fostered" them long ago. These days such mental habits are promoted by modern science, while Islamic patterns of thought nowadays follow different patterns.

On the mystical side of things, "The more genuine schools of Sufism have, no doubt, done good work in shaping and directing the evolution of religious experience in Islam;" but their patterns of thought are ill-suited to the modern world.[34] The Sufi methods for knowing God are useless for this day and age.

Thus there is an "urgent demand" to reconsider Islamic religious philosophy. We need to learn—or, rather, rediscover or *reconstruct*—a better way of thinking. It would draw from Sufism's insight into religious experience, draw from modern scientific patterns of concrete thought, and integrate both to the detriment of neither.[35] In both respects it would ultimately

33. Iqbal, *Reconstruction*, v.
34. Iqbal, *Reconstruction*, v.
35. Not that religious thought is *not* concrete. The term "concrete" does not refer to physicality so much as to the reality and immediacy of an experience. See his reference to concrete religious experience in, e.g., *Reconstruction*, 5.

return to the conception of knowledge taught in the Qur'an.[36] Iqbal aims to begin this work here, and he notes that the moment is timely insofar as science itself has learned "to criticize its own foundations," leading to the decline of materialism and the promise of "hitherto unsuspected mutual harmonies" between science and religion.[37]

Experience Religious and Otherwise

Iqbal argues that religious experience is a form of human experience and, accordingly, a possible source of knowledge. This analysis relies on a way of thinking about what knowledge actually is. Let us first consider two definitions of knowledge suggested by Iqbal and link both of them to religious experience. Then we must consider how Iqbal develops his religious empiricism to account for the testing of a religious doctrine in future experience.

Chapter I of the *Reconstruction* considers "the character of knowledge and religious experience."[38] One definition of knowledge suggested by the text is a fairly simple formula: Experience plus interpretation equals knowledge. Iqbal says there are two branches of knowledge and two varieties of experience on which they are based. Scientific knowledge results from interpreting sensory experience. Religious knowledge results from interpreting religious experience. In one succinct remark he captures this notion: "The facts of religious experience are facts among other facts of human experience and, in the capacity of yielding knowledge by interpretation, one fact is as good as another."[39]

This is the central idea of religious empiricism: There is such a thing as religious experience, and it is a potential source of knowledge. Implicit is an argument from science for the possibility of religious knowledge. Roughly, the argument goes something like this: Scientific knowledge derives from experience plus interpretation, and since there is such a thing as religious experience which can be interpreted, it is possible that religion can be knowledge no less than science.[40]

Another account of knowledge appears even earlier in the text and brings us closer to Iqbal's ultimate goal: "knowledge is sense-perception

---

36. On this aspect of the *Reconstruction* see Koshul, "Seeing, Knowing, Believing." This and other articles in *Iqbal Review* were previously available at AllamaIqbal.com, but unfortunately I no longer know how to locate them there.
37. Iqbal, *Reconstruction*, v–vi.
38. Iqbal, *Reconstruction*, 8.
39. Iqbal, *Reconstruction*, 16.
40. I consider this argument further in the next chapter of this book.

elaborated by understanding."[41] This may appear to be the experience-plus-interpretation formula applied merely to the sensory side of experience, but this is not quite right. This is, rather, a description of a *higher* form of knowledge than what we get when we interpret either religious or sensory experience by themselves. The ultimate goal of knowledge is to understand that which we experience with our five senses in the light of religious insight—to understand the physical world as a creation and revelation of God. Quoting from the Qur'an, Iqbal explains how it gives evidence that this is just what God created us to do![42]

And this, of course, connects to the traditions the integration of which is the whole point of the *Reconstruction*. Modern science focuses on sensory experience, and religious mysticism on religious experience. Not only are both justifiable on empirical grounds, but both can indeed be reconciled and integrated. And, what's more, they need each other. God has taught us to look for knowledge of him where science now seeks knowledge: our sensory experience of the physical world. Moreover, the completion of that knowledge of the physical world which science begins can only be found in religious insight. Science only gives us "sectional views of reality," but religion aims to understand the whole.[43]

Completing his religious empiricism requires a look at the testing of a religious doctrine. Science subjects its theories to future testing. So also religion, its empirical counterpart. "Religious experience . . . is essentially a state of feeling with a cognitive aspect, the content of which cannot be communicated to others, except in the form of a judgment."[44] Religious experience is an entirely personal matter in its *origin*, but public in its *product*: a proposition, a statement, a theory. What should someone make of such a proposition who has not herself *had* that experience? An important question with an important answer: "Happily we are in possession of tests which do not differ from those applicable to other forms of knowledge. These I call the intellectual test and the pragmatic test."[45] The intellectual test is work for a philosopher. It is a consideration of human experience generally to consider whether it is consistent with the conclusions of religious experience. Iqbal applies this test in chapter II of the *Reconstruction*, arguing that modern science and the philosophical interpretations of its discoveries point towards a universe which is in fact consistent with that taught by religion: It

41. Iqbal, *Reconstruction*, 12.
42. Iqbal, *Reconstruction*, 13–14.
43. Iqbal, *Reconstruction*, 41–42.
44. Iqbal, *Reconstruction*, 26–27.
45. Iqbal, *Reconstruction*, 27.

is not a universe of mere matter; "the ultimate nature of Reality is spiritual, and must be conceived as an ego."[46] The pragmatic test is not the work for a philosopher as such to perform, although he may analyze it. It is rather the work of a prophet and his followers. The pragmatic test is to see whether a prophet's work has led to good results in the world; "The pragmatic test judges it by its fruits."[47] Iqbal considers the results of Islam in chapter V,[48] considering "the cultural world that has sprung out of the spirit of" a prophet's message; this, in the case of the history of Islam, is a good one. This, it seems to Iqbal, is a solid justification of Islamic religious experience by its fruits.

With such an empirical foundation laid, Iqbal completes the groundwork for a reconstructed Islamic philosophy true to its religious heritage and fit for a modern, scientific world. The analysis is rich and multifaceted. Although it is the subject for a broader study of Iqbal than this one, it is important to understand that the epistemology suggested in the *Reconstruction* leads here—to new directions for Islamic thought including Iqbal's philosophy of time, understanding of free will, his social and political philosophy, and so on.[49]

COMPARISON AND CONTRAST

Various scholars have noted the connections between James and Iqbal.[50] No wonder, since Iqbal himself cites James a number of times in the

46. Iqbal, *Reconstruction*, 61.
47. Iqbal, *Reconstruction*, 27.
48. Iqbal, *Reconstruction*, 124–45.

49. For example, for an overview of Iqbal's integrated philosophies of time, free will, and social reform, see Diagne, *Open to Reason*, 88–97. On the social and political philosophy of Iqbal, see Diagne, *Islam and Open Society*. Since the initial publication of this chapter, I have gone through *The Reconstruction* myself in some detail online; the interested reader can look it up in the Allama Iqbal's *The Reconstruction of Religious Thought in Islam* playlist at TeacherOfPhilosophy on YouTube and Rumble.

50. In an interesting article on Iqbal and C. S. Pierce (another American pragmatist), Peter Ochs observes that Iqbal draws from the *Varieties* on prayer and that James's "work introduced Iqbal himself to the psychology and epistemology of American pragmatism." Ochs, "Iqbal, Peirce and Modernity." Similarly, Richard Gilmore considers Iqbal's relation to Pierce but also mentions his citation of James in Gilmore, "Pragmatism and Islam in Pierce and Iqbal," 88–111. Nicholas Adams focuses on understanding Iqbal's approach to western philosophy, briefly mentioning James; Adams, "Iqbal and the Western Philosophers." Asif Iqbal Khan notes that "Iqbal makes use of a kind of pragmatic method to justify the conclusions drawn by him;" in a footnote Khan elaborates: "Incidentally, James and Iqbal shared many convictions and beliefs. Both sport diversity of interest and are not much bothered by the need for method in their thought. It is possible to work out a significant area of influence under which Iqbal

Reconstruction. What is less well understood is how Iqbal follows James in developing an empiricism which takes religious experience into account. They both look to experience as the source of knowledge, considering the parity of religious experience and the sensory experiences foundational to science. They both look to further experience to test the conclusions drawn from religious experience, with a particular attention to the fruits of religious belief.

Although we cannot hope to be thorough in a short study, let us consider some of the major connections, looking first at the similarities and at Iqbal's citations of James, and then at the major difference.

Similarities

We may note five major similarities between James's and Iqbal's religious epistemologies. After considering them it would do to look at some of the evidence that these connections involve a direct influence of the former on the latter.

First, each of them is committed to the idea that knowledge comes from experience.

Second, each of them extends his understanding of empiricism beyond the traditional understanding of its boundaries. Sensory experience is not the only kind that counts. Religious experience also counts.

Third, they both argue that religion is partly justified on empirical grounds by looking to its origins in experience. Religious experience testifies to the likelihood of a reality outside our ordinary experience of the physical world.

Fourth, they both argue that religious belief derived from past experience ought to be tested in future experience.[51]

Fifth, they both argue that religion's ultimate empirical justification must come by looking at its fruits. James looks to the personal life-change associated with religious conversion, a fruit well known from already past experience. Iqbal looks to the past cultural contributions of Islam as

---

formulated some of his views strikingly in line with those of James." See Khan, "The Problem of Method in Iqbal's Thought." Khan later gives a more detailed study of James and Iqbal on the psychology of religion, albeit with little emphasis on epistemology; Khan, "James and Iqbal."

51. Proudfoot on James is remarkably similar to Iqbal's two tests: "Any belief must be tested by examining its reasonableness in the light of other beliefs already held and its consequences for ordering experience." Proudfoot, "William James on an Unseen Order," 58.

evidence, another look to the past. Both look hopefully to the future where religion may yield a much better world.[52]

There are other similarities in metaphysics. Both James and Iqbal resist materialism,[53] and both understand reality to have an ultimate mental rather than physical aspect.[54] Both defend the idea that we have free will.[55] And so on. Here, however, our priority is the epistemological and methodological similarities.

And these are no coincidence. Although Iqbal draws on many sources, James is a significant tributary to his thought. Let us look over the references to James in the *Reconstruction*. The first mention of James is in chapter I where Iqbal notes the similarity of medieval Islamic scholar Ibn Khaldun's thought to James's in the *Varieties*.[56] (Iqbal almost immediately notes his disagreement with James on the nature of "mystic experience.")[57] Elsewhere he similarly notes a similarity of Ibn Rushd (Averroes) to James.[58] Iqbal also cites "the great American psychologist, Professor William James" on the meaning and function of prayer.[59] Later he notes James's clever idea that our experience of the world is a continuous "stream" rather than a set of discrete units.[60] However, he objects, saying that consciousness as we experience it is not as James described, but rather shows the self as a constant presence directing consciousness. In another passage Iqbal mentions James's critique of an argument against life after death, but in turn critiques James's suggestion as an insufficient assurance of immortality.[61]

These references show that Iqbal is a reader of James and in dialogue with James, who had some degree of influence on him. The most important reference to James in the *Reconstruction* is the decisive third one. Paving the

---

52. See, for example, Lecture VIII in James's *A Pluralistic Universe*, the conclusion to "The Moral Philosopher and the Moral Life" in *The Will to Believe and Other Essays*, and Iqbal, *Reconstruction*, 179–80.

53. A memorable passage from James is found in the discussion of how Beethoven played on strings, when reduced to a materialistic explanation, is "a scraping of horses' tails on cats' bowels." James, "The Sentiment of Rationality" in *The Will to Believe and Other Essays*. For Iqbal's resistance to materialism, I suggest *Reconstruction*, chapter II.

54. See James, *A Pluralistic Universe* and Iqbal, *Reconstruction*, 61.

55. See James, "The Dilemma of Determinism" in *The Will to Believe and Other Essays* and Iqbal, *Reconstruction*, chapter IV.

56. Iqbal, *Reconstruction*, 17.

57. Iqbal, *Reconstruction*, 18.

58. Iqbal, *Reconstruction*, 112.

59. Iqbal, *Reconstruction*, 89.

60. Iqbal, *Reconstruction*, 102.

61. Iqbal, *Reconstruction*, 113.

way for his introduction of the pragmatic test of religious belief, Iqbal cites James.[62] Giving a succinct summary of James's idea from the beginning of the *Varieties* that the physical causes of religious experience do not matter, he then quotes James on what *does* matter in evaluating religious experience: "... by their fruits ye shall know them and not by their roots."[63]

Does this show that James's radical empiricism is the source of Iqbal's own version of religious empiricism? Certainly not; indeed, Iqbal would consider his own analysis a failure had he not drawn it from the Qur'an.[64] It does, however, show that at least one crucial aspect—the testing of a religious belief by its fruits—of his religious empiricism comes through James. In short, James's religious empiricism is very similar to Iqbal's in many respects, and while the former is not the sole source of the latter, it is an important source.

Different Directions in Interpretation

Iqbal and James are still rather different philosophers. It seems to me that there is one major difference in their religious epistemologies. Perhaps the only one, but it's a big one: They go in rather different directions in the interpretation of religious experience.

Recall that James in Lecture XX of *Varieties* summarizes the religious position "that there is *something wrong about us* as we naturally stand" and that "*we are saved from the wrongness* by making proper connection with the higher powers." He then suggests as a philosophical hypothesis that religious experience is what happens when we access a region of consciousness continuous with our own conscious minds but ordinarily beyond them. Whether this region is continuous with the God described by one of the traditional religions, with something else, or with nothing at all is a separate question. We are free to answer it as we may. James is characteristically eloquent:

> [H]ere mysticism and the conversion-rapture and Vedantism and transcendental idealism bring in their monistic interpretations and tell us that the finite self rejoins the absolute self, for it was always one with God and identical with the soul of the

62. Iqbal, *Reconstruction*, 23–24.

63. Khan notes that the *Varieties* "was an inspiration as well as a work which he used substantially in working out his own view of religion." Khan, "James and Iqbal."

64. For that matter, as Adams explains, Iqbal considers that the best of western philosophy was itself a development of Quranic ideas; see Adams, "Iqbal and the Western Philosophers."

world. Here the prophets of all the different religions come with their visions, voices, raptures, and other openings, supposed by each to authenticate his own peculiar faith.

Those of us who are not personally favored with such specific revelations must stand outside of them altogether and, for the present at least, decide that, since they corroborate incompatible theological doctrines, they neutralize one another and leave no fixed result. If we follow any one of them, or if we follow philosophical theory and embrace monistic pantheism on non-mystical grounds, we do so in the exercise of our individual freedom, and build out our religion in the way most congruous with our personal susceptibilities.

We face a choice of what "over-belief," in James's terminology, to have concerning that higher region of consciousness. We may choose philosophically or choose to follow one of the traditional religious views on the subject. James nods to one particular philosophical approach, the strategy favored by the Hegelians which leads towards monistic pantheism. As we have seen, his own considered over-belief is more along the lines of a hybrid of polytheism and pantheism—a view of all reality as touched with divine mind, but in a pluralistic rather than a monistic universe.

That is *his* choice. Put simply, the difference with Iqbal is that he makes a *different* choice. Iqbal's analysis of religious experience is explicitly tied to one specific religious tradition. He appeals to Islam, applies his pragmatic test to its prophetic origins, and recommends its spiritual and social insights for building a better world.

The conclusion to Iqbal's chapter II vividly depicts Iqbal's and James's parting of ways.[65] Like James, he nods to the Hegelian-style philosophy. This approach, Iqbal explains, tends towards pantheism. This is because philosophy can't help systematizing, and pantheism is the natural result of any systematization of the insight that ultimate reality is mind. Iqbal recommends we *not* take the philosopher's path; "the aspiration of religion soars higher than that of philosophy." We need not an intellectual account, but a relationship with the divine—"living experience, association, intimacy." So Iqbal points to prayer instead of to systematizing philosophy—and in context of an explanation and defense of Islam for the modern world.

Not that James's philosophy is systematizing in the manner of the Hegelians, or that he objects to prayer. (Indeed, he closes his essay "The Moral Philosopher and the Moral Life" with an eloquent exhortation to prayer.) James also thinks we need "living experience, association, intimacy."

---

65. Iqbal, *Reconstruction*, 60–61.

So it appears that James's and Iqbal's divergent approaches to religious empiricism are not in dramatic conflict. However, ultimately they do go in two separate directions.

And here I, personally, have one final point to offer. I, a Nicene Christian, go in a third direction. This too, so far as I can tell, is a permissible choice by James's lights. (James does air some concerns with traditional theism from time to time, for example in Lecture I of *A Pluralistic Universe* where he suggests that "philosophic theism makes us outsiders and keeps us foreigners in relation to God;" I think this difficulty is avoided in orthodox Christianity by the doctrine of the incarnation.) James says of Pascal in "Will to Believe" that he unduly limits our choices. Perhaps the divergence of James and Iqbal is similar; we do have other options consistent with religious empiricism.[66] The prophets Moses and Jesus may also be subjected to Iqbal's pragmatic test, and many other philosophers of religion (for example, to name only one of the more recent and famous ones, Richard Swinburne) have offered their own analyses of religious empiricism. In short, James and Iqbal have some interesting (and, it seems to me, insightful) things to say, but they are not the whole story.

CONCLUSION

So what have we learned? Allama Iqbal, twentieth-century Islamic philosopher of the Subcontinent, shows some influence of William James, nineteenth- and twentieth-century American philosopher. They both develop empirical accounts and defenses of religious belief. They both argue that a thoroughgoing empiricism must consider religious experience as a legitimate form of experience and a possible source of knowledge. They both argue that a religious belief is tested by its fruits. James's analysis comes about in the course of his development of radical empiricism, which leads ultimately to his articulation of a philosophical interpretation of the data of experience. Iqbal's analysis is part of his attempt to reconstruct traditional Islamic thought in the modern world.

And why does this matter? For many reasons, perhaps not the least of which is that it is interesting. We might also take from his influence on Iqbal a lesson on William James—that he is a global and not a merely American philosopher. And perhaps we can better appreciate how creative is Iqbal's

---

66. I would also note that the experiences on which the Christian faith rests, in particular the resurrection event, are not that type of "inner experience on which religious faith ultimately rests" according to Iqbal (*Reconstruction*, v). They are outer and public experiences.

philosophical approach integrating not only elements of religious mysticism and modern science but also a range of modern western philosophers.

However, I think the primary benefit of understanding the commonalities of James and Iqbal is the enrichment of our understanding of the topic of faith and reason. The conversation concerning the relationship of faith and rationality features diverse characters and perspectives. These two interesting participants are well worth knowing, and their insights and arguments are worth keeping in mind as that perennial discussion continues.

But there is more to say about empirical faith, which we must consider in the next chapter.

WORKS CITED

Adams, Nicholas. "Iqbal and the Western Philosophers." *Iqbal Review* 49.4 (2008) online at AllamaIqbal.com.

Algaier, Ermine L. "Reconstructing James's Early Radical Empiricism: The 1896 Preface and the 'The Spirit of Inner Tolerance.'" *William James Studies* 11 (2015) 46–63.

Brown, Hunter. *William James on Radical Empiricism and Religion*. Toronto: University of Toronto Press, 2000.

Campbell, James. *Experiencing William James: Belief in a Pluralistic World*. Charlottesville, VA: University of Virginia Press, 2017.

Diagne, Souleymane Bachir. *Islam and Open Society: Fidelity and Movement in the Philosophy of Muhammad Iqbal*. Translated by Melissa McMahon. Dakar: Codesria, 2010.

———. *Open to Reason: Muslim Philosophers in Conversation with the Western Tradition*. Translated by Jonathan Adjemian. New York: Columbia University Press, 2018.

Gilmore, Richard. "Pragmatism and Islam in Pierce and Iqbal: The Metaphysics of Emergent Mind." In *Muhammad Iqbal: Essays on the Reconstruction of Modern Muslim Thought*, edited by Chad Hillier and Basit Koshul, 88–111. Edinburgh: Edinburgh University Press, 2015.

Hollinger, David A. "James, Clifford, and the Scientific Conscience." *The Cambridge Companion to William James*, edited by Ruth Anna Putnam, 69–83. Cambridge: Cambridge University Press, 2006.

Iqbal, Sir Muhammad. *The Reconstruction of Religious Thought in Islam*. 1974. 11th ed. New Delhi: Kitab Bhavan, 2011.

James, William. "The Dilemma of Determinism." In *The Will to Believe and Other Essays in Popular Philosophy*. Available at https://gutenberg.org/files/26659/26659-h/26659-h.htm.

———. "The Moral Philosopher and the Moral Life." In *The Will to Believe and Other Essays in Popular Philosophy*. Available at https://gutenberg.org/files/26659/26659-h/26659-h.htm.

———. *A Pluralistic Universe: Hibbert Lectures at Manchester College on the Present Situation in Philosophy*. Available at https://www.gutenberg.org/cache/epub/11984/pg11984-images.html.

———. Preface. In *The Will to Believe and Other Essays in Popular Philosophy*. Available at https://gutenberg.org/files/26659/26659-h/26659-h.htm.

———. "The Sentiment of Rationality." In *The Will to Believe and Other Essays in Popular Philosophy*. Available at https://gutenberg.org/files/26659/26659-h/26659-h.htm.

———. "The Will to Believe." In *The Will to Believe and Other Essays in Popular Philosophy*. Available at https://gutenberg.org/files/26659/26659-h/26659-h.htm.

Khan, Asif Iqbal. "James and Iqbal (A New Approach to Psychology of Religion)." *Iqbal Review* 37.3 (1996) online at AllamaIqbal.com.

———. "The Problem of Method in Iqbal's Thought." *Iqbal Review* 35.1 (1994) online at AllamaIqbal.com.

Koshul, Basit Bilal. "Seeing, Knowing, Believing: Iqbal on Faith in the Modern World." *Iqbal Review* 47.4 (2006) online at AllamaIqbal.com.

Lamberth, David. *William James and the Metaphysics of Experience*. Cambridge: Cambridge University Press, 1999.

Niebuhr, Richard R. "William James on Religious Experience." In *The Cambridge Companion to William James*, edited by Ruth Anna Putnam, 214–36. Cambridge: Cambridge University Press, 1997.

Ochs, Peter. "Iqbal, Peirce and Modernity." *Iqbal Review* 49.4 (2008) online at AllamaIqbal.com.

O'Connell, Robert J. *William James on the Courage to Believe*. Bronx, NY: Fordham University Press, 1997.

Proudfoot, Wayne. "William James on an Unseen Order." *The Harvard Theological Review* 93.1 (2000) 51–66.

Sabine, George H. "Radical Empiricism as a Logical Method." *The Philosophical Review* 14.6 (1905) 696–705.

Slater, Michael R. *William James on Ethics and Faith*. Cambridge: Cambridge University Press, 2009.

Smith, John E. "Radical Empiricism." *Proceedings of the Aristotelian Society* 65 (1964–65) 206–18.

5

Can Faith Be Empirical?

Two fundamental questions in the study of science and Christian belief concern faith and empiricism.[1] Can a religious mode of believing also be an empirical mode of believing? What are the empirical characteristics of Christian faith specifically?

William James speaks in favor of empirical faith: "Let empiricism once become associated with religion, as hitherto, through some strange misunderstanding, it has been associated with irreligion, and I believe that a new era of religion as well as of philosophy will be ready to begin."[2] Similarly, the Dalai Lama, Sarvepalli Radhakrishnan, Allama Iqbal, Eliezer Berkovits, and C. S. Lewis—notable twentieth-century philosophers representing the religions of Buddhism, Hinduism, Islam, Judaism, and Christianity[3]—concur that their religious doctrines are truths we can know through experience. Their analyses, if correct, show that religion is thoroughly compatible with empirical modes of belief, give arguments for the possibility of religious empirical knowledge, and show that Christianity measures up well by empirical epistemological standards. Moreover, its doctrines even admit of the possibility of verification and falsification, and it is not reliance on faith

---

1. The biggest change to this chapter since its initial publication in *Science and Christian Belief* is that I have improved the account of those who think of knowledge as following the pattern of experience-interpretation-testing.

2. James, *A Pluralistic Universe*, Lecture VIII.

3. Such, at least, was their intention, and they seem to me to have been largely successful, although no doubt imperfect. (I have disagreed with Lewis myself on some points of Christian theology.)

so much as the particular method of testing which distinguishes Christian belief from science.

There is more than one sense of the word "empiricism." The theory that all our ideas originate in sensory experience is called "empiricism,"[4] as is the tradition in early modern British philosophy that was devoted to this idea.[5] In the quote above, James is talking about three other things. One is the *descriptive* theory that we get knowledge from experience—and that not limited to *sensory* experience. Another is the *normative* theory that, since we get knowledge from experience, we should submit our beliefs to rigorous scrutiny in light of evidence from experience. Finally, there is the way of life of someone who tries to *follow* that normative theory. I am interested in these senses of "empiricism," especially the latter two. It seems to me—following James and these others—that we may identify three major characteristics of a person whose thought life is marked by empiricism: Her beliefs are adopted based on evidence from experience, she seeks to test her beliefs in future experience, and she holds her beliefs with a degree of caution in case future experience should turn up evidence against them. If Lewis et al. know anything much about their respective religions, then these religions are highly compatible with empiricism. Religious belief can be based on empirical evidence, can seek and respond to experiences that support or undermine it, and can be held tentatively in case future

---

4. In this paper I develop the ideas of the aforementioned philosophers and apply their empirical epistemological standards to Christian theology. Their positions presume that we human beings experience reality and can gain knowledge about reality from that experience. A closer look at the meaning, significance, and reasonableness of this presumption along with other debates about the nature of experience, the meaning of "empiricism," and so on are outside the scope of this paper. The interested reader might begin to study these matters by consulting some of the following sources. For essays on the nature of philosophy, see Haug, *Philosophical Methodology: The Armchair or the Laboratory?* On the idea that reality exists independently of our minds, see Plantinga, "How to Be an Anti-Realist," 47–70, as well as McDowell, *Mind and World.* On twentieth-century and contemporary theories of empiricism, see Quine, "Two Dogmas of Empiricism," 20–43; Bealer and Strawson, "The Incoherence of Empiricism," 99–14; and van Frassen, *The Empirical Stance.*

5. Bacon, Hobbes, Locke, Berkley, and Hume held that all our ideas, and hence all knowledge, derive from sensory perception—contrary to the epistemology of continental European rationalist philosophers like Leibniz and Descartes. Even after Kant tried to integrate the insights of rationalism and empiricism, traditions descended from empiricism continued to focus on the idea that knowledge comes from experience. Logical positivism followed Hume and developed the idea that the only meaningful statements about a world outside the mind are those which can be tested in sensory experience. One notable idea from American pragmatists such as James and Dewey is the expansion of the category of "experience" beyond mere sensory experience—an influence on my own views.

experience should reveal evidence against it. Even dogmatic religious faith can be empirical, although there is a degree of tension between a fully empirical attitude and a faith which is "dogmatic" in the sense of an absolute or unquestioned commitment.

Of course, some religious traditions consider experience a source of knowledge alongside and sometimes, as in traditional Methodism, subservient to authoritative sources of knowledge. Although this demonstrates some degree of consistency between religious belief and empiricism, my concern is with the direct overlap of empirical attitudes and a posture of faith in particular testimonies of religious authority; a religious belief (or a system of religious beliefs) which is accepted by faith can *also* be accepted empirically, and Christianity is no exception. The fact that some religious traditions use experience as an *additional* source of knowledge or as a means of better understanding knowledge derived from faith is beside the point. Moreover, I will not delve into the contemporary literature on the epistemology of religious experience. William Alston, Richard Swinburne, Kai-man Kwan, and others have done some fine work on the idea that religious experience can be a source of rational belief or even knowledge.[6] Others have considered the commonalities of science and theology.[7] One thing more is needful in the defense of the Christian faith. We could do with a direct look at the twentieth-century philosophers who represented the world's great religions in their encounters with modern empiricism as they consider these three characteristics of empiricism. This article considers their insights, with a little help from Augustine and James. I will begin with Buddhism, Hinduism, Islam, and Judaism. Then I will show that Christianity can have these three aspects of empiricism and explain some of the salient empirical features of Christian theology. Lastly, in a concluding section, I will summarize and offer some clarifications of my position.

EASTERN RELIGIONS, ISLAM, AND JUDAISM

We begin with the Dalai Lama and Radhakrishnan, philosophers representing Buddhism and Hinduism and pointing to the origin of religious belief in experience, efforts to test it, and tentativeness in case future experience should turn up evidence against it. Radhakrishnan has an interesting

---

6. Alston, *Perceiving God*; Swinburne, *The Existence of God*; Kwan, *The Rainbow of Experiences*. For a good introduction to this field, see Webb, "Religious Experience," Section 3.

7. Such as Johnson, *Epistemology and Biblical Theology* and *Biblical Knowing*. Also Torrance, *Reality and Scientific Theology* and *Theological and Natural Science*.

analysis of how that testing works—following, he says, a two-step process of logical investigation and application to future experience. Moreover, both treat their religious beliefs as entirely subject to modification in light of future experience since nothing in their religious beliefs is fixed; the doctrines to which they are committed may be modified without the religion changing in any crucial way.

In a talk on what Buddhism and neuroscience can do for each other, the Dalai Lama says that Buddhism has always recognized experience as a source of knowledge overriding all others: "... in the Buddhist investigative tradition, between the three recognized sources of knowledge—experience, reason and testimony—it is the evidence of the experience that takes precedence, with reason coming second and testimony last."[8] A thorough empiricism is always open to old conclusions, including the most important religious doctrines, being corrected by future experience.[9] The generalized thought-pattern here, which we will see in other thinkers, is from fact to interpretation—an interpretation recognized as fallible, correctable in light of future experience.

Representing the Hindu tradition is Sarvepalli Radhakrishnan, a philosopher-king in the twentieth century—or at least a philosopher who was president of India. Radhakrishnan explains that Hinduism has no "fixed intellectual beliefs," but always subordinates "dogma to experience."[10] Faith is a kind of "spiritual perception," fallible and in need of testing.[11] All deliverances of perception are subject to a twofold testing process; after being sifted through logic, they are sent back to experience for further testing.[12] Radhakrishnan claims that even the most sacred Hindu scriptures, the Vedas, do not give us any non-negotiable belief; such fixed doctrine as Hinduism possesses is not *in* the Vedas, but *about* them—the doctrine that they are records of spiritual perceptions: "They are not so much dogmatic dicta as transcripts from life. They record the spiritual experiences of souls strongly endowed with the sense for reality. They ... express the experiences of the experts in the field of religion."[13] (Similarly, a scientist may take it as unquestioned dogma that the data in a report on an experiment really do originate in the experiences of the scientist performing it.) We have an

8. Gyatso, "Science at the Crossroads."

9. Siderits is similar, taking Buddhism as a non-dogmatic set of beliefs and practices based on reason rather than authority; Siderits, *Buddhism as Philosophy*.

10. Radhakrishnan, *The Hindu View of Life*, 15.

11. Radhakrishnan, *The Hindu View of Life*, 16.

12. Radhakrishnan, *The Hindu View of Life*, 16.

13. Radhakrishnan, *The Hindu View of Life*, 17.

inalienable "right to inquire and sift the evidence."[14] The Vedic doctrines derive from experience, and are subjected to the test of future experience: "The truths revealed in the Vedas are capable of being re-experienced," and we can test them "by means of logic but also through life."[15] In sum, "The Hindu philosophy of religion starts from and returns to an experimental basis . . . ."[16] This is the same thought-pattern as the Dalai Lama's talk, although Radhakrishnan here is a little clearer than the Dalai Lama there on how the whole process works: We move from the facts of experience to an interpretation of those facts, and we then take that interpretation back to the facts for testing.

Simply put, even the most thoroughgoing empiricism poses no problem for a religious outlook lacking both essential and unquestioned doctrines. That's no problem for the Dalai Lama or Radhakrishnan, nor for some western dogma-less religious outlooks such as those of Unitarianism, John Dewey in *A Common Faith*,[17] and James, who tells us that empiricists consider all religious doctrines subject to correction by later experience.[18]

We now turn to Abrahamic religions. Allama Iqbal, representing Islam, argues that religious knowledge can be rooted in experience and, moreover, tested. Eliezer Berkovits represents Judaism and focuses on the particular experiences of the historical events at Sinai. Berkovits suggests that this sort of religious belief may be confirmed in *future* experience.

A brief word of introduction: Sir Muhammad Iqbal (1877–1938), a British knight and national poet of Pakistan, wrote poetry in Urdu and Persian, wrote philosophy in Persian and English, and is the only major philosopher I know of after whom an international airport has been named (Allama Iqbal International in Lahore, Pakistan). Iqbal argues that experience may encounter divine reality, resulting in the data necessary for empirical religious knowledge. Iqbal's *The Reconstruction of Religious Thought in Islam* attempts to integrate the insights of modern science and religious mysticism, especially Sufism. Knowledge, he says, is born of reflection based on experience. Scientific knowledge is born of reflection on sensory experience, and religious knowledge is born of reflection on religious experience. He says, "The facts of religious experience are facts among other facts of

---

14. Radhakrishnan, *The Hindu View of Life*, 18.
15. Radhakrishnan, *The Hindu View of Life*, 17.
16. Radhakrishnan, *The Hindu View of Life*, 17.
17. Dewey, *A Common Faith*
18. James, *The Will to Believe and Other Essays*, 17.

human experience and, in the capacity of yielding knowledge by interpretation, one fact is as good as another."[19]

Here is a more formal reconstruction of Iqbal's argument:

1. Science is a branch of knowledge.

2. That which is knowledge has sufficient warrant to be knowledge.

3. Science derives its warrant from a combination of experience and reflection on experience.

4. So experience and reflection on experience is a possible source of sufficient warrant for knowledge.

5. There is such a thing as religious experience that can be reflected on.

6. So religious experience and reflection on it is a possible source of sufficient warrant for knowledge.

Iqbal's premises, if true, are good reason to think his conclusion is true. One possible objection is that there may be no such thing as experience with a divine reality: So-called "religious" experiences are mere delusions! It seems to me that we may let experience determine whether this is the case; more precisely, whether at least some of the experiences people call "religious" are actual encounters with a divine reality should be determined by considering those experiences.[20] Prior to that investigation, we need merely take Iqbal's argument as aiming at the *possibility* of an experience of the divine, and rephrase premise 5: *It is possible that there is such a thing as an experience in which a human being encounters a divine reality and that this experience can be reflected on.*

Of course, we need not be talking about one's *own* experience. Scientific knowledge draws from experience, but most of us rely on the experiences of others for our scientific knowledge. Non-professional scientists rely entirely on the experiences of others for their scientific knowledge, but can still have knowledge from science. I know, for example, that electrons exist and that polio vaccinations prevent polio. Even a professional scientist relies largely on the experiences of others (on which more anon).

There is another objection in the area: Mystical or subjective religious experiences are not accessible to all observers. Fair enough. Insofar as Iqbal's argument pertains to such experiences, this would limit the degree of warrant available for the resulting beliefs. Hence a belief with an empirical origin ought, ideally, also to be tested. Iqbal agrees. At the end of

---

19. Iqbal, *Reconstruction*, Lecture I.

20. Larmer reaches the same conclusion about miracles in Larmer, *The Legitimacy of Miracle*.

chapter 1 of the *Reconstruction*, he introduces two tests of religious beliefs. The *intellectual* test would see whether a religious belief coheres with everything else we know from experience, and the *pragmatic* test would see whether a prophet's revelation has led to good results. Iqbal devotes chapter 2 of his book to analyzing religion in light of modern science, and chapter 5 to analyzing the fruits of Islam. Another version of the same pattern of thought we saw in the Dalai Lama and Radhakrishnan: We go from the facts of experience to an interpretation of those facts, and then we move on to test those interpretations.

In any case, Iqbal's argument is not relevant only to mystical or subjective experiences; the experiences of God alleged by the Abrahamic religions are for the most part historical events in which humans encountered the divine, often recognizing it as such by accompanying miracles.

This leads us to Berkovits. In a 1961 article Berkovits asks, "What is Jewish philosophy?"[21] He explains that there is a "common denominator"[22] in genuinely Jewish philosophy—the building of its doctrines "not on ideas but on certain facts and events."[23] These include the exodus, the giving of the Torah at Sinai, and the establishing of the Hebrew nation.[24] These are historical facts, "events themselves having occurred, the facts having entered into history . . . ."[25] These historical experiences are the foundation of the Jewish religion. Judaism is not *a priori*. So also in his *God, Man, and History* (1959), Berkovits explains that "The foundation of religion is not the affirmation that God *is*, but that God is concerned with man and the world . . . ."[26] We can *know* that God is concerned "by the appropriate proof," which is not "metaphysical"[27] but empirical: We know by our experience of God's help in response to our entreating.[28] The same empirical pattern pertains to God's existence, relevance, Word, and instructions. It even involves sensory perception: "At Sinai, you knew God . . . by actual experience, in which all of your senses were involved."[29]

Berkovits suggests that the biblical encounter with God is not merely a historical event. The occurrence at Sinai is fixed history, but the same God

21. Berkovits, "What Is Jewish Philosophy?," 117–30.
22. Berkovits, "What Is Jewish Philosophy?," 119.
23. Berkovits, "What Is Jewish Philosophy?," 120.
24. Berkovits, "What Is Jewish Philosophy?," 120–21.
25. Berkovits, "What Is Jewish Philosophy?," 120.
26. Berkovits, *God, Man, and History*, 15.
27. Berkovits, *God, Man, and History*, 15.
28. Berkovits, *God, Man, and History*, 15–16.
29. Berkovits, *God, Man, and History*, 17.

may be experienced today: "that 'the Eternal, he is God' is revealed in an event, that this knowledge was experienced—and that it remains capable of being experienced—is of course what is meant by 'the living God,' Judaism's incomparable discovery."[30] The idea here seems to be that religious knowledge may be verified in contemporary experience, to which we will return later.

CHRISTIANITY

Christian theology will not entail quite the same epistemology as other religions. Christianity presumes a verbal revelation from God; Christians expect, as John 1:18 says, to know God through Jesus Christ; and so on. Others have studied the particularities of biblical and Christian epistemology.[31] Yet the epistemological particularities of Christianity do not preclude that Christian theology has the empirical traits of rootedness in past experience, the seeking of testing in future experience, and a degree of tentativeness in case future experience should disconfirm the beliefs. In this section I will first review the idea that knowledge, including empirical knowledge, can be faith. Then I will explain how Christian theology can have these traits of empiricism.

Knowledge, Including Empirical Knowledge, Depends on Faith

It is an old idea that an article of faith can be an instance of knowledge. Besides James and our other thinkers, Thomas F. Torrance has written of the commonalities between science and theology as studies dealing with our experience of objective reality.[32] This is very proper. However, one crucial point is best made by considering Augustine—that trust in authority can be a source of knowledge, and is indeed a source of empirical knowledge on which science no less than Christian theology is reliant.

Faith is trust. This is the first definition in the English dictionary,[33] and the Latin *fides* and the Greek *pistis* concur. Faith and knowledge overlap because belief based on a reliable authority can be an instance of both faith *and* knowledge.

30. Berkovits, *God, Man, and History*, 17.

31. For example, Johnson, *Biblical Knowing and Epistemology and Biblical Theology* as well as "Knowledge by Ritual" and *Scripture's Knowing*.

32. Torrance, *Reality and Scientific Theology* and *Theological and Natural Science*, among other books.

33. faith, MerriamWebster.com.

It is helpful to keep in mind that arguments from authority are not necessarily fallacious. They are good or bad depending on their content, and most importantly on whether it is reasonable to suppose that the authority really has the expertise presumed by the argument.[34] An argument from a *reliable* authority speaking within his area of expertise is generally a good argument, and any other argument from authority a bad one. We must also remember that science is not the epistemological opposite of faith: one relying entirely on reason, one not at all. We may set aside the argument that science is not a matter of objective reason alone[35] and even the fact that religious faith often relies on reason to varying degrees.[36] The crucial point is that science, like a typical religion, depends on faith—*on trust.*

Of course, scientific experiments can be repeated; in principle at least, all of the data supporting scientific knowledge can be tested, much of it *is* tested, and many scientists have done some of the testing themselves. By and large, however, science relies on trust; no individual scientist has tested enough data *not* to. Nor would he have time to do so, nor would it be prudent thus to use his time if he did. Say a chemist wants to know chemistry without relying on trust at all; he will have to begin *from the very beginning* and repeat *all* of the experiments that led to the current state of chemical knowledge *multiple times each*. He would likely die of old age before catching up with the present state of chemical knowledge. His hard work would be useless unless others were willing to take his word for it at least *some* of the time on how his experiments had turned out.

Thus scientific knowledge, even for scientists, relies heavily on trust in the testimony of reliable witnesses. The rest of us are entirely dependent on their testimony for our scientific knowledge. The same is true of other areas of knowledge, as Augustine shows.[37] In *history*, we know by trust that Socrates died in Athens after being condemned by the Athenian jury. In *geography*, we know that Harare, Zimbabwe, exists; most readers of this article know it only by trust; although *I* have been to Harare, I rely on trust for my knowledge of the existence of Moscow. In the category of *social and familial* knowledge, I know who my parents are by faith alone. If I underwent DNA testing, my knowledge would still depend on trust, unless, like our incredulous chemist, I were to spend my entire life collecting the data and replicating the experiments underlying genetic science!

---

34. Howard-Snyder, Howard-Snyder, and Wasserman, *The Power of Logic*, 509–12.

35. Kuhn, *The Structure of Scientific Revolutions*.

36. For example, Thomas Aquinas's *Summa Theologiae* is one of the most impressive works of systematic reasoning ever written.

37. Augustine, *On the Profit of Believing* and *Confessions*, Book VI, chapter 5.

In short, faith, or trust, is a necessary source (or, rather, a conveyor) of knowledge, and a major source (or conveyor) of empirical knowledge. Accordingly, insofar as it is possible to experience God or any other reality in which religious belief is interested, trust in this testimony can be an empirical source (or conveyor) of *religious* knowledge. That this is so is, as we have seen, said by some religious philosophers. We now turn to the same themes in C. S. Lewis.

Christian Theology Is Rooted in Experience

Perhaps the most influential twentieth-century Christian philosopher, C. S. Lewis, writes in *Mere Christianity* of the sources of Christian doctrine in experience. He says:

> And that is how Theology started. People already knew about God in a vague way. Then came a man who claimed to be God; and yet he was not the sort of man you could dismiss as a lunatic. He made them believe Him. They met Him again after they had seen Him killed. And then, after they had been formed into a little society or community, they found God somehow inside them as well: directing them, making them able to do things they could not do before. And when they worked it all out they found they had arrived at the Christian definition of the three-personal God.[38]

The essential doctrines of Christianity have an empirical basis: the experiences of those who knew the living, miracle-working, crucified, and resurrected Messiah of the Hebrew religion. That itself is a rather important experience of the divine.[39] Its power to contribute to empirical religious knowledge is compounded by the daily religious experience of the community of early Messiah-followers. Notice how Lewis parallels Berkovits in placing the origins of religious knowledge in historical events, and also on the possibility of interacting with the same God *after* those historical events have passed. Notice how Lewis's account mirrors Iqbal's claim that reflection on religious experience can produce knowledge: "when they worked it all out" they had discovered knowledge of the Trinity. Warrant rooted in

---

38. Lewis, *Mere Christianity*, 163.

39. Radhakrishnan is wrong that Christianity relies on only one religious experience, "the immediate certitude of Jesus as one whose authority over conscience is self-certifying and whose ability and willingness to save the soul it is impossible not to trust." *The Hindu View of Life*, 19. The resurrection is a more important religious experience, but, as Lewis shows, we cannot name *only* one.

reflection on experience of the divine is precisely the origin of Christian theology. Iqbal shows that religious belief can be rooted in experience, and he gives a criterion for its being knowledge; Lewis shows that Christian belief has that origin and meets that criterion. In short, despite differences in history, culture, and theology, these three religious philosophers are working with very similar ideas, and their conclusions converge on the empirical respectability of religious belief, with all emphasizing its experiential origin, Lewis and Iqbal emphasizing reflection on experience, and Lewis and Berkovits emphasizing historical events and a religious community's continuing encounters with the God responsible for those events.

In our day we are heirs to the historical testimony, not ourselves eyewitnesses. Still, as we have seen, empirical knowledge typically depends in large part on trust in eyewitnesses. The biblical events of which Lewis speaks are not things we believe without knowledge just because our belief relies on the testimony of witnesses. Rather, as Augustine shows, the origin of Christian theology in eyewitness testimony would confirm that we *can* have knowledge here, just as I can have scientific, historical, geographical, and familial and social knowledge derived from eyewitness testimony. And Christian theology *does* have such origins, as others have shown.[40]

A third source of empirical warrant for Christian theology is easily incorporated into Lewis's account. The experiences of the Hebrew prophets and their hearers resulted in a number of detailed predictions of the Messiah which the early church understood fit their own experiences of the Messiah (as Paul points out; 1 Cor 15:4).

Christian Knowledge Can Be Tested

One possible weakness of religious empirical knowledge confronts us. All else being equal, a belief derived from experience which *cannot* be tested is less secure than a belief which *can*. Its truth is less probable; it has a lesser degree of warrant, and if it is knowledge then it is a poorer sort of knowledge.

By way of comparison, *my* knowledge of science, since I am not a scientist, depends entirely on trust. But a professional scientist's scientific knowledge is not dependent *entirely* on trust, for she does some testing on her own. Moreover, *my* scientific knowledge has the advantage that it is usually not reliant on trust in only a few, but relies on many who have replicated the relevant experiments. Moreover, if I should ever want to test

---

40. On which, see the likes of Bauckham, *Jesus and the Eyewitnesses*; Wright, *The Resurrection of the Son of God*; Craig, *Assessing the New Testament Evidence*; and Loke, *Investigating the Resurrection*.

my knowledge, I may be able to replicate some of the experiments myself, or have someone I trust do it for me.

In short, knowledge derived from experience is better off if it can be *tested*. Can religious empirical knowledge be tested? Iqbal, for one, says so. However, while I agree on the importance of his intellectual and pragmatic tests, I will not focus on them here, instead considering the processes of verification and falsification.

So—can Christian theology be tested? Yes. Before explaining why, it will first be necessary to summarize my own working views of the nature of empirical warrant in science, which I consider to involve distinct processes of verification and falsification. Then I will consider the verification of Christian theology, showing that some points of Christian theology can be subjected to tests for verification. Next, I will consider the falsification of Christian theology, showing that certain doctrines can be subjected to tests for falsification.

Accordingly, Christian belief can have that second characteristic of empiricism, that its adherents seek warrant for their beliefs in future experience. In Radhakrishnan's terms, Christian theology is drawn from experience and may be tested logically before being returned to experience for confirmation.

The Forms of Scientific Warrant

Science is a highly refined method of gaining empirical knowledge, and it makes a helpful comparison for other varieties of empirical belief. The nature of scientific reasoning is a major topic of discussion in the philosophy of science, and I will not attempt to bring any disputes to a close here.[41] A brief statement of my own working understanding will suffice for our purposes. Roughly, science is the practice of learning about the world through observing, theorizing, conducting controlled experiments, and revising. A genuinely scientific theory is one which does not fit all possible accumulations of data based on sensory experience. The experimental component of scientific practice brings a theory into contact with experiences and relevant data likely to *fit* it (if the theory is correct) or *not* fit it (if it turns out to be incorrect). The predictions one can make on the basis of a theory are especially useful in identifying what sort of data are relevant.

41. On this discussion see Kuhn's challenge to the unmixed objectivity of science as well as Popper's analysis of falsification in *The Logic of Scientific Discovery*. Also useful is A. J. Ayer's *Language, Truth, and Logic*, a classical statement of logical positivism and a good source on the idea that scientific statements are characterized by verifiability.

There are, however, distinct ways a theory may be tested against a set of relevant data; it may be either verified or falsified. Roughly, verification is what happens when a scientist finds new data that fit a theory, and falsification is what happens when she finds new data that do *not*. The former is the finding of evidence *for* it, the latter the finding of evidence *against*. Although it is no doubt possible to test some theories for verification and falsification at the same time, not every theory can be both falsified and verified by the same test, if it can be both verified and falsified at all. The theory that the Vikings never visited the Punjab could be falsified by new archaeological evidence, say by the remains of a Viking longboat on the banks of the Indus, but it cannot be verified in this way. The theory that the Vikings *did* visit Canada can easily be verified by archaeological evidence, but would be very difficult to falsify. Moreover, a theory that can be subjected to tests for falsification and verification at the same time may be verified but not yet falsified—as was that well-known example, the theory that all swans are white, for quite some time.

Although Thomas Kuhn does not believe in absolute falsification,[42] I need not come to terms with this question. The mere finding of strong evidence against a theory is close enough to the falsifying of it for the purposes of my analysis of empiricism and faith. The important point is simply that distinct processes take place in the empirical testing of a theory against relevant data: confirmation from the data (what I am, perhaps a bit loosely, calling "verification"), and disconfirmation ("falsification").

Verification

So verification and falsification are distinct processes, and both are important to empirical testing. Can Christian knowledge derived from experience be either verified or falsified? It can. Here I will first explain one important characteristic of the verification of some religious beliefs, a point explained nicely by James and Lewis. Then I will consider Lewis's remarks on the verification of religious belief in corporate religious experience and, lastly, the verifiability of religious belief in historical claims.

James explains one reason the verification of religious belief might be possible, but might not proceed in the same manner as the verification of scientific knowledge:

> The more perfect and more eternal aspect of the universe is represented in our religions as having personal form . . . and any

---

42. Kuhn, *Structure of Scientific Revolutions*, 145.

> relation that may be possible from person to person might be possible here.... We feel, too, as if the appeal of religion to us were made to our own active good-will, as if evidence might be forever withheld from us unless we met the hypothesis half-way. To take a trivial illustration: just as a man who in a company of gentlemen made no advances, asked a warrant for every concession, and believed no one's word without proof, would cut himself off by such churlishness from all the social rewards that a more trusting spirit would earn—so here, one who should shut himself up in snarling logicality and try to make the gods extort his recognition willy-nilly, or not get it at all, might cut himself off forever from his only opportunity of making the gods' acquaintance.[43]

Religious truth might be verifiable after all, but under certain conditions. God, like any other person, might require us to trust more than the currently available evidence requires. Yet this may be only temporary. The evidence may come from God, as it did from Shakespeare's Beatrice to Benedick and from him to her, *after* our belief in it—perhaps even *because of* our belief in it.

Lewis independently reached the same insight, concurring in James's use of the analogy from human persons to divine:

> Theology is, in a sense, an experimental science.... I mean that it is like the other experimental sciences in some ways, but not in all. If you are a geologist studying rocks, you have to go and find the rocks. They will not come to you, and if you go to them they cannot run away. The initiative lies all on your side.... But suppose you are a zoologist.... That is a bit different from studying rocks. The wild animals will not come to you: but they can run away from you. Unless you keep very quiet, they will. There is beginning to be a tiny little trace of initiative on their side.
>
> Now a stage higher; suppose you want to get to know a human person. If he is determined not to let you, you will not get to know him. You have to win his confidence. In this case the initiative is equally divided—it takes two to make a friendship.
>
> When you come to knowing God, the initiative lies on His side.[44]

This is one of the key differences between science and religion. Science depends on replicable experiments, which works best when there is the

---

43. James, *Will to Believe*, 27–28.
44. Lewis, *Mere Christianity*, 164.

possibility of some degree of control over that which is being tested. Human control over divine reality is just not possible. So it would be a mistake to say that scientific belief differs from religious belief simply because one is subject to testing and one is not; rather, one is normally subject to *controlled* testing, and the other is not. (Notice that I am talking about having some *control* over the object of study; I am not talking a "controlled" experiment in the sense of an experiment using a "control" group.)

Lewis extends the analogy, saying that God will not verify knowledge of himself to just any man. God cannot "show Himself to a man whose whole mind and character are in the wrong condition."[45] Lewis:

> You can put this another way by saying that while in other sciences the instruments you use are things external to yourself (things like microscopes and telescopes), the instrument through which you see God is your whole self. And if a man's self is not kept clean and bright, his glimpse of God will be blurred—like the Moon seen through a dirty telescope.[46]

God's initiative in verifying religious belief depends in part on the state of those trying to verify it. Willingness to believe is not enough if we want to know God in present experience; we also have to be *good*. Lewis explains that man, made in the image of God, can know God best when they—no longer *he*, but *they*—are living like they are meant to:

> God can show Himself as He really is only to real men. And that means not simply to men who are individually good, but to men who are united together in a body, loving one another, helping one another, showing Him to one another. For that is what God meant humanity to be like; like players in one band, or organs in one body.[47]

Lewis thus suggests another key difference between science and religion. Not only is religion less subject to *controlled* testing than science usually is, but the verification of religious belief can only be successfully attempted by a holy and loving community. Verification of scientific knowledge rarely if ever depends on any moral qualities of a community of scientists.

Verification takes place—in the life of the church when it is living holily. They will perceive that God exists in their communal Christian experience: "Consequently, the one really adequate instrument for learning about God, is the whole Christian community, waiting for Him together. Christian

---

45. Lewis, *Mere Christianity*, 164–65.
46. Lewis, *Mere Christianity*, 164–65.
47. Lewis, *Mere Christianity*, 165.

brotherhood is, so to speak, the technical equipment for this science—the laboratory outfit."[48] In this holy life the community of believers experience God; and that experience fits their religious faith. To be precise, under these conditions their experience provides data consistent with their religious beliefs. As Berkovits says, the living God is one we may still encounter.

Finally, and much more briefly, the historical aspect of some religions opens them up to a considerable degree of verifiability. This is particularly salient to the Abrahamic traditions, many of whose historical claims are open to a significant degree of verification from relevant data sets accumulated from history or archaeology. Insofar as these religions *entail* these historical claims, then, those religions are at least partially verifiable. And insofar as an adherent of such a religion takes such claims on faith, at least those particulars of her faith are verifiable. Various points of Christian belief are verifiable, and a great many have been verified, from the existence of the Hittite empire to the biblical characters whose tombs have been discovered.

Falsification

Can Christian theology be falsified? I think so, for at least two reasons. First, universal claims made by religious theories of inerrancy or infallibility open up these religious views to falsifying counterexamples. Second, those religions which include or rely on historical claims are often falsifiable by historical or archaeological data. The central claim of the Christian religion, the resurrection of Jesus the Messiah, is a particularly striking example of a falsifiable religious doctrine.

The doctrine, particularly important to various branches of the Abrahamic religions, of an infallible or inerrant authority is falsifiable. Perhaps not every strictly theological or moral claim made by a religious authority is falsifiable. Consider, however, that the doctrine that an authority is inerrant constitutes a universal denial of *any* errors in that particular authority. Such a doctrine is falsifiable if only that authority should make a disprovable claim about something which can be empirically investigated. Within Christianity *alone*, this opens up at least two major doctrines to the possibility of falsification: the doctrine of biblical inerrancy and the Roman Catholic doctrine of magisterial infallibility.

Take biblical inerrancy. Though it goes back at least as far as the church fathers,[49] it has more recently been presented as the doctrine that the Bible is

---

48. Lewis, *Mere Christianity*, 165.

49. See, for example, Book XII of Augustine's *Confessions* where he commits himself to the authority of the Bible's meaning as intended by its authors. Note, however, that Augustine is open to a biblical passage meaning more than that intended by its author.

without error according to its original meaning, that being located within the intentions of the human authors.[50] But if that intent includes any falsifiable claim, such as one that might possibly conflict with modern science, then not only *that* claim but *the entire doctrine* of biblical inerrancy is falsifiable.

Indeed, many believe that the doctrine of biblical inerrancy has *already been falsified*. They think it is disproved by the incompatibility of one or more biblical teachings and the findings of science. Let us look at one typical example. Inerrancy may be falsified against a set of data pertaining to the Hebrew language, ancient literature, and geology. All that is required for falsification is that that particular set of data strongly supports two propositions: that the original meaning of Genesis 1–3 is that the earth was created by God in a mere six days, and that the earth itself is in fact far too old to have been created in a mere six days.[51] For the record, I myself do not think that that set of data supports both of these claims; I do not think that the doctrine of biblical inerrancy has been falsified. However, I am in agreement with those who think that science *has* falsified biblical inerrancy in thinking that *the logical possibility* of this sort of thing is entailed by the very meaning of inerrancy.

By the same reasoning, any other claim of infallibility in a Holy Book, a prophet of God, or the theological or moral pronouncements of a church or a Pope is likewise falsifiable—if only that authority makes some claims intersecting with science, history, or any other field where empirical data may conflict with those claims. For that matter, even claims that are not falsifiable in and of themselves can serve to falsify a claim about infallibility if any two such claims should contradict—if the Bible clearly says both "X" and "Not X," we can be sure that the Bible is wrong on *something*, whether or not we have any ability to test the claim "X."

Finally, and more generally, any historical religious claim, such as are common in the Abrahamic religions, which can fail to fit some accumulation of relevant archaeological or historical data is falsifiable. Insofar as such a religion *entails* such a historical claim, the religion *itself* is falsifiable. And any such religious claim is a falsifiable religious belief for anyone who takes that particular belief on faith.

The Christian gospel includes one particularly important historical claim: the resurrection of Jesus the Messiah, identified by Paul in 1 Cor 15

---

50. The International Council on Biblical Inerrancy; "The Chicago Statement on Biblical Inerrancy."

51. To be a bit more precise, it seems to me that a falsification of biblical inerrancy would require that the multiplied probability of these two propositions exceed the probability of biblical inerrancy given whatever evidence supports it.

as the *sine qua non* of the Christian faith. Remarkably, this central doctrine is eminently falsifiable. It always has been *in principle*: All it takes is persuasive evidence of the bones of Jesus in some tomb. It is falsifiable *in practice*, though it would be difficult to find and confirm right set of bones after all this time. In the earliest days the falsification of this doctrine would seem to have been remarkably easy. To be precise, the resurrection survives *this* test for falsification: *Did Jesus's judges and executioners produce the body or, if his ragtag band of followers had overcome the national and imperial peacekeeping apparatus and made off with the body, did they extract its location by bribes or torture and then locate and display it?*[52]

This test is still relevant. True, this particular test for falsification is reliant on the lack of such falsifying evidence in the historical record. This diminishes the strength of the test by making it dependent on trust in the currently available historical sources. This, however, does *not* mean the test is insignificant; after all, I can know the falsity of the proposition "All swans are white" although I myself have not seen a black swan and rely on the testimony of others. What diminishes the strength of this test for falsification is *not* that our knowledge of how the test went relies on *trust*. What diminishes its strength is that what we learn from that trust is difficult to verify and that this particular test for falsification is impossible to *repeat*. All else being equal, a test for falsification which *can* be repeated and whose results are easily verified is better than one which lacks these characteristics. All the same, this particular test is somewhat significant in and of itself, and it also serves as an important refutation of the misperception that religious belief and falsifiable belief are never the same thing.

In summary, religious beliefs rooted in experience can be subjected to future testing, although not to tests that can be performed by an individual tester regardless of moral character, or to repeatable and controllable tests like a typical scientific theory.[53] This testing may provide verification, or perhaps falsification. Accordingly, not only does Christian theology derive largely from experience, but it also can also have a second major characteristic of empiricism: It can be held by one who seeks to test and, hopefully, confirm these beliefs in future experience. Since various Christian beliefs are verifiable or falsifiable, a Christian can easily approach future experience with the possibility of this testing in mind.

---

52. There are other possible tests for falsification, such as whether there is any very good historical evidence that the New Testament's depiction of Jesus's character is seriously inaccurate.

53. Arguably neither can some theories in science, such as ideas in theoretical physics testable only by continuing consistency with observations. Resolving this matter, however, is outside the scope of this chapter.

Christian Theology Can Be Held Tentatively

A third characteristic of empiricism is that an empiricist believes with a degree of caution, mindful of the possibility that future experience will produce evidence against his beliefs. Christian faith can have this characteristic of empiricism. Here we must confront the objection that a religion with dogmas cannot have this trait of empiricism. Let us first review some of the available senses of the word "dogma," then look at the limited compatibility of empiricism and the unquestioning acceptance of or absolute commitment to Christian theology, and finally look at the full compatibility of empiricism and Christian dogma in the sense of a settled, accepted, or official belief.

"Dogma" can mean different things. Three uses are particularly relevant for our investigation, those suggesting irrational belief, stubborn and unquestioning belief, and settled or official belief. For example, we see in *Merriam-Webster* that a "dogma" might be "a point of view or tenet put forth as authoritative without adequate grounds," the result of trust without reason.[54] (The derivatives of "dogmatism" and "dogmatic" often have this connotation of irrational or unreasoned belief.) Alternatively, and turning to Dictionary.com, we see that "dogma" can mean "prescribed doctrine proclaimed as unquestionably true by a particular group."[55] Or, returning to *Merriam-Webster*, "dogma" might simply be "something held as an established opinion," i.e. an official or established teaching.[56]

Christianity, of course, is a religion with dogmas; but does that mean irrational trust, unquestioning belief, or established teaching? Based on what we have already seen, plainly not irrational trust. Suppose that Christianity is "dogmatic" in the sense of requiring an absolute commitment—a commitment to beliefs objections to which I am rigidly refusing to entertain. A thoroughgoing empiricism will hold beliefs tentatively. This sort of "dogmatism" would rule out such tentativeness (and with it one motivation to seek more evidence in future experience). Yet this sort of religious belief may still have a strongly empirical aspect. Such a dogmatic believer might simply think that his religion requires an absolute commitment to a given doctrine which happens to be warranted by the empirical evidence. He might conclude that the empirical evidence warrants acceptance of the belief yet also conclude that the nature of the doctrine requires a commitment with no turning back, perhaps an absolute commitment *beyond* that which

---

54. dogma, MerriamWebster.com.
55. dogma, Dictionary.com.
56. dogma, MerriamWebster.com.

is strictly warranted by the evidence. (This, I think, was one of Kierkegaard's points about faith and reason—not that Christianity is unreasonable but that it requires a total commitment when reason at its best can provide only partial evidence.) Such an attitude to faith may be compared to marriage. A young man might consider the proposition "Miss S. R. is the woman who should be my wife" to have a 93% probability as warranted by the empirical evidence. But Miss S. R. might require a total commitment and a whole ring, not 93% of a ring and 93% of a commitment! He may eagerly wish to test his beliefs about Miss S. R. but still consider the vow, once entered, to stick to the marriage till death parts them to be unbreakable. Similarly, religious commitment can be "dogmatic" in this sense, and *largely* empirical. Such a believer may seek to *test* his beliefs in future experience. He may simply believe that, once the commitment is made, there is no turning back.

Alternatively, let us consider that third sense of the term "dogma," which may be more properly applied to Christianity. The point of saying that a religion has dogmas, after all, is not necessarily that its adherents are not allowed to *question* their theology; it may only be that if they should *reject* certain points of their theology, then they will no longer be members of that religion! In other words, Christian dogma is simply settled or fixed belief. A believer could say, "I accept the teachings of the Nicene Creed / the Roman Magisterium / the Westminster Confession / the Baptist Faith and Message. I am not *certain* they are true, but I think they are warranted by the empirical evidence. I suppose I could change my mind someday in light of new evidence." In this sense of the term, a Christian's faith can be entirely empirical, yet include dogmas. (Still, I'd recommend the Christianity of the previous paragraph—"no turning back," as the old hymn says!)

In summary, Christian faith is fully compatible with that third characteristic of empiricism, that beliefs are held with a degree of caution in case future experience should turn up evidence against them. If we presume that Christian faith must be held unquestioningly, then one or the other would have to give at least a little. Between acceptance of this sort of religious "dogma" and this particular characteristic of empiricism, a tension remains.

CONCLUSION

In short, evidence for religious belief may be rooted in experience to a degree comparable to other forms of empirical knowledge, reliance on faith being a point in common rather than a contrast between religion and other empirical varieties of belief. Religious knowledge may seek testing in future experience, albeit with limitations on the degree of control over the subject matter. Even dogmatic religion and empirical tentativeness are compatible. Christianity in particular remains a largely empirical theology in origins, content, and structure and is justified on empirical grounds assuming the accuracy of the epistemologies of Augustine, James, the Dalai Lama, Radhakrishnan, Iqbal, Berkovits, and Lewis. The commonalities in epistemic standards held by James and Lewis, by Lewis and Iqbal, by Iqbal and Radhakrishnan, and so on are empirical epistemic standards, and the arguments of these philosophers, if successful, justify Christian theology by those standards.

Now I do not think that religious belief is ever *entirely* empirical in its *origins*, or that any knowledge is. Gaining knowledge from experience relies, as David Hume showed,[57] on our knowing some principles (such as the legitimacy of inductive reasoning) which cannot themselves be known from experience. Unlike Hume, and more like Thomas Reid,[58] I think we *do* know these principles. So I do not think of empirical knowledge as entirely independent of *non*-empirical knowledge, for it has non-empirical foundations. If we were to tweak the descriptive definition of empiricism from the introduction to this article so as to involve the claim that *all* knowledge derives from experience *alone*, then I would reject "empiricism." Moreover, I am open to the possibility of religious knowledge that is warranted independently of the evidence (though not necessarily independently of experience), such as in our day Alvin Plantinga has described.[59]

Nor do I claim that religious belief or knowledge is entirely empirical in its *structure*. Again, I doubt whether *any* knowledge is. Knowledge is a system, aptly described by some as a web. Warrant is transferred throughout the system in many ways, and enters the system at many points. Susan Haack has described this aspect of knowledge quite well,[60] John Zeis has applied her insights to religious knowledge,[61] and I have summarized these matters elsewhere.[62] Here I need only add that in a system of empirical knowledge some confirmation processes may be *non*-empirical. For example, checking a physicist's mathematical equations for accuracy is a non-empirical process relevant to their confirmation, and physics is nevertheless (on the whole) a system of empirical knowledge.

---

57. Hume, *Enquiry Concerning Human Understanding*, Sections IV–V.
58. Reid, *Inquiry into the Human Mind*.
59. Plantinga, *Warranted Christian Belief*.
60. Haack, "Double-Aspect Foundherentism," 113–28 and "Précis," 7–11.
61. Zeis, "A Foundherentist Conception," 133–60.
62. Boone, "Inferential, Coherential, and Foundational Warrant," 377–98.

So also with faith. If, for example, an a priori argument for the existence of God, perhaps a version of the ontological argument, were to succeed, it would constitute a point of non-empirical confirmation of a system of religious knowledge—which system might nevertheless be largely empirical. Here, also, we may place one very important word of caution. Christian faith requires submission to the authority of Christ and of Scripture (and, some say, of the church). Indeed, empirical evidence for Jesus as Savior, God, and Messiah *requires* trust in him. Thus a point of theology derived solely from such a theological authority is accepted by faith—yet not (or not directly) by experience.

In sum, although there are differences between religion and science, they do not amount to a dichotomy of religion and empiricism. Religious belief *can*, and often *does*, have the empirical traits of being rooted in past experience, tested in the present, and tentative. And, if these things are false, then so are the accounts of Buddhism given by the Dalai Lama, of Hinduism by Radhakrishnan, of Islam by Iqbal, of Judaism by Berkovits, and of Christianity by Lewis! Christianity in fact measures up well by these standards of empirical epistemology and even admits of a significant degree of verifiability and falsifiability. Discussions of science and Christian theology would benefit from keeping these matters well in mind.

But if faith should be empirical, and if it should be based on trust, is this trust a kind of knowledge? Let's talk about that.

WORKS CITED

Alston, William. *Perceiving God: The Epistemology of Religious Experience*. New York: Cornell University Press, 1991.

Augustine. *Confessions*. Translated by F. J. Sheed. Introduction by Peter Brown. 2nd ed. Edited and notes by Michael P. Foley. Indianapolis: Hackett, 2006.

———. *On the Profit of Believing*.

Aquinas. *Summa Theologiae*. Translated by Fathers of the English Dominican Province. Available at https://www.newadvent.org/summa/.

Ayer, A. J. *Language, Truth, and Logic*. New York: Dover, 1952.

Bauckham, Richard. *Jesus and the Eyewitnesses: The Gospel as Eyewitness Testimony*. Grand Rapids: Eerdmans, 2006.

Bealer, George, and P. F. Strawson, "The Incoherence of Empiricism." *Proceedings of the Aristotelian Society* 66 (1992) 99–14.

Berkovits, Eliezer. *God, Man, and History*. 1959. New ed. Jerusalem: The Eliezer Berkovits Institute for Jewish Thought at the Shalom Center, 2004.

———. "What Is Jewish Philosophy?" *Tradition: A Journal of Orthodox Jewish Thought*, 3.2 (1961) 117–30.

Boone, Mark J. "Inferential, Coherential, and Foundational Warrant: An Eclectic Account of the Sources of Warrant." *Logos & Episteme* 5.4 (2014) 377–98.

faith. MerriamWebster.com. http://www.merriam-webster.com/dictionary/faith (accessed April 6, 2016).

Craig, William Lane. *Assessing the New Testament Evidence for the Historicity of the Resurrection of Jesus*. Lewiston, NY: Edwin Mellen, 1989.

Dewey, John. *A Common Faith*. New Haven, CT: Yale University Press, 1934.

Dogma. Dictionary.com. http://www.dictionary.com/browse/dogma (accessed March 10, 2018).

dogma. MerriamWebster.com. http://www.merriam-webster.com/dictionary/dogma (accessed May 9, 2016).

Faith. MerriamWebster.com. http://www.merriam-webster.com/dictionary/faith (accessed April 6, 2016).

Gyatso, Tenzin. "Science at the Crossroads." His Holiness the 14th Dalai Lama of Tibet. http://www.dalailama.com/messages/buddhism/science-at-the-crossroads (accessed January 1, 2017).

Haack, Susan. "Double-Aspect Foundherentism: A New Theory of Empirical Justification." *Philosophy and Phenomenological Research* 53.1 (1993) 113–28.

———. "Précis of 'Evidence and Inquiry: Towards Reconstruction in Epistemology.'" *Synthese*, 112.1 (1997) 7–11.

Haug, Matthew, ed. *Philosophical Methodology: The Armchair or the Laboratory?* London: Routledge, 2013.

Howard-Snyder, F., D. Howard-Snyder, and R. Wasserman. *The Power of Logic*. 5th ed. New York: McGraw-Hill, 2012.

Hume, David. *An Enquiry Concerning Human Understanding*. Available at https://www.gutenberg.org/files/9662/9662-h/9662-h.htm

The International Council on Biblical Inerrancy. *The Chicago Statement on Biblical Inerrancy*. Chicago, 1978.

Iqbal, Muhammad. *The Reconstruction of Religious Thought in Islam*. 1974. 11th ed. New Delhi: Kitab Bhavan, 2011.

James, William. *A Pluralistic Universe: Hibbert Lectures at Manchester College on the Present Situation in Philosophy*. Available at https://www.gutenberg.org/cache/epub/11984/pg11984-images.html.

———. *The Will to Believe and Other Essays*. New York: Dover, 1956.

Johnson, Dru. *Biblical Knowing: a Scriptural Epistemology of Error*. Eugene, OR: Cascade, 2013.

———. *Epistemology and Biblical Theology: From the Pentateuch to Mark's Gospel*. London: Routledge, 2018.

———. "Knowledge by Ritual: A Biblical Prolegomenon to Sacramental Theology." *Journal of Theological Interpretation* Supplement 13. Warsaw, IN: Eisenbrauns, 2016.

———. *Scripture's Knowing: A Companion to Biblical Epistemology*. Eugene, OR: Cascade, 2016.

Kuhn, T. S. *The Structure of Scientific Revolutions*. 4th ed. Chicago: University of Chicago, 2012.

Kwan, Kai-man. *The Rainbow of Experiences, Critical Trust, and God: A Defense of Holistic Empiricism*. London: Bloomsbury, 2011.

Larmer, Robert. *The Legitimacy of Miracle*. Lanham, MD: Lexington, 2014.

Lewis, C. S. *Mere Christianity*. 1952. New ed. New York: HarperCollins, 2001.

Loke, Andrew Ter Ern. *Investigating the Resurrection of Jesus Christ: A New Transdisciplinary Approach.* London: Routledge, 2020.

McDowell, John. *Mind and World.* Cambridge: Harvard University Press, 1996.

Plantinga, Alvin. "How to Be an Anti-Realist." *Proceedings and Addresses of the American Philosophical Association* 56.1 (1982) 47–70.

———. *Warranted Christian Belief.* New York: Oxford University Press, 1993.

Quine, Willard Van Orman. "Two Dogmas of Empiricism;" *The Philosophical Review* 60 (1951) 20–43.

Radhakrishnan, Sarvepalli. *The Hindu View of Life.* London: George Allen & Unwin, 1926.

Reid, Thomas, *An Inquiry into the Human Mind.* Edited by Jonathan Bennett. Available at https://www.earlymoderntexts.com/assets/pdfs/reid1764.pdf

Siderits, Mark. *Buddhism as Philosophy: An Introduction.* Farnham, UK: Ashgate, 2007.

Swinburne, Richard. *The Existence of God.* Oxford: Oxford University Press, 1979.

Torrance, Thomas F. *Reality and Scientific Theology.* Reprint, Eugene, OR: Wipf and Stock, 2001.

———. *Theological and Natural Science.* Reprint, Eugene, OR: Wipf and Stock, 2002.

van Frassen, Bas C. *The Empirical Stance.* New Haven, CT: Yale University Press, 2004.

Webb, Mark. "Religious Experience." *The Stanford Encyclopedia of Philosophy* (2001). https://plato.stanford.edu/entries/religious-experience.

Wright, N. T. *The Resurrection of the Son of God.* London: SPCK, 2003.

Zeis, John. "A Foundherentist Conception of the Justification of Religious Belief." *International Journal for Philosophy of Religion* 58 (2005) 133–60.

6

Trust: Biblical and Otherwise

THE BIBLE MAKES A distinction between faith and sight. As I will explain in more detail in the *next* chapter, I think this is a distinction between belief by trust, which in the New Testament is considered a form of knowledge, and belief based on direct firsthand acquaintance with the facts. In *this* chapter, I will do some preliminary work showing that the biblical idea of knowledge by trust makes a lot of sense, and is explained by some important philosophers; in this case, as is my wont, I will focus on Augustine and William James.

Philosophical analyses of epistemology can sometimes be a helpful conceptual tool for understanding the Bible, as others have suggested.[1] Of course, if we read the Bible with the standards of the philosophers in mind, we may end up misunderstanding it, for it is not a work of philosophy. However, it can sometimes be helpful to employ some conceptual tools borrowed from the philosophers in the study of Scripture. This is a fallible enterprise, but it has often been a *good* enterprise—or at least the enterprise of some very influential theological thinkers. Names like Ambrose, Augustine, Anselm, and Aquinas come to mind as well as, more recently, Jean-Luc Marion and Kevin J. Vanhoozer. I dabble in this sort of thing myself.

And, when the New Testament authors specify that we have faith but not sight, they also teach us that we *do* have knowledge. For this faith is

---

1. Johnson, *Biblical Knowing; Epistemology and Biblical Theology; Knowledge by Ritual*; Johnson, *Scripture's Knowing*; Kennard, *Epistemology and Logic in the New Testament*. One difference between myself and these is that I rely less on the likes of Michael Polanyi and Thomas Kuhn (Johnson's luminaries) or Wittgenstein, Locke, and Pierce (Kennard's) than on Augustine and James.

simply trust in reliable authorities. As Augustine and James help to show, in the New Testament knowledge by faith is in this respect very like other forms of knowledge. It is an idea with remarkable similarities to that found in various fields of secular inquiry such as science, history, and geography.

In this chapter I shall briefly review the alleged dichotomy of faith and knowledge. I shall look at the everyday workings of knowledge, explaining why there is an overlap of reason and faith, since faith is simply trust, and why knowledge and faith can be the same thing. I shall then introduce a good way of looking at knowledge: a credit system.

However, I think it is best to begin this study with *a story*. I wrote the following paragraphs in the year 2017 (having since edited them very minimally and mostly for clarity):

> At the time of the writing of this paragraph, I am between jobs. Technically, I am unemployed. But there's a reason for that. I worked for four years as an assistant professor of philosophy at Forman Christian College in Pakistan before my name was found on a document in the possession of a local terrorist organization. So my family and I spent the past academic year—the fifth at FC College—packing and looking for a new job. Shortly after we returned to Texas I was blessed with a job offer at Hong Kong Baptist University—another liberal arts university in Asia with a Christian heritage. HKBU, thankfully, allowed me the option of a contract beginning in January of 2018. It is now August of 2017, and my wife and I have a few months to sort through our footlockers, our crate from Pakistan, and our storage unit—and repack for moving to Hong Kong! I prefer to think of this time as a sabbatical rather than unemployment—an opportunity to do some reading, some writing on Augustine, and some writing on other projects such as this one. I'm not worried about my family's financial situation because we're not likely to go into debt, because I think future income is more important than how much money I have *now*, and because my future salary is going to be a raise as compared to my last job.
>
> In essence, I am living on trust. I trust that our visas will be granted. I trust that, come December, the airline we select will get us safely from Texas to Hong Kong. I trust the contract I signed to hold water. I trust that I will be paid for my work in January sometime around early February. I have faith that these things will happen.
>
> I have not seen my seat on the airliner, or the campus of HKBU, or our new home in Hong Kong, or the money in the checking account I will eventually set up in Hong Kong. I would

be a fool to say "I'll believe it when I see it." I believe it *now*, and I *act* on that belief—packing, preparing for my spring semester courses, and so on.

I am walking by faith, not by sight.

But I also *know* that these things are so. My trust is paradigmatically rational; I am trusting in such things as the safety standards of modern aircraft, the professionalism of university employees such as the ones who hired me, and the solidity of a well-written employment contract. I know that the day will come when my family and I leave from George Bush Intercontinental in Houston, that I will start teaching at HKBU in January, and that I will get paid. Chances are pretty good that I know all this about as well as the storeowners from whom you purchased groceries sometime in the last week know that the credit card company will pay them on your behalf, as well as the credit card company knows that you will pay them back, and as well as you know that you will be paid by your employer for your work this month. We walk by *knowledge* when we walk by trust, or by faith, in those with good faith and good credit. That's life.

Of course, I am not *certain*—inasmuch as I could die in a car accident tomorrow, our flight might be one of those rare ones that plunges into the sea, and so on. Nor are you, the grocer, or the credit card company *100%* certain; but you have a rational belief on which you are acting and which you may reasonably call knowledge.

And this, of course, has everything to do with the Bible.

But first let's consider how this idea of knowledge is not only downright *normal*, but also very philosophical.

FAITH VERSUS KNOWLEDGE?

The New Testament speaks of our having faith rather than sight: "Jesus said to him, 'Have you believed because you have seen me? Blessed are those who have not seen and yet have believed'" (John 20:29 ESV). These words may suggest that Christianity is about faith and not about knowledge. We might reason to this conclusion from the premise that all knowledge is sight. Thus Christians *believe*, but do not *know*. This would be a mistake. I will not say that it is a typical mistake in Bible scholarship, although perhaps Bible scholars could do a better job explaining what the Bible says on these matters, and I hope that my next chapter can help to rectify that. What bothers me is more of a deep-seated, widespread *cultural* problem, and I hope that this chapter will help to provide some readers with the wherewithal to respond to it.

The separation of faith from knowledge ranges from the view James attributes to a schoolboy—"Faith is when you believe something that you know ain't true"[2]—to more peaceful attempts at separation such as Immanuel Kant's[3] claim that "I must, therefore, abolish knowledge, to make room for belief" in propositions that might well be true. I have often heard from my own students and even from seminary students that faith and knowledge are separate categories. On one occasion, I recall a churchgoer endorsing this description of faith from *Miracle on 34th Street*: "Faith is believing in things when common sense tells you not to."[4] How many Christians have opined that what God wants—or what is exemplified in the Bible—is "blind faith"? How many secular folk have viewed the choice between Christian faith and unbelief as a choice between reason and a suspension of reason, and chosen the former?[5] In one illustrative case, a scholar claims that Buddhism relies on reason; Christian faith, he says, means "a set of beliefs that one accepts out of a conviction that is not based on rational argumentation, a matter of the heart rather than the head."[6] And, of course, the dichotomy is recognized by other famous academics such as Steven Pinker, Alex Rosenberg, and Richard Dawkins.[7] And then there is *The Hitchhiker's Guide to the Galaxy*'s magnificent remark:

> "I refuse to prove that I exist," says God, "for proof denies faith, and without faith I am nothing."[8]

I have encountered the same premise—that genuine faith cannot be based on reason—in objections to a Christian's employment of cosmological

---

2. James, "Will to Believe."

3. Kant, *The Critique of Pure Reason*, Preface to the second edition.

4. Seaton, *Miracle on 34th Street*.

5. Just to name one example, I heard faith described in just this way by podcast host Todd Feinburg and physicist Michael Stopa in "Episode 147."

6. Siderits, *Buddhism as Philosophy*, 5. Siderits furthermore suggests that faith is an "emotional commitment" for which "reason and logical investigation are or little or no use;" Siderits, *Buddhism as Philosophy*, 6. Again, he suggests that faith is "a commitment for which no reasons can be given;" Siderits, *Buddhism as Philosophy*, 7. (Siderits's book, I might add, is at any rate a very fine study of its titular topic, Buddhism and philosophy!)

7. As cited by Howard-Snyder, "Propositional Faith," 368.

8. Adams, *Hitchhiker's Guide to the Galaxy*, 54. The passage in which this remark appears includes an amusing parodic argument which attempts to prove that God does *not* exist on the basis of the incompatibility of faith with some very good evidence *for* the existence of God!

arguments for the existence of God at a philosophy café; I was left with the impression that some people were downright *offended* that anyone would presume to give evidence for his religious beliefs.

It is sometimes more specifically said that the empirical way of believing is not the religious way of believing—that religion and empiricism are separate or even conflicting ways of believing. The idea is present in some influential chapters in the history of modern philosophy, including Kant and the logical positivists. Let us, briefly, take a closer look at Kant. Kant actually wrote of religion built on a purely rational foundation and "within the limits of reason alone." However, as far as I can understand Kant, he did not consider this religion to be a variety of *knowledge*—merely rational belief. Moreover, the rationality of religious belief is, in Kant's view, quite independent of experience. The logical positivists agreed with him on the dichotomy of empiricism and religion; their difference was in *not* recognizing a rational *non*-empirical foundation for religion. At the present time the idea of a dichotomy of empiricism and religion seems a very part of contemporary *culture*, not merely an academic theory. One episode of *Star Trek: The Next Generation* is a good example: Lieutenant Worf informs Data that the identity of Kahless "is not an empirical matter" because "it is a matter of faith."[9] Many a time I have heard from my students that science and religion are epistemological opposites because, of the two, only science relies on evidence; that they are different because religion is inherently dogmatic and science is not; that religion is inherently unempirical because it relies on authority; and so on. They often took these matters to be plain and obvious. Those expressing the same thoughts on social media are legion.

My personal speculations suggest at least two causes for this notion's being so widespread. One is the influence of those modern philosophers. Another is that it is, in part, a side effect of the creation/evolution controversy: Some have (mistakenly) thought that this dispute was a straightforward case of religion vs. empirical science, and simply concluded that the religion in question—usually Christianity or a branch thereof—has nothing to do with empiricism.

In any case, these are all different expressions of the idea that faith, Christian faith in particular, is separate and distinct from knowledge. This way of thinking is, of course, all very logical in that the premises (that knowledge is incompatible with faith and that biblical religion involves faith) support the conclusion. However, one of the premises is false: Not all knowledge is separate and distinct from faith. Quite a bit of what we

---

9. Kolbe, "Rightful Heir." Ironically, empirical methods revealed exactly who this character was.

know is by faith and, when we walk by that knowledge, we walk by faith and not by sight. Furthermore, the New Testament distinguishes faith from sight, but it does not separate faith from knowledge. New Testament faith is simply one kind of knowledge, and sight another kind. In the typical New Testament usage, faith is knowledge by trust in reliable testimony, and sight is firsthand knowledge. The distinction in the New Testament between faith and seeing is thus only a separation of one way of knowing from another way of knowing.

In this respect, the gospel proclaimed in the New Testament is (at least according to the New Testament) an instance of knowledge not unlike other kinds of knowledge. We'll get to the New Testament in the next chapter. For now, let's look at some philosophy.

THE EVERYDAY WORKINGS OF KNOWLEDGE

The everyday workings of secular knowledge show that reason and faith can be the same thing. They also show that we *can* know by faith, and often *do*. This is a normal way—we might even say it is *the* normal way—of knowing, in science and other fields of knowledge no less than in theology. Augustine helps to show us why this is the case, and James's idea of knowledge as a credit system is a helpful way of understanding the integral role faith plays in the acquisition of knowledge.[10]

In short, we need to resist the hype that teaches that faith and knowledge have nothing to do with one another. In many realms of knowledge we do not know firsthand but by faith or trust. Let us begin with regular English, and then move on to Augustine and James.

Reason and Faith Can Be the Same Thing

Even using plain old English and prior to any advanced studies in philosophy or theology, it is reasonable to say that reason and faith overlap. Let us begin with some definitions of our relevant terms. I suggest this as a

---

10. Johnson, in *Biblical Knowing*, analyzes the everyday workings of knowledge, with an emphasis on philosophy of science. He argues that these show that knowledge relies in large part on reliable authority, and on seeing the world in light of its testimony by obeying its commands. He also says that this is the biblical way of knowing. Similarly, Kennard in *Epistemology and Logic in the New Testament* draws numerous connections between Jewish epistemic canons, philosophical epistemic canons, and the New Testament's logic and epistemology.

working definition of *reason*: the proper operation of the mind, consistent with the rules of logic, with the purpose of gaining knowledge.[11]

And as a working definition of *faith*, I suggest: trust. This is not at all original. The first definition of "faith" in the online dictionary is "confidence or trust in a person or thing."[12] One could also consult some forerunner terms: The Latin *fides* means trust, credit, belief, or faith, and the relevant sense of the Greek *pistis* is "state of believing on the basis of the reliability of the one trusted, *trust, confidence, faith*."[13]

Now *one of the proper operations of the mind is to trust reliable testimony*. When consistent with the rules of logic, therefore, trust in reliable testimony is one of the workings of reason. And, thus, faith is sometimes reason—at least by our rough-and-ready definitions.

So the ancient question is easy to answer. *Is religious faith rational?* It certainly is *not* rational whenever we accept as reliable a testimony which we should *not* treat as reliable. But it is rational whenever we treat a testimony as reliable which we *should* treat as reliable.[14]

But we need take a closer look at this question. Let us consider the economic sense of *fides*. It can mean "credit." Can *credit* be rational? This question may strike us as a confused mix-up of economic and mental categories. But the economic property of *being given credit* is the state of *being trusted*, and so there is at least a correspondence here: For everyone who is extended credit, someone is trusting. Is that trust rational?

Of course, there is such a thing as extending *bad* credit. But much credit is good, and is extended prudently and rationally to someone with creditworthiness. So the extension of credit *does* admit of rationality, and frequently is rational. When the Visa Corporation extends credit to you, it extends *monetary* credit—it expects you to pay the money you owe. Why shouldn't the same be true of the religious variety of faith or credit? This would be an extension of *epistemic* rather than monetary credit—trusting the object of faith to tell the truth. What we need for religious faith or credit to be rational is reliable testimony about God. For example, we might have reliable testimony from God Himself (or Themselves), or from a prophet, a church, or a holy book which we can reasonably think to be reliable (and

---

11. For example, see dictionary definitions of reason as "proper exercise of the mind" and "the sum of the intellectual powers" at Merriam-Webster or "normal or sound powers of mind; sanity" at Dictionary.com. reason, MerriamWebster.com; reason, Dictionary.com.

12. Faith, Dictionary.com.

13. Arndt, Danker, Bauer, and Gingrich; "πίστις, εως, ἡ."

14. Not that faith and reason are always the same thing, or the same in every respect. More on that in other chapters of this book—and, God willing, in my *next* book!

preferably, as historic Christianity and the other Abrahamic religions tend to think, infallible).

Perhaps a Venn diagram would be in order. Consider two overlapping circles, the leftward circle denoting things that are reason and the rightward circle denoting things that are faith. An X in each region denotes a mode of believing. The leftward X, in the reason circle but not in the faith circle, denotes rational belief which is *not* based on trust—like when I know that 2 + 2 = 4. The middle X, in the overlapping regions of both circles, represents rational belief which *is* trust—like when I believe my employer will pay me. The rightward X, in the faith circle but not the reason circle, represents *ir*rational belief which *is* based on trust—like following Jim Jones and drinking the Kool-Aid.

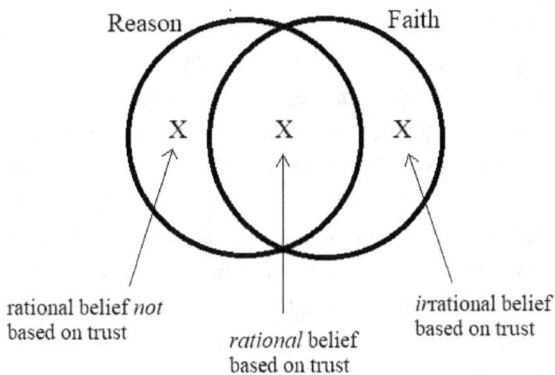

rational belief *not* based on trust

rational belief based on trust

*ir*rational belief based on trust

We Know By Faith

Faith as a variety of reason, an operation of the mind for gaining knowledge, is in fact frequently successful. The nature of much (if not most) of our knowledge shows this.

For a start, we should note that it is only a myth that an argument from authority is necessarily fallacious.[15] The typical argument from authority is good or bad depending on its content—primarily on what sort of knowledge the authority is supposed to have, and whether it is reasonable to suppose that the authority really *has* it. So an argument from a *reliable* authority is generally a good argument, but an argument from an *un*reliable or untrustworthy authority is a bad argument.

---

15. See Howard-Snyder, Howard-Snyder, and Wasserman, *The Power of Logic*, chapter 10, section 2. (I confess to not having taught from the fifth edition as a result of working overseas; in my region of Asia the only available textbook was from a different publisher!)

We must also dispense with the idea that science is the epistemological opposite of faith: one relying entirely on reason, one not at all. Religious faith often relies on reason to varying degrees, up to and including Thomas Aquinas's summary of Christian theology, the *Summa Theologiae*—probably the most impressive bit of systematic reasoning in human history. And, if Thomas Kuhn is even partly correct, science is not a matter of objective reason alone.[16]

But the more important point here is that science depends on faith, perhaps almost as much as your average religion. That is to say—it depends *on trust*. Of course it is true, as a critic would likely say, that scientific experiments can be replicated. But who replicated them? Chances are pretty good that the critic did not replicate them; someone else did that. And if the critic himself *did* replicate some experiments, did he *repeat* the replication (since science relies on the repeatability of experiments) in order altogether to avoid having to take someone else's word for it?

Using chemistry as an example, here is the end-point of this exercise. If you want to know something in chemistry without relying on trust, you will have to begin *from the very beginning* and repeat *all* of the experiments that led to the current state of chemical knowledge: *all* of them, *multiple times each*. You would die of old age before you caught up with the present state of chemical knowledge. And all of your hard work would be useless unless others had the good sense you lacked and were willing to take your word for it at least some of the time when you said that your experiments had turned out the way they had.

Thus, even for scientists, scientific knowledge relies heavily on the testimony of other scientists. As for the scientific knowledge of those of who *aren't* scientists, we are left where Scott Adams puts us in the Introduction to *Don't Stand Where the Comet Is Assumed to Strike Oil*: depending on the word of people (most of whom we've never met) who simply *tell us* how things are.[17] None of this means that I do not know, for example, that electrons exist. Rather, since I really *do* know that they exist, my scientific knowledge relies on trust.

Augustine, the church father and founder of medieval philosophy, in *On the Profit of Believing* and *Confessions* (Book VI, chapter 5), lists these sorts of examples:[18]

---

16. Kuhn, *Structure of Scientific Revolutions*.

17. Adams, *Don't Stand Where the Comet*.

18. Although, at least in his earlier texts, he tends to emphasize a belief's quality as *rational* and as *practical* rather than as *knowledge*.

- Do you know that Caesar became emperor of Rome about 50 BC? Yes; you know it by faith—by *pistis*, by *fides*, by *trust*—in the testimony of historians.

- Do you know that Harare, Zimbabwe, exists? Yes. But if you haven't *been* there, then you know it by faith—by *pistis*, by *fides*, by *trust*—in the testimony of geographers or of others who have been there. (Trust me—it's real, and the jacaranda trees are lovely.)

- Do you know who your parents are? You know that also by faith—by *pistis*, by *fides*, by *trust* in what they told you.

On this last point my students have thought of DNA tests, but, as I explain to them, they would need not only to perform the test themselves, but to start from the very beginning of genetic science and reinvent it singlehandedly if the goal is to know who their parents are without taking *someone's* word for *something*.

Knowledge as a Credit System

The credit system is a good way of thinking about knowledge. Here's William James on a related subject, truth:

> Truth lives, in fact, for the most part on a credit system. Our thoughts and beliefs "pass," so long as nothing challenges them, just as bank-notes pass so long as nobody refuses them. But this all points to direct face-to-face verifications somewhere, without which the fabric of truth collapses like a financial system with no cash-basis whatever. You accept my verification of one thing, I yours of another. We trade on each other's truth. But beliefs verified concretely by SOMEBODY are the posts of the whole superstructure.
>
> Our account of truth is an account of truths in the plural, of processes of leading, realized in rebus, and having only this quality in common, that they PAY. They pay by guiding us into or towards some part of a system that dips at numerous points into sense-percepts, which we may copy mentally or not, but with which at any rate we are now in the kind of commerce vaguely designated as verification.[19]

Now I would amend James on a few points. I say these things about *knowledge*—not about *truth*. Moreover, confirmation of a belief may involve the

---

19. James, *Pragmatism*, Lecture VI: Pragmatism's Conception of Truth.

surviving of tests for falsification as well as verification.[20] Furthermore, confirmation is not necessarily limited to confirmation from strictly *sensory* experience. Like some philosophers of religion including Allama Iqbal,[21] C. S. Lewis,[22] and, if I am not mistaken, James himself, I think religious experience which is not necessarily limited to the sensory may be a source of confirmation. Indeed, I would not restrict the sources of confirmation to *experience*. There may be such a thing as *a priori* verification stemming from, for example, being able to test a belief system for internal coherence—similar to the relevance of checking math when evaluating a theory in physics.

Nevertheless, there are some insights in James's remarks. When James is talking about truth he is also talking about knowledge, since all things known are true things. James is saying this: *Knowledge, even scientific knowledge, is a system or network of beliefs, and it operates on a credit system—a system of trust in the testimony of others. And that credit system depends on the beliefs in the system being subjected to direct confirmation at various points.* It seems to me that James is precisely correct about this. Knowledge is like an economic system in at least two respects. It relies on trust, and it relies on the possibility of cashing in at times. Neither paper money nor the number of dollars linked to my electronic banking account has any value unless it is possible to exchange them for something concrete. A dollar bill, in James's day, might be passed around in a thousand exchanges, but it had value only because it *could* be exchanged for gold. In our day (even without a gold standard), a dollar bill might be passed around in a thousand exchanges, but it has value only because its owner knows he can use it in the *next* exchange, to buy something else he needs (a car, a computer, a cup of tea, etc.). In the case of knowledge, a belief may be passed on a number of times, say from one scientist to another, from the second one to a professor, from the professor to a college student, and from the student to a friend or child. Yet knowledge would be worthless if it was not possible to cash in; someone ought to be able to repeat the original experiments. Quite a bit of what I know relies on my trust in scientists, historians, geographers, friends, family, the authors of the Bible, and more. It is necessary that various points of the system of

---

20. Roughly, I take verification to be the finding of relevant evidence consistent with a belief, and falsification the finding of relevant evidence *in*consistent with it. Commonly, a test for verification will also be a test for falsification. However, verification and falsification are not quite the same thing, and one of the big debates in philosophy of science concerns their respective roles. Some, such as the logical positivists, thought that science relies on verification; Karl Popper thought that science does not rely on verification at all, but solely on falsification.

21. Iqbal, *The Reconstruction*, Lecture I.

22. Lewis, *Mere Christianity*, 163.

belief are such that someone can run experiments modeled after Mendel's to confirm what biologists tell me about genetics, to visit Tokyo to confirm what the geographers say about Japan, to look for archaeological evidence relevant to the biblical account of first-century Jerusalem, and so on.

This idea of knowledge is a largely social one. Knowledge is an individual matter inasmuch as it is something an individual can *have*. But it is social in that no one can have very *much* of it except as the result of the cooperative effort of a large group of people relying on each other for the evidence which warrants their beliefs. This reliance is credit, or trust, or faith. When it is not *good* credit, *reasonable* trust, and *rational* faith, it is foolish credulity rather than knowledge. When the credit is good, the trust reasonable, the faith rational, and the beliefs true, this reliance is a form of knowledge.[23]

Perhaps some readers will suspect that I am attacking the legitimacy of science. To the contrary, I *presume* the legitimacy of science. I am only pointing out that science is rooted in trust; and, since science is a type of knowledge, other beliefs rooted in testimony can *also* be knowledge. We have plenty of reliable testimony: science, history, geography, and (for most of us at least) our parents. Like Augustine says, we live most of our lives by this testimony.

CONCLUSION

Certain ideas about knowledge may cloud our understanding of the New Testament. These include the dichotomy of reason and faith, the dichotomy of faith and knowledge, and the notion that all knowledge is the same sort of thing as seeing for yourself. In fact, reason and faith overlap, faith and knowledge overlap, and all things captured by the metaphor of sight are knowledge but not vice versa. Faith is trust, and trust in trustworthy authorities is a way of knowing in our everyday experience—in fields such as geography, history, science, and economic transactions—no less than in the Bible.

To that greatest of all books we now turn.

WORKS CITED

Adams, Douglas. *The Hitchhiker's Guide to the Galaxy*. 1979. Reprint, New York: Del Rey, 2009.

---

23. Assuming this is not a Gettier case. Roughly, a Gettier case is a situation in which I have a warranted belief, but in which the warrant does not lead me to the truth and yet the belief is still true—by sheer luck. I explain Gettier cases in more detail in chapter 2 of this book.

Adams, Scott. *Don't Stand Where the Comet Is Assumed to Strike Oil*. Kansas City: Andrews McMeel, 2004.

Augustine. *Confessions*. Translated by F. J. Sheed. Introduction by Peter Brown. 2nd ed. Edited and notes by Michael P. Foley. Indianapolis: Hackett, 2006.

———. *On the Profit of Believing*. Available at https://www.newadvent.org/fathers/1306.htm.

faith. Dictionary.com. http://www.dictionary.com/browse/faith (accessed August 16, 2017).

Feinburg, Todd, and Michael Stopa. "Episode 147: Happy Trump Year!!!" *Harvard Lunch Club*. Ricochet.com; available at https://ricochet.com/podcast/harvard-lunch-club/happy-trump-year/; November 7, 2017.

The Holy Bible. English Standard Version.

Howard-Snyder, Daniel. "Propositional Faith: What It Is and What It Is Not." *American Philosophical Quarterly* 50.4 (2013) 357–72.

Howard-Snyder, Frances, Daniel Howard-Snyder, and Ryan Wasserman. *The Power of Logic*, 4th ed. New York: McGraw-Hill, 2008.

Iqbal, Muhammad. *The Reconstruction of Religious Thought in Islam*. 1974. 11th ed. New Delhi: Kitab Bhavan, 2011.

James, William. *Pragmatism: A New Name for Some Old Ways of Thinking*. New York: Longmans, Green, and Co., 1907.

———. "The Will to Believe." In *The Will to Believe and Other Essays in Popular Philosophy*. Available at https://gutenberg.org/files/26659/26659-h/26659-h.htm.

Johnson, Dru. *Biblical Knowing: A Scriptural Epistemology of Error*. Eugene, OR: Cascade, 2013.

———. *Epistemology and Biblical Theology: From the Pentateuch to Mark's Gospel*. London: Routledge, 2018.

———. *Knowledge by Ritual: A Biblical Prolegomenon to Sacramental Theology*. Journal of Theological Interpretation Supplement 13. University Park, PA: Eisenbrauns, 2016.

———. *Scripture's Knowing: A Companion to Biblical Epistemology*. Eugene, OR: Cascade, 2016.

Kant, Immanuel. *Critique of Pure Reason*. Translated by Paul Guyer and Allen D. Wood. Cambridge: Cambridge University Press, 1998.

Kennard, Douglas. *Epistemology and Logic in the New Testament: Early Jewish Context and Biblical Theology Mechanisms That Fit within Some Contemporary Ways of Knowing*. Eugene, OR: Wipf and Stock, 2016.

Kolbe, Winrich. "Rightful Heir." *Star Trek: The Next Generation*, May 17, 1993.

Kuhn, Thomas. *The Structure of Scientific Revolutions*, 3rd ed. Chicago: University of Chicago Press, 1996.

Lewis, C. S. *Mere Christianity*. 1952. New ed. New York: HarperCollins, 2001.

reason. Dictionary.com. http://www.dictionary.com/browse/reason?s=t (accessed July 2, 2018).

reason. MerriamWebster.com. http://www.merriam-webster.com/dictionary/reason (accessed July 2, 2018).

Seaton, George, Director. *Miracle on 34th Street*. 20th Century Fox, 1947.

Siderits, Mark. *Buddhism as Philosophy*. Indianapolis: Hackett, 2007.

7

Blessed Are Those Who Have Not Seen by Faith

Knowledge, Faith, and Sight in the New Testament

SOME GOOD WORK HAS recently been done on biblical epistemology.[1] Dru Johnson and Douglas Kennard come to mind.[2] But there is more to be done, and in this chapter I aim to make a modest contribution towards a fuller picture of the biblical theory of knowledge. The New Testament speaks of our having faith rather than sight: "Jesus said to him, 'Have you believed because you have seen me? Blessed are those who have not seen and yet have believed'" (John 20:29).[3] Does this mean that Christianity is about separating faith from knowledge? Not at all. Rather, the New Testament understanding is that faith is a way of knowing by trust in reliable authority.

---

1. The major changes made to this chapter since its initial publication in *Evangelical Quarterly* involve its deepened discussion of the description of faith in Hebrews.

2. Dru Johnson analyzes the everyday workings of knowledge, with an emphasis on philosophy of science, in *Biblical Knowing* and in *Epistemology and Biblical Theology*. He explains that knowledge involves seeing the world in light of what we learn from reliable authority. Similarly, Kennard in *Epistemology and Logic in the New Testament* links Jewish and philosophical rules for gaining knowledge with the New Testament's logic and epistemology. See Johnson, *Biblical Knowing*, *Epistemology and Biblical Theology*, *Knowledge by Ritual*, and *Scripture's Knowing*; and Kennard, *Epistemology and Logic in the New Testament*.

3. Unless otherwise indicated, Scripture translations are from the ESV.

When the New Testament authors specify that we have faith but not sight, they also teach us that we *do* have knowledge. The passages distinguishing faith and sight distinguish not faith and knowledge, but knowledge that relies on trust in reliable authority and firsthand knowledge. Sight is often used a figure of speech, a use of synecdoche to be precise, for this firsthand knowledge. Synecdoche, a variation of metonymy, is the use of the name of a part to stand for the whole.

In this article I shall analyze the epistemology of the New Testament passages that distinguish faith from sight. First I shall briefly review some passages in the New Testament which present Christian theology as *known* truths about God. Then I shall give a brief overview of my understanding of the New Testament distinction between faith and sight. Then I shall take a brief look at passages from Peter and John distinguishing faith and sight, and then make a closer examination of passages from Paul and the author of Hebrews.

THE NEW TESTAMENT: FAITH IS KNOWLEDGE

The New Testament writers persistently treat faith and knowledge as overlapping.[4] The picture would be rather complex if we were to paint it fully—with nature, miracles, prophecy, apostleship, the inward testimony of the Holy Spirit, and more all playing a part.[5] Central to this picture is the idea that faith is placed in an eminently reliable authority—"God, who never lies" (Titus 1:2), speaking to us of matters or by means of acts "in which it is impossible for God to lie" (Heb 6:18). According to the biblical perspective God's credit is very, very good, as known from his mighty works of redemption, as stated in Ps 136; God's credit is very, very good, as known from his promises kept, according to Josh 23.

Here are just a few examples of New Testament writers claiming that some faith is also knowledge.

In Luke's preface to his gospel, he explains that he has researched the matter in a manner resembling that of a historian or a journalist, in order that his readers may know that the histories of Jesus are accurate: "it seemed good to me also, having followed all things closely for some time past, to

---

4. In this chapter I am more interested in New Testament exegesis than textual or other forms of criticism. I will take the New Testament claims at face value—not, for example, challenging the traditional accounts of authorship. Although I leave to others the work of tracing their effects, critical theories such as a two-author theory of the Petrine epistles would no doubt, if correct, weaken my case to some degree.

5. I hope to explain more adequately in my next book.

write an orderly account for you, most excellent Theophilus, that you may have certainty concerning the things you have been taught" (Luke 1:3-4).

In Romans 1, Paul explains that some truths about God are *knowable* to all from creation, and indeed *are known* to all who do not suppress that knowledge. He says:

> For the wrath of God is revealed from heaven against all ungodliness and unrighteousness of men, who by their unrighteousness suppress the truth. For what can be known about God is plain to them, because God has shown it to them. For his invisible attributes, namely, his eternal power and divine nature, have been clearly perceived, ever since the creation of the world, in the things that have been made. So they are without excuse. (Rom 1:18-20)

Again, in 1 Corinthians Paul appeals to the foundations of Christian theology in the dual evidences of fulfilled prophecy and eyewitness testimony to the great miracle of the resurrection of the Messiah:

> For what I received I passed on to you as of first importance: that Christ died for our sins according to the Scriptures, that he was buried, that he was raised on the third day according to the Scriptures, and that he appeared to Cephas, and then to the Twelve. After that, he appeared to more than five hundred of the brothers and sisters at the same time, most of whom are still living, though some have fallen asleep. Then he appeared to James, then to all the apostles, and last of all he appeared to me also, as to one abnormally born. (1 Cor 15:3-8)

John, in his gospel, says that the miracles of Jesus, as recorded by eyewitnesses, are evidence that he is the Messiah: "Jesus performed many other signs in the presence of his disciples, which are not recorded in this book. But these are written that you may believe that Jesus is the Messiah, the Son of God, and that by believing you may have life in his name" (John 20:30-31). Again, John in his first letter explains that his testimony and that of other apostles is that of eyewitnesses—and also *ear*witnesses and *hand*witnesses:

> That which was from the beginning, which we have heard, which we have seen with our eyes, which we looked upon and have touched with our hands, concerning the word of life—the life was made manifest, and we have seen it, and testify to it and proclaim to you the eternal life, which was with the Father and was made manifest to us—that which we have seen and heard

we proclaim also to you, so that you too may have fellowship with us; and indeed our fellowship is with the Father and with his Son Jesus Christ. And we are writing these things so that our joy may be complete. (1 John 1:1–4)

2 Peter explains that fulfilled prophecy accompanied by eyewitness testimony to the glory of God bestowed on Jesus evidences Christian doctrines:

> For we did not follow cleverly devised myths when we made known to you the power and coming of our Lord Jesus Christ, but we were eyewitnesses of his majesty. For when he received honor and glory from God the Father, and the voice was borne to him by the Majestic Glory, "This is my beloved Son, with whom I am well pleased," we ourselves heard this very voice borne from heaven, for we were with him on the holy mountain. And we have the prophetic word more fully confirmed.... (2 Pet 1:16–19a)

FAITH AND SIGHT

Jesus tells Thomas that it is blessed to believe without seeing. Paul tells us that we walk by faith rather than by sight. The author of Hebrews tells us that faith is in that which we do not see. If, then, New Testament faith is knowledge, why do we have this consistent theme in the New Testament, the separation of faith and sight? Don't we *know* everything we *see*? And vice versa? If some bit of theology is *known*, shouldn't it also be *seen* to be true?

We should probably not expect to find that New Testament theology is always perfectly neat and tidy according to modern standards for categorizing things like faith, sight, knowledge, reason, and so on. Nor are the New Testament categorizations of faith and *works* always neat and tidy, allowing for precise definitions and causing things to fall into neat stacks in little boxes. The New Testament *was* written in language, after all, and language is rarely, if ever, all that neat and tidy. (Nor, for that matter, is life.) Faith and works, for example, may be *contrasted* in one place (such as in Paul), *linked* in another (most obviously in James, but also, as I read him, in Paul), and shown to be more or less the *same* thing in a third place (such as in the letter to the Hebrews, as we will see below)! It will suffice to employ reasonably precise definitions and reliable generalizations corresponding for the most part with New Testament language.

To return to our question, let us consider John 20. In John 20:25 Thomas says he will not *believe* (*pisteuō*) without seeing and touching. In 20:27 Jesus tells him to be *believing* (*pistos*) rather than *unbelieving* (*apistos*), and in 20:29 he observes that Thomas now *believes* (*pisteuō*) because he has seen. So faith *can* operate in the presence of sight. Similarly, in the opening of John's first letter we see that John believes having seen. So there is a *contrast* or a *distinction*, but not an absolute *dichotomy* between faith and sight in the New Testament.

Here are four New Testament passages that distinguish faith and sight:

- 1 Pet 1:8: "Though you have not seen him, you love him. Though you do not now see him, you believe in him. . . ."
- John 20:29: "Jesus said to him, 'Have you believed because you have seen me? Blessed are those who have not seen and yet have believed.'"
- 2 Cor 5:7: ". . . for we walk by faith, not by sight."
- Heb 11:1: "Now faith is the assurance of things hoped for, the conviction of things not seen."

There are at least two relevant senses of sight here: the literal and the use as a synecdoche for firsthand knowledge. One obvious sense of the term in these passages is *literal* sight—that which we do with our eyes. This appears to be the meaning in 1 Peter, and also in John 20 where Thomas wants to see and touch. Probably the same meaning is intended in Heb 11 as well. Perhaps this is also the case in 2 Cor 5; Paul in verses 1–4 has been talking about his eschatological hope, perhaps including the believer's resurrection body, which is something that (and with which) we would no doubt be able to see.

But there is another meaning. Thomas wants to *touch* as well as to see. Jesus lets him, and then observes that he has *seen*. There is something which includes both of these ways Thomas has known—seeing and touching—but for which seeing is used as a name. This is knowing *firsthand*, without relying on trust. Sight is a synecdoche for firsthand knowledge. This is no doubt the meaning used in 2 Cor 5, inasmuch as the fulfillment of these eschatological promises is something we would know firsthand, and that not merely by *seeing*. Christ means this in John 20. Hebrews 11 seems also to have this secondary meaning (on which more in good time).

The New Testament distinction between faith and sight is thus a distinction between two ways of knowing: by rational trust, and firsthand. It is not a separation of faith and knowledge; this, happily, is an error rarely if ever made in the commentaries, although from what I can tell they tend not to expound on the New Testament idea of sight as one but not the only mode of knowing.

This particular biblical idea of knowledge is a bit different from some ideas of knowledge which have captured the attention of Christian thinkers. For example, Alvin Plantinga's analysis does not emphasize our knowledge of God via trust in reliable testimony, but rather the direct and unmediated knowledge of God by means of the *sensus divinitatis*.[6] With the greatest respect for Plantinga and his epistemology, the biblical account of knowledge considered here could do with a little more attention.

A more detailed inspection of these passages will confirm our interpretation.

PETER

Peter tells his readers that they "have not seen him" and "do not now see him." The first thing to note is that 2 Pet 1:16–21 claims that Peter and the other apostles *did* see. Second, 1 Pet 1:18–19 refers to some of the related theology as information *known*: ". . . knowing that you were ransomed from the futile ways inherited from your forefathers . . . with the precious blood of Christ." Of course, this Christ is the one the readers love, and the ransoming is the reason they love him. The word for "knowing" here is *eidō*, from *oida*, a word unambiguously connoting knowledge.[7] A third clue presents itself from the well-known 1 Pet 3:15: ". . . but in your hearts honor Christ the Lord as holy, always being prepared to make a defense to anyone who asks you for a reason for the hope that is in you; yet do it with gentleness and respect." The word *apologia*, a defense or explanation or reason, is "a speech of defense,"[8] difficult to achieve if the author's idea of gospel faith has nothing to do with reason or evidence.

Putting together these clues from the Petrine epistles, a picture of their religious epistemology emerges. Faith in and love for the Christ believers have not seen is secondhand knowledge depending on reliable testimony—namely, on the witness of those who *have* seen. In virtue of their reliable testimony, they do know that Christ really did these wonderful things on

---

6. Among other writings, Plantinga, *Warranted Christian Belief*. The difference between Plantinga's analysis and mine is perhaps most evident on pages 265–66 where he looks at two of the same New Testament passages and concludes that faith is a direct knowledge of God produced by the Holy Spirit. I do not contest the sort of knowledge Plantinga describes, but I think that is another sort which is described here.

7. On the senses of *oida*, see Arndt, Danker, Bauer, and Gingrich, "οἶδα."

8. Arndt, Danker, Bauer, and Gingrich, "ἀπολογία, ας, ἡ."

their behalf. They must respond with love and faith and hope, following him and being prepared to explain to others the evidence they have for this love, faith, and hope.

JOHN

John 20:24 tells us Thomas did not see the risen Jesus the first time he appeared. The other disciples tell him (20:25) *they* have seen, but he says he will not believe until he also sees and touches. Days later, Jesus meets him and tells him to see and touch. Verse 27: "Do not disbelieve, but believe." Thomas believes, and Jesus tells him, "Blessed are those who have not seen and yet have believed."

Now consider what John says immediately after: "Now Jesus did many other signs in the presence of the disciples, which are not written in this book; but these are written so that you may believe that Jesus is the Christ, the Son of God, and that by believing you may have life in his name" (John 20:30–31). Only twenty-four verses later he says that his readers also *know* what they believe: "This is the disciple who is bearing witness about these things, and who has written these things, and we know that his testimony is true" (John 21:24). So when John quotes Jesus as saying that faith without sight is blessed, it seems that he is not (or is not primarily) pointing to "a source of knowledge that transcends our ordinary perceptual faculties and cognitive processes . . . ."[9] Rather, John is emphasizing a very ordinary way of knowing—knowing through reliable testimony—and thus he appeals to his own status as a witness passing knowledge on to us. Not only life but also knowledge comes by this belief. John's readers have not, like Thomas, seen and touched; yet, he considers, they also may believe and know. So there is some knowing without seeing. And that *seeing* would be a variety of firsthand knowledge—that which comes by firsthand, physical experience.

PAUL

Here is the passage from Paul's letter to the Corinthians in context:

> For we know that if the tent that is our earthly home is destroyed, we have a building from God, a house not made with hands, eternal in the heavens. For in this tent we groan, longing to put on our heavenly dwelling, if indeed by putting it on we may not be found naked. For while we are still in this tent, we

---

9. Plantinga, *Warranted Christian Belief*, 266.

groan, being burdened—not that we would be unclothed, but that we would be further clothed, so that what is mortal may be swallowed up by life. He who has prepared us for this very thing is God, who has given us the Spirit as a guarantee.

So we are always of good courage. We know that while we are at home in the body we are away from the Lord, for we walk by faith, not by sight. Yes, we are of good courage, and we would rather be away from the body and at home with the Lord. So whether we are at home or away, we make it our aim to please him. (2 Cor 5:1–9)

What is Paul talking about here? Certainly some area of personal eschatology: He is talking about death and about being with God afterwards. The primary reason for Paul's hope seems to be our place in heaven, although "heavenly dwelling" or at least "further clothed" may refer to the heavenly body after the coming resurrection of the dead.

In any case, verse 7 tells us that we live not by sight but by faith. The object of faith, that in which we *have* faith, appears to be either the God in whose presence we would like to be but are not *yet*, or else the main topic of this passage—Paul's eschatological hope.

Consider the basis of this faith in verse 5: God "has given us the Spirit as a guarantee" of the keeping of these promises and the fulfilling of these desires. The Holy Spirit is the *arrabōn*. This word, *arrabōn*, is an economic term, a business term. It means "payment of part of a purchase price in advance, first installment, deposit, down payment, pledge."[10] In Paul's way of thinking, the Holy Spirit is a down-payment making the credit the Christian places in God's promises a solid decision. This trust is rational and has a strong claim to being knowledge, much like comparable economic knowledge by trust. I know I will be paid for my work, the credit card corporation knows, on the basis of my good credit, that I in turn will pay my debt to them, and the Christian knows that these eschatological promises will be kept.

Of course, this presumes that believers really do *have* the down-payment, and that they *know* they do. In Paul's view the Corinthian believers know they have the Holy Spirit by the wonders He does among them (1 Cor 12), by the wonders done when the Holy Spirit came on the church in the first place (Acts 2), by His power gradually to heal them of sin (Gal 5:16–24),[11] and by the miracles done among them when Paul first came to

---

10. Arndt, Danker, Bauer, and Gingrich, "ἀρραβών, ῶνος, ὁ."

11. Moser, in an effort to improve on Plantinga's neglect of arguments for his theological views, suggests that the Christian's ability to love better is evidence of God's working in her life; Paul Moser, "Man to Man," 369–77.

them with the gospel (2 Cor 12:12).[12] Acquaintance with the Holy Spirit provides an important ongoing confirmation of the truth of the gospel. Thus David Garland: "How do Christians know that the promise of a heavenly existence is real? Paul's answer is that the experience of the transforming and uplifting power of the Holy Spirit now in their lives is the one piece of empirical evidence that shows that God's promises are real."[13] And Colin Kruse: "Paul's hope rests not only upon the objective knowledge that it is God who is preparing him for a glorious future, but also upon the subjective experience of the Spirit which believers enjoy."[14] That eschatological belief which Paul here says is by faith rather than sight is part of a system of theological belief which is, at certain points, subject to direct confirmation.

All of this, in Paul's way of thinking, makes this trust in this particular bit of eschatology a rational faith—without sight. And that makes it a faith which is also knowledge, assuming that the beliefs are *true*.[15] So the New Testament says that we *do* know what we *see*, but we do *not* see everything we *know*—because some knowledge is by trust rather than sight. Our knowledge here is not firsthand knowledge, which is why it is not the same thing as "sight." Speaking of his eschatological hope for "the redemption of our bodies," Paul in Rom 8:23-25 says that this hope is not seen. Sight in Rom 8 is plainly a synecdoche for firsthand knowledge, inasmuch as this redemption is something Paul's reader would expect to know *firsthand* by *experiencing* it. This experience would include the full range of the experience of *being* these redeemed persons with redeemed bodies—including but

---

12. A summary not of the theology of these verses, but only of the epistemology we can derive from them.

13. Garland, *2 Corinthians*, 264.

14. Kruse, *2 Corinthians*, 158.

15. This is a bit of an oversimplification. Epistemologists have known at least since Plato wrote the *Meno* that knowledge requires that a proposition be true and believed, and also a third thing to connect belief to truth—a thing often described in terms of rationality, justification, evidence, or warrant. The epistemology I am describing here is the biblical way of satisfying *this* requirement. However, these three elements are not quite enough, as Gettier cases show. A *Gettier case*, named for Edmund Gettier, is a situation in which I have a warranted belief, but in which the warrant does not lead me to the truth—and yet by sheer luck the belief is true! The interested reader might consult Gettier, "Is Justified True Belief Knowledge?," 121-23, and Zagzebski, "The Inescapability of Gettier Problems," 65-73. An additional complication comes from Johnson's claim that biblical knowledge involves recognizing the authorities God appointed, but also *acting* on their instructions and *looking* at the world in light of what they say; *Biblical Knowing*, 3. He also claims that the activity knowledge involves works by ritual; *Knowledge by Ritual*. I make no objection to this. In Johnson's terms, my analysis considers only that first requirement for biblical knowledge, the recognizing that an authority is reliable and appointed by God.

not limited to sight. Sight is a synecdoche for firsthand knowledge, and even without it in Rom 8 those "who have the firstfruits of the Spirit" know that this will take place.

Let us return to our text. Consider 2 Cor 4:13-14: "Since we have the same spirit of faith according to what has been written, 'I believe, and so I spoke,' we also believe, and so we also speak, knowing that he who raised the Lord Jesus will raise us also with Jesus and bring us with you into his presence." Perhaps we are tempted to take 2 Cor 5:7 as our operative definition of faith and to presume that New Testament faith means believing without seeing, and thus believing without knowing. But then what would we do with 2 Cor 4:13-14?

A better approach is to do it the other way around. 2 Cor 4:13-14 clearly states that believing the gospel coincides with knowing that certain promises of God will be kept. Paul here seems to be speaking of the apostles as such, not of his readers. But why should they lack knowledge who have heard from the witnesses who knew, since we who have heard from the witnesses who knew in the areas of science, geography, and history derive some knowledge from their testimony?[16] Perhaps we could take this as a clue to the New Testament idea of faith—that it overlaps with knowledge. Then, upon reading in 5:7 that we walk by faith rather than sight, we can conclude that this particular variety of knowledge is independent of sight.

In fact, 4:13-14 encapsulates what we have seen already from looking at chapter 5: Faith is a mode of knowing, not firsthand, that God's mercies are waiting for the believer after death. Johnson's paraphrase in light of "a broader biblical connotation of faith" is appropriate: "We walk by trusting authentic authority and not merely by sight."[17]

Johnson's further commentary on this passage is rewarding. To walk by faith rather than sight is not like walking with our eyes closed and knowing where we go by ears alone. It is more like using our ears to know which way to go and using our eyes to apply that knowledge to each step.[18] Johnson adds, "Faith and sight are not opposed to one another. Trusting the correct guides, docents, or prophets is the first step that enables our eyes to see."[19] My only quibble is that in this passage Paul is speaking of sight as it relates to the object of faith, not as it relates to the ground on which we are walking or the life we are living. Sight is firsthand knowledge, faith is knowledge by

---

16. Augustine's line of reasoning in *Confessions* 6 and *On the Usefulness of Believing*. For a more detailed look at the differences between scientific and religious trust, see chapter 5 of this book.

17. Johnson, *Biblical Knowing*, 3.

18. Johnson, *Biblical Knowing*, 1-3.

19. Johnson, *Biblical Knowing*, 3.

trust, and we walk in the light of our good theology which we know in the latter way rather than the former. It seems C. K. Barrett is not quite correct that in this passage "Faith does not proceed on the basis of an objectively authenticated Christ" in the resurrection but rather "trusts the absent and undemonstrable Christ, whose history has already vanished into the past and whose coming lies in the unknown future."[20] Faith in this passage could indeed be traced to the resurrection insofar as it relies on the promises of Christ whose reliability is confirmed by the resurrection. Granted that the future which is not seen is largely unknown, it seems that Paul considers this particular component of it to be known by trust in reliable promises and by down-payments. And it seems that the immediate basis of this faith is not Christ but the *arrabōn* of the Holy Spirit, who according to Paul is neither absent nor indemonstrable nor unknown.

THE AUTHOR OF HEBREWS

"Now faith is the assurance of things hoped for, the conviction of things not seen" (Heb 11:1). Is this verse really all about a way of believing, an attitude of mind, a trait of assent? Is this verse saying that "faith is a hope that is absolutely certain that what it believes is true, and that what it expects will come," that faith is "the hope which looks forward with utter certainty"?[21] Or is it saying that faith is an inner process instigated by the Holy Spirit that confers warrant directly on our theology such that faith itself is the evidence or warrant for unseen truths?[22] Should a scholarly discussion about how we should interpret this verse focus on the "subjective" aspect of my inner assurance versus an "objective" aspect—the way in which this faith grants me a present experience of future realities?[23]

The first thing to notice about this passage is the soteriological sense of "the conviction of things not seen." We may have misunderstood this passage most of our lives. It is, in Greek, "the *elegchos* of unseen *pragmatōn*." *Elegchos* can mean "the act of presenting evidence for the truth of someth[ing], *proof, proving*;" alternatively, it can mean "the act of charging a pers[on] with wrongdoing" or expression of strong disapproval, *reproof, censure, correction*."[24] *Pragma*, the nominative singular of *pragmatōn* (the geni-

20. Barrett, *The Second Epistle to the Corinthians*, 158.
21. Barclay, *The Letter to the Hebrews*, 144–45.
22. Plantinga, *Warranted Christian Belief*, 265.
23. Scholarly debate to this effect cited by David Allen, who seems to favor *both* views, in Allen, *Hebrews*, 543.
24. Arndt, Danker, Bauer, and Gingrich, "ἔλεγχος, ου, ὁ."

tive plural of *pragma*), means "that which is done or happens, *deed, thing, event, occurrence, matter*."[25] 2 Timothy 3:16 reads in the Majority Text, "All Scripture is breathed out by God and profitable for teaching, for *elegchos*, for correction, and for training in righteousness" (with other texts reading *elegmon*). Here the sense would seem to be "reproof" (as the ESV and some other translations handle *elegmon* or *elegchos* in 3:16) or "conviction." The use of *elegchos* in this way is anticipated in Septuagint uses such as the reproofs in Prov 1, verses 23, 25, and 30. Similar is the infinitive of the verb *elegcho* in Titus 2:9, the imperative in Titus 1:13 and 2:15, and the imperative in 2 Tim 4:2. This is likely the case in Heb 11:1 as well; *elegchos* is the change required of us by the unseen *pragmatōn*.[26] These *pragmata* are, mostly likely and quite literally, *deeds*. In Heb 6:18 the same form, *pragmatōn*, is used to refer to two of God's unchangeable deeds—his promise and his oath. The primary referent in 11:1 is *the deeds of Christ*. The author of Hebrews has just described the mighty sin-purifying deeds of Christ in Heb 9:23–25, and he references heavenly deeds, deeds done in "holy places" which are not "made with hands." The author comments on the same deeds again in chapter 10.[27] In 10:1 *pragmatōn* refers to these acts, of which the Mosaic sacrifices were symbolic. These are, plainly, deeds we do not *see* with our eyes. We do not know them firsthand in that or any other way. But, we are told, we *do* know them by the reliable testimony of Christ and of those who testified to him and to those deeds. (11:39–40 shows that the faith of Old Testament saints looked forward to the same deeds of Christ, which to them were *future* deeds.) This, it seems, is the primary referent of *pragmatōn*.

However, there are secondary senses.[28] 11:3 extends the sphere of reference of *pragmatōn* to other past deeds, the creation of the universe by God; the earlier clause, referencing things we *hope* for, extends the reference to *future* deeds of God in the eschaton. 11:7 speaks (with no use of *pragma*) of unseen things on which Noah had been instructed and on which he had acted—the concern of his faith, events which were for him at the time still in the future. With reference to these particular future events faith allows us to see them, and the author of Hebrews says so in verse 13: The heroes of faith died not yet receiving the promises, yet seeing them from afar and welcoming them. In verse 27 we are told that Moses saw God by faith. A

---

25. Arndt, Danker, Bauer, and Gingrich, "πρᾶγμα, ατος, τό."

26. Bruce makes the same observation; Bruce, *The Epistle to the Hebrews*, 277.

27. "The use of the word *pragma*, from which we get the English word 'pragmatic', points back in Hebrews to what the writer said about the accomplishment of Christ as our High Priest, Hebrews 10:1–18." Packer, "Hebrews 11, 1–2."

28. "But the word *pragma* also refers today to spiritual realities around us and points forward to all the promises of God that lay in the future." Packer, "Hebrews 11, 1–2."

close examination of this use of the language of *seeing* in the New Testament is outside the scope of this paper. It must suffice to observe that this appears to be a non-literal, but *not* synecdochal, use of sight—as a metaphor for knowing or understanding *well*, yet by other means than physical eyesight, as in the line from the old hymn, "by faith we can see it afar."[29]

So, taking into consideration these referents of *pragmatōn* in Heb 11:1, faith is first of all the reproof of the unseen deeds of Christ. It is the life-change required of us in response to those deeds. The work of Christ requires us to live differently, to live in light of them. Secondarily, insofar as *pragmatōn* references future deeds, faith is the life-change required of those who look forward to them. All of these unseen things involve our redemption; they are the *pragmata*, the matters—or, more properly, the actions—taken by God for our redemption. Although I think a more literal translation of *pragmatōn* in 11:1 is appropriate, my interpretation does not depend on it. It depends on the contextual clarification from chapters 9 and 10 of the deeds of Jesus, and on the straightforward reading of the text as declaring that the work of Jesus reproves us into a life of repentance and faithfulness.

The immediate context also helps to clarify. Recall the verse right before 11:1.[30] Hebrews 10:39: "But we are not of those who shrink back and are destroyed, but of those who have faith and preserve their souls." This verse is a call to a way of life following Christ. It is something like a coach's pep talk: "*We* are not those who give up now, in the time of trial. *We* are those who persevere!" Hebrews 10:38 refers to "my righteous one," who "shall live by faith." Now, in 10:39, the author states that faith requires us to live in a particular way. At last, in 11:1, the author gives his definition of faith, and it is a description of this way of life: Faith is the life-change required by the unseen deeds of Christ.

Consider also Heb 11:6: "And without faith it is impossible to please him, for whoever would draw near to God must believe that he exists and that he rewards those who seek him." This verse links three things: believing in *God* (using both the noun *pistis*/faith/trust/faithfulness and the verb *pisteuō*/believe/trust/have faith in), believing in the *relevance* of God to my behavior and its consequences, and *acting* like we believe in God. These three things are *barely* distinguishable and *completely* inseparable, as we also find in the Old Testament such as when Ps 53:1 connects disbelief in God to evil behavior.

29. An aspect of Heb 11:1 and 11:27 pointed out by Marvin Vincent as well as by Bruce, *The Epistle to the Hebrews*, 277; Vincent, *Vincent's Word Studies*, Heb 11:1.

30. Donald Guthrie on Heb 11:1: "There is no break between this verse and the previous one;" Donald Guthrie, *Hebrews*, 225.

So it seems that Heb 11:1 is not exclusively (if even primarily) epistemic, but is soteriological and practical.[31] It is not standing alone at the beginning of chapter 11 as the verse to which we should go for a statement of the epistemic characteristics of biblical faith—for an understanding of what sort of a belief it is and what relationship it bears to reason and evidence. Hebrews 11:1, rather, is to be taken in conjunction with chapter 9 and with 10:39 as one of the first places to which we *should* go for a statement of the *practical* characteristics of faith.[32] This teaching is much like that of the epistle to James. Faith involves works; it is expressed through works, or we might even say that it *is* a work. Hebrews 11:1 is saying that faith is the life-change required of a believer by the unseen deeds of Christ. (Johnson emphasizes the participatory and ritual aspect of the life-change and its characteristic of *testing* God's promises by acting on them.)[33] The author of Hebrews is not painting a picture of faith as an operation of the human mind performed on some *thing* which we believe. The work of faith is perhaps more usefully considered under a picture where the action is going in the opposite direction: Faith is the action performed *on us* by the deeds of the Messiah, reproving us to repent and follow him. It calls us to, using the alternative translation of *pistis*, a life of faith*fulness*. It is probably a good idea to classify *pragmatōn*—the genitive plural of *pragma* meaning "of deeds"—as what scholars of biblical Greek would call a *subjective genitive* rather than an *objective genitive*, meaning that in the phrasing "the reproof of unseen deeds" the reproof is not done *to* but done *by* the deeds.

Now I am not saying that Heb 11:1 is not *at all* about modes of belief. In fact, the *rest* of chapter 11 indicates that 11:1 is *also* about modes of belief. Faith involves things we "must believe" (11:6). These heroes of faith did not see that in which they had faith, for they "did not receive what was promised" (11:39). So 11:1 is about a particular mode of belief as well as a particular mode of life; faith is the life lived in response to the work of Christ inasmuch as one believes in that unseen work without having seen it. After all, why should a connection of faith and works be separate from a distinction between one kind of belief and another? A separation of belief

---

31. Allen helpfully reviews three scholarly theories on "the nature of faith in Hebrews, especially ch. 11." These are the view that faith in Hebrews is "an ethical quality," and two views focused on the object of faith as a belief. One of these is future eschatological events and the other is Christ. Allen favors the third view. I myself think the correct and complete answer would incorporate all three. Allen, *Hebrews*, 541–42.

32. George Guthrie, citing Philip Hughes, is emphatic of the prominent active aspect of the *elegchos* clause; George Guthrie, *NIV Application Commentary: Hebrews*, 374–75.

33. Johnson, *Scripture's Knowing*, 83.

and life is foreign to the Bible's teachings. We have not found that 11:1 is not at all about faith and sight—only that it *is* about works, more so than is commonly appreciated. We have also found that 11:1 defines faith as the life-change required by the unseen deeds of Christ.

Moreover, this lack of sight is in no way a lack of knowledge. Nothing in the verse ties all knowledge to seeing. Rather, this passage links attributes of knowledge to faith. Hebrews 11:3: "By faith we understand that the universe was created by the word of God, so that what is seen was not made out of things that are visible." This, the author presumes, we have learned from reliable authority—in this case, Moses in the Torah. This understanding, from *noeō*, might be taken to mean mere *comprehension* of a statement, not knowledge that the statement is *true*. But let us rewind a bit to an earlier moment in the text, Heb 10:26: We must not "go on sinning deliberately after receiving the knowledge of the truth." This "knowledge" is *epignōsis*, which may be translated simply as "knowledge."[34] And how did a believer get *this* knowledge? She got her knowledge of *creation* from the testimony of a prophet, Moses, and she gets *this* knowledge from the Son of God, by whom God "in these last days" has spoken (Heb 1:2). This, it seems, is the most important "objective" aspect of faith in Heb 11:1—not that faith gives the believer a present experience of her future hope (although this is not an unbiblical notion), but that it is based on objective facts known by trust in reliable and confirmed authority.

Perhaps we might interpret Heb 11:1 in light of 10:26 and 11:3—at least when it comes to determining the epistemic characteristics of faith. This would hardly be a novel way of thinking. It would merely be a bit Augustinian, for Augustine held that understanding comes by faith. Thus Donald Guthrie on verse 3: "But the words *By faith we understand* show that knowledge is not independent of faith."[35]

So Heb 11:1 is about faith in relation to works, yet is also about faith in relation to sight and about faith in relation to knowledge. And what, in sum, does it say about the relationship of faith, sight, and knowledge? Let us recall chapter 9, which speaks of certain deeds of Christ which are heavenly and not physical. This is why they are, quite literally, unseen as far as our bodily eyes are concerned. So 11:1 refers to *literal* sight. It is also a synecdoche for firsthand knowledge. For any of the heroes of faith surveyed in chapter 11, when he eventually should "receive what was promised" (11:39), would know by more than his physical eyes alone. So Heb 11:1 says that

---

34. Arndt, Danker, Bauer, and Gingrich, "ἐπίγνωσις, εως, ἡ."
35. Donald Guthrie, *Hebrews*, 227.

faith involves a life-change, and it also tells us that gospel faith is faith in that which we do know but do *not* know firsthand.[36]

The astute reader will perhaps be dissatisfied that I have not yet said anything about the earlier phrase from 11:1, which defines faith as "the *hypostastis* of things hoped for." This *hypostasis* could mean "guarantee of ownership/entitlement, *title deed*"[37]—suggestive of the Pauline *arrabōn*. Or it could mean "a plan that one devises for action, *plan, project, undertaking, endeavor*," which I suggest is the sense here, as it is in Heb 3:14.[38] Faith is the believer's steadiness of mind or conviction with respect to those things she hopes for. The sense of the passage is not such as to exclude any possibility of doubt,[39] but rather to forbid the believer to waver in her commitment. Faith is the commitment and conviction that sticks to Christ no matter what.[40] Faith is not (or is not primarily) the source of warrant for Christian theology,[41] but the commitment to stick with that theology which is warranted in other ways. So, again, the emphasis is on a commitment which constitutes a life-change. Of course, the commitment is based on the knowledge of what Christ has accomplished, and looks forward to what is yet to come; the believer does not (yet) have firsthand knowledge of that fulfillment, for what she only *hopes* for she does not yet have (as Paul says in Rom 8:24). The *hypostasis* is a mental state, but one with a profound practical application.[42]

---

36. Indeed, there may even be an economic aspect of the passage much like that of 2 Cor. 5:7, as Kenneth Wuest explains; Wuest, *Hebrews in the Greek New Testament*, 193. Bruce (*Epistle to the Hebrews*, 277) is skeptical, and George Guthrie supports him; George Guthrie, *NIV Application Commentary: Hebrews*, n. 4, 374. Allen very helpfully introduces various scholars on this topic; Allen, *Hebrews*, 542–43.

37. Arndt, Danker, Bauer, and Gingrich, "ὑπόστασις, εως, ἡ." Arndt, Danker, Bauer, and Gingrich are also optimistic about *hupostasis* as the "realization" of the unseen realities as a possible meaning of Heb 11:1.

38. On which latter point Bruce concurs; *The Epistle to the Hebrews*, 277.

39. See Barclay above, at footnote 21.

40. Donald Guthrie: "Faith is the act of commitment on the part of the believer . . . ;" Donald Guthrie, *Hebrews*, 226. George Guthrie: "Thus, we can translate this part of the verse: 'Now faith is the resolute confidence . . . .'" George Guthrie, *NIV Application Commentary: Hebrews*, 374.

41. See Plantinga above, at footnote 22.

42. Indeed, the *elegchos*, as Vincent observed long ago, is "included in *hypostasis*"; Vincent, *Vincent's Word Studies*. Thus the life-changing reproof of the unseen deeds of Christ is part of the conviction relating to the things we hope for.

CONCLUSION

In New Testament epistemology faith involves trust, and trust in reliable authority is a way of knowing. Sight is a synecdoche for firsthand knowledge, whereas the way of knowing the gospel on which most Christians rely is the way of trusting in reliable authority. Various New Testament authors concur on this. Paul in particular suggests that the credit we place in God's eschatological promises is confirmed by the down-payment of the Holy Spirit, much like the credit the bank places in a creditworthy customer who takes out a loan—knowing that the outstanding commitment will be met. Moreover, the author of Hebrews does not tell us that faith is a confidence in what we do not know, but a commitment to live by the gospel and its promises, a gospel *known* to be true, but not known *firsthand*.

In short, Jesus is not saying that we are blessed if we believe blindly and without any good evidence, but that those are blessed who have not seen and yet have known by faith!

This knowledge focuses on Jesus the Messiah, but leads to a knowledge of the Bible, which we must consider in the next chapter.

WORKS CITED

Allen, David L. *Hebrews*. The New American Commentary, vol. 35. Nashville: Broadman & Holman, 2010.

Arndt, William, Frederick W. Danker, Walter Bauer, and F. Wilbur Gingrich. "ἀπολογία, ας, ἡ." *A Greek-English Lexicon of the New Testament and Other Early Christian Literature*. Chicago: University of Chicago Press, 2000. *Logos Bible Software*. Faithlife Corporation.

———. "ἀρραβών, ῶνος, ὁ." *A Greek-English Lexicon of the New Testament and Other Early Christian Literature*. Chicago: University of Chicago Press, 2000. *Logos Bible Software*. Faithlife Corporation.

———. "ἔλεγχος, ου, ὁ." *A Greek-English Lexicon of the New Testament and Other Early Christian Literature*. Chicago: University of Chicago Press, 2000. *Logos Bible Software*. Faithlife Corporation.

———. "ἐπίγνωσις, εως, ἡ." *A Greek-English Lexicon of the New Testament and Other Early Christian Literature*. Chicago: University of Chicago Press, 2000. *Logos Bible Software*. Faithlife Corporation.

———. "οἶδα." *A Greek-English Lexicon of the New Testament and Other Early Christian Literature*. Chicago: University of Chicago Press, 2000. *Logos Bible Software*. Faithlife Corporation.

———. "πίστις, εως, ἡ." *A Greek-English Lexicon of the New Testament and Other Early Christian Literature*. Chicago: University of Chicago Press, 2000. *Logos Bible Software*. Faithlife Corporation.

———. "πρᾶγμα, ατος, τό." *A Greek-English Lexicon of the New Testament and Other Early Christian Literature.* Chicago: University of Chicago Press, 2000. *Logos Bible Software.* Faithlife Corporation.

———. "ὑπόστασις, εως, ἡ." *A Greek-English Lexicon of the New Testament and Other Early Christian Literature.* Chicago: University of Chicago Press, 2000. *Logos Bible Software.* Faithlife Corporation.

Augustine. *Confessions.* Translated by F. J. Sheed. Introduction by Peter Brown. 2nd ed. Edited and notes by Michael P. Foley. Indianapolis: Hackett, 2006.

———. *On the Usefulness of Believing.*

Barclay, William. *The Letter to the Hebrews: Translated with an Introduction and Interpretation by William Barclay.* Edinburgh: The Saint Andrew Press, 1955.

Barrett, C. K. *The Second Epistle to the Corinthians.* London: Adam and Charles Black, 1973.

Bruce, F. F. *The Epistle to the Hebrews.* Grand Rapids: Eerdmans, 1990.

Garland, David E. *2 Corinthians.* The New American Commentary, vol. 29. Nashville: Broadman and Holman, 1999.

Gettier, Edmund L. "Is Justified True Belief Knowledge?" *Analysis* 23.6 (1963) 121–23.

Guthrie, Donald. *Hebrews.* Grand Rapids: Eerdmans, 1983.

Guthrie, George H. *The NIV Application Commentary: Hebrews.* Grand Rapids: Zondervan, 1998.

The Holy Bible. English Standard Version.

Johnson, Dru. *Biblical Knowing: A Scriptural Epistemology of Error.* Eugene, OR: Cascade, 2013.

———. *Epistemology and Biblical Theology: From the Pentateuch to Mark's Gospel.* London: Routledge, 2018.

———. *Knowledge by Ritual: A Biblical Prolegomenon to Sacramental Theology.* Journal of Theological Interpretation Supplement 13. Winona Lake, IN: Eisenbrauns, 2016.

———. *Scripture's Knowing: A Companion to Biblical Epistemology.* Eugene, OR: Cascade, 2016.

Kennard, Douglas. *Epistemology and Logic in the New Testament: Early Jewish Context and Biblical Theology Mechanisms That Fit within Some Contemporary Ways of Knowing.* Eugene, OR: Wipf and Stock, 2016.

Kruse, Colin G. *2 Corinthians.* Downers Grove, IL: InterVarsity, 2015.

Packer, David. "Hebrews 11,1–2." *NightTimeThoughts.org.* http://nighttimethoughts.org/?p=42 (accessed November 6, 2017).

Plato. *Meno.* Translated by G. M. A. Grube. In *The Complete Works of Plato*, edited by John M. Cooper. Indianapolis: Hackett, 1997.

Plantinga, A. *Warranted Christian Belief.* New York: Oxford University Press, 2000.

Vincent, Marvin R. *Vincent's Word Studies*, Heb. 11:1. https://www.studylight.org/commentaries/vnt/hebrews-11.html (accessed November 6, 2017).

Wuest, Kenneth S. *Hebrews in the Greek New Testament for the English Reader.* Grand Rapids: Eerdmans, 1947.

Zagzebski, Linda. "The Inescapability of Gettier Problems." *The Philosophical Quarterly* 44.174 (1994) 65–73.

8

Inerrancy Is Not a Strong or Classical Foundationalism

DISCUSSIONS OF BIBLICAL AUTHORITY and hermeneutics have long considered epistemology, that branch of philosophy that studies the nature, origins, and structure of knowledge. Stanley Grenz and John Franke have said that inerrantist theology is linked to a particular view of the structure of knowledge, *classical foundationalism* or *strong foundationalism* (hereafter the latter).[1] The general idea of strong foundationalism is that knowledge has a foundation in well warranted beliefs that do not derive any warrant from other beliefs and that, moreover, all our other beliefs depend on these foundational ones for their warrant. Alvin Plantinga further posits as an essential trait of strong foundationalism its unduly restrictive criterion for a foundational belief—that it be self-evident, evident to the senses, or incorrigible.[2]

Grenz's and Franke's view is no stranger to criticism.[3] However, it appears that a criticism emerging from a careful study of the structure of knowledge has not yet been made. The doctrine of inerrancy has almost

---

1. The major sources include Grenz, *Renewing the Center*; Franke, "Recasting Inerrancy," 259–85; and Grenz and Franke, *Beyond Foundationalism*.

2. Among other sources, Plantinga, "Is Belief in God Properly Basic?," 41–51 and Plantinga, "Reason and Belief in God," 60.

3. For critiques concerning truth, objectivity, evangelism, and the viability of weak foundationalism see Kurka, "*Before* 'Foundationalism,'" 145–65; Mohler, "Response to John R. Franke," 288; and Vanhoozer, "Response to John R. Franke," 304.

nothing to do with strong foundationalism. Inerrancy does not require any view of the structure of knowledge, and notable sources including the Chicago Statement on Biblical Inerrancy (hereafter CSBI) tout inerrancy in ways inconsistent with most forms of strong foundationalism. There are three types of warrant—what I call inferential, coherential, and foundational warrant. Different views of the structure of knowledge are different accounts of how these types of warrant are arranged. Strong foundationalism has it that knowledge has a foundation in beliefs warranted by foundational warrant alone. If inerrancy is a strong foundationalism, then the doctrine itself must be alleged to be warranted in this manner, or else built on beliefs that are. Critics seem to not fully appreciate this point, not explaining the relation of inerrancy to basic beliefs and instead observing that inerrantists build on Scripture as a foundation.

The biggest problem with tying inerrancy to strong foundationalism is that more than one variety of warrant is said to support the doctrine. Notable sources point to warrant of the foundational variety, derived from the Holy Spirit's testimony about the Bible, and also to inferential warrant, often said to derive from the authority of Christ; coherential warrant is also a factor. This would render inerrancy incompatible with most forms of strong foundationalism, although there is at least one interesting exception (on which more in good time). There are smaller problems. Inerrancy does not necessarily entail *any* view of the structure of knowledge; in particular, the inference from the authority of Christ need not rely on any particular view of the structure of knowledge, or may rely on strong or weak foundationalism or neither. Moreover, by Plantinga's definition any inerrantist appeal to the Holy Spirit as directly warranting inerrancy clashes with strong foundationalism's criterion for a belief's having foundational warrant.

In short, that inerrancy resembles strong foundationalism is correct only to the extent that inerrancy posits Scripture as a solid foundation for theology. The structure of the doctrine does not commit it to any such epistemology, and some proponents employ epistemologies incompatible with most forms of strong foundationalism.

In what follows I shall first explain the building blocks of knowledge and some major views of the structure of knowledge. Then I shall consider the charge that inerrancy is a strong foundationalism. Then I shall review some justifications for biblical inerrancy and explain why inerrancy is not a strong foundationalism. I will close with some remarks on the prospects for a strongly foundationalist inerrancy.

THE STRUCTURE OF KNOWLEDGE

Knowledge is a system of beliefs; it has a structure, an arrangement. Knowledge is always true belief; I can only know what I believe, and if I believe something false my belief is error rather than knowledge. Plato explains that we need a third thing to tie belief down to the truth (*Meno* 96d–98b). That thing, as Plantinga puts it, is *warrant*, that "quality or quantity enough of which, together with truth and belief, is sufficient for knowledge."[4] Warrant frequently involves evidence or justification; a belief is justified by other beliefs. But justification does not spontaneously arise; those justified beliefs had to get their warrant from somewhere; the process of justification needs a beginning.

Thus, epistemologists have discovered two other varieties of warrant. After explaining these, I shall explain why a good view of the structure of knowledge requires taking all three into consideration, and this at all levels of that structure. *Coherentism* and most forms of *strong foundationalism* are failures, while *foundherentism* and *weak foundationalism* are at least viable. (I have explained this material in more detail elsewhere, and it is recommended for the reader with a particular interest in epistemology.)[5]

Three Varieties of Warrant

Inferential warrant is easily understood. A belief often has evidentiary support from other beliefs. When a belief or a set of beliefs is warranted and provides good enough support for another belief, at least some of that warrant is extended to the supported belief.

Inferential warrant is derivative; a belief gets it from other warranted beliefs, whose own warrant must either be inferential, or not. If it is inferential, it too comes from other warranted beliefs. This process cannot go on into infinity, since we do not have an infinite number of beliefs. So inferential warrant must be rooted in some other variety of warrant.

Hence *foundational* warrant is that which is *not* derivative. A belief has it without getting it *from* anywhere. Beliefs arising directly from sensory experience ("I see something blue," "I feel pain"), truths of reason ("2 + 2 = 4," "If all men are mortal and Socrates is a man then Socrates is mortal"), and other commonsense beliefs ("The evidence of the senses can be trusted," "The world outside my mind exists") are examples of beliefs with foundational warrant. I know them, but not by inference from other beliefs.

---

4. Plantinga, *Warrant and Proper Function*, v.
5. Boone, "Inferential, Coherential, and Foundational Warrant," 377–98.

There is a third way a warranted belief can be connected to the system of knowledge. If a belief is consistent with a system of warranted belief, especially one closely concerning the topic of the belief, it is (all else being equal) more likely to be true than one not thus consistent. Accordingly, this consistency confers another variety of warrant on a belief: *coherential* warrant.

All Three Varieties Are Necessary

All three of these types of warrant are necessary, and an accurate and thorough theory of the structure of knowledge must account for all three and acknowledge that beliefs with foundational warrant have the other kinds.

To deny that inferential warrant is a part of the structure of knowledge is to deny that we know anything based on evidence. So obviously inferential warrant is necessary.

Inferential and coherential warrants are both derivative, and they must have something from which to derive—namely, foundational warrant. The beliefs of a person in the Matrix, or of the philosopher's famed brain-in-a-vat, may have as much inference and coherence as my beliefs or yours. But his beliefs do not track reality; their warrant is illusory, and he lacks knowledge. Our beliefs, which *do* track reality, are different from his mainly in having foundational warrant.

Coherential warrant is also important. A system of beliefs could hardly be *knowledge* if it had a high degree of inconsistency. Even beliefs with foundational warrant need coherential warrant. Say I look out the window and my perceptual faculties, generally reliable and functioning properly at the time, lead me to believe that there is an animal in the yard. Plantinga would say (rightly, I think) that such a belief has foundational warrant. Say, furthermore, that the belief I form is "There is a sparrow outside my window." Say that on another occasion the same thing happens for the belief "There is a tyrannosaurus rex outside my window." This belief is less warranted than the other because of the coherential warrant the former enjoys—since my beliefs tell me that, although sparrows are a common animal around here, dinosaurs, sadly, are not.

Coherentism and Strong Foundationalism

Since all three varieties of warrant are part of the structure of knowledge, the correct account of its structure must include them. Classical coherentism intentionally leaves out foundational warrant, positing that the warranting process never actually *begins* anywhere.[6] Accordingly, coherentism is mistaken.[7]

Strong foundationalism is likewise mistaken, or at least most versions of it are. Let us first take a closer look at the relevant terms. *Foundationalism* is the theory that there are such things as *properly basic beliefs*, beliefs with enough foundational warrant to be known on its strength alone.[8]

It can be difficult to nail down just one definition of *strong foundationalism*, although by most definitions Descartes's foundationalism will be the strongest. The strength of a foundationalism comes in degrees, and in fact a foundationalism may be strong in at least three senses. Plantinga's approach suggests the first—the fewer beliefs, or varieties of belief, recognized as properly basic, the stronger the foundationalism. Second, the more certain the basic beliefs are, the stronger the foundationalism; indeed, the special epistemic status attributed to basic beliefs is sometimes treated as the essence of strong foundationalism.[9] Third, the *less often* a foundationalism recognizes beliefs which have foundational warrant but not enough to be known without some other kind of warrant, or properly basic beliefs which also happen to have coherential or inferential warrant, the *stronger* it is.[10]

Strong foundationalism thus implies that a basic belief may be warranted by foundational warrant alone; inferential and coherential warrant lend no support to basic beliefs. Strong foundationalisms are typically wrong because our beliefs with foundational warrant often *do* have inferential or coherential warrant, and often *need* it. The other forms of warrant work closely with foundational warrant. Susan Haack has done some good work explaining this,[11] and John Zeis has applied her work to religious epistemology.[12] Zeis uses a convenient illustration, which I here modify to fit my own life: I remember some years ago running into my friend John at the

---

6. Laurence BonJour's earlier work is a fine example of coherentism; BonJour, *The Structure of Empirical Knowledge* and "Can Empirical Knowledge Have a Foundation?," 1–13.

7. For more on this see Boone, "Inferential, Coherential, and Foundational Warrant," 388–97.

8. I discuss this and two alternative definitions of foundationalism in Boone, "Inferential, Coherential, and Foundational Warrant," 390–92.

9. For example, Poston, "Foundationalism," 4.a.i; however, note that Poston turns to the third sense when defining *weak* foundationalism (4.a.iii).

10. For an alternative definition of classical foundationalism, see Richard Fumerton's working definition as "foundationalism committed to *internalism*" ("Classical Foundationalism," 4).

11. Haack, "Double-Aspect Foundherentism," 113–28; "Précis," 7–11; and "Reply to BonJour," 25–35.

12. Zeis, "A Foundherentist Conception," 133–60.

Dallas-Fort Worth International Airport. Plantinga would correctly say that my belief here has foundational warrant; however, it matters to its warrant that I know, independently of the memory, of such a place as the D-FW airport and of such a person as John. I also know that some years ago I flew through D-FW on American Airlines on the way to San Francisco for a meeting of the Evangelical Philosophical Society, where I delivered a paper on Plantinga's epistemology. I also remember that John and I were in the same graduate school program. I have a vague memory that he read a paper at the same conference. In the absence of all this I would probably write off my memory as some confused dream. From that particular memory alone, my belief derives insufficient warrant for knowledge or rational belief, but the strong coherential warrant derived from all these other beliefs makes a big difference in favor of the belief. Typical strong foundationalisms, denying this, are accordingly mistaken.

Recall Plantinga's more restrictive definition of strong foundationalism: the view that only beliefs self-evident, incorrigible, or evident to the senses can have foundational warrant—a too-short list of properly basic beliefs. Plantinga's critique is not on the grounds that strong foundationalism has the wrong account of the structure of knowledge. The problem is with how beliefs in the structure's *foundation* are warranted. Plantinga gives various reasons this view is mistaken.[13] Here is another, borrowed from the history of philosophy. Hume observed that knowledge gained from experience requires some principle or principles *by which* we gain knowledge from experience—for example induction or the uniformity of nature.[14] These are not evident to the senses (being themselves the knowledge we bring *to* the senses in order to learn from them), nor incorrigible (being dubitable), nor self-evident like "2 + 2 = 4" is self-evident (and were not evident to Hume, though he did recommend believing them).

Before going on, we need to take a look at one promising account, Timothy McGrew's "classical foundationalism" in *The Foundations of Knowledge*.[15] McGrew argues that knowledge is rooted in incorrigible beliefs about our mental states, and he employs in his chapter 7 an interesting probabilistic argument that these mental states can ground knowledge of the world outside the mind. If I understand it rightly, his account is not subject to my major objection to strong foundationalism, at least as concerns basic beliefs, for the basic beliefs he identifies concern awareness of our mental

---

13. Plantinga, "Is Belief in God Properly Basic?" and "Reason and Belief in God." See also Beilby, *Epistemology as Theology*, 47.

14. Hume, *Enquiry Concerning Human Understanding*.

15. McGrew, *The Foundations of Knowledge*.

states, which does not require inferential or coherential warrant, although these would still be necessary for beliefs just a few levels up. (Indeed, I think McGrew might well agree with me on that much; I take it that his account of mutual support among beliefs would preclude a foundationalism strong in the third sense from applying anywhere except to basic beliefs.)[16] McGrew's is a promising account, assuming the chapter 7 argument is solid, although this is not the place to put that argument to the test. (We will return to McGrew's account in relation to inerrancy later.)

Foundherentism or Weak Foundationalism

Two major theories on the structure of knowledge are viable. Roughly, foundherentism is the theory that some beliefs have foundational warrant, but none have *enough* of it to be *known* without some help from the other varieties of warrant.[17] On a viable model of *weak* foundationalism, at least *some* beliefs with foundational warrant have *enough* of it to be known; but *some* beliefs with foundational warrant, including the ones that *can* be known on its strength alone, can *also* be warranted by inferential or coherential warrant.

Foundherentism and weak foundationalism, then, agree that all three varieties of warrant matter, and that even beliefs with foundational warrant can enjoy other varieties. Their only salient disagreement is whether *some* beliefs with foundational warrant sometimes have *enough* of it to be known on its strength alone. One of these theories is likelier to be true than coherentism or most forms of strong foundationalism.

And what is the connection of all this to biblical inerrancy? Let's find out.

DOES INERRANCY ENTAIL A STRONG FOUNDATIONALISM?

The charge that inerrancy is a strong foundationalism is ambiguous. On the one hand, it may mean that inerrantists have had a strong foundationalist epistemology, perhaps treating inerrancy as a properly basic belief or trying to base it on other properly basic beliefs. How inerrantists are supposed to have attempted this is not entirely clear. On the other hand, the

---

16. McGrew, "How Foundationalists Do Crossword Puzzles," 333–50.

17. For more detailed presentations of foundherentism, see the aforementioned articles by Haack, Zeis, and Boone.

charge may be simply that inerrantists attempt to build their theology on the foundation of the Bible much as a strong foundationalist would attempt to build knowledge on the solid foundation of basic beliefs. If this is the case, inerrancy may have nothing to do with foundationalism beyond this point of comparison, and why exactly that particular point of comparison would be a problem is unclear. Inerrancy, if true, guarantees that the Bible is a solid foundation for theology. But this does not make inerrantists into strong foundationalists; whether they are depends on why they accept the Bible's authority.

In *Renewing the Center*, Grenz gives us a fair description of strong foundationalism, often referring to it simply as "foundationalism." He notes that it is motivated by the desire to escape from uncertainty, and rightly associates it with Enlightenment figureheads Locke and Descartes.[18] He states that according to foundationalism "reasoning moves in only one direction—from the bottom up, that is, from basic beliefs or first-principles to resultant conclusions."[19] This is actually Haack's definition of foundationalism, and a fine definition of *strong* foundationalism as I use the term.[20] As Grenz tells the tale, Enlightenment theology followed Enlightenment foundationalism, tending towards deism.[21] Then Enlightenment theology was abandoned, by some in favor of blind Christian faith and by others in favor of a "skeptical rationalism."[22] A new theological perspective emerged in the 1800s.[23] This was a theology aimed at satisfying the demands of strong foundationalism and employing the Bible as the foundation. The doctrine that every proposition in the Bible is true was used as the foundation for all knowledge. Thus began what we now think of as fundamentalism or inerrantist evangelicalism. So contemporary inerrancy was infected with strong foundationalism from its beginning and, indeed, developed precisely because of the presumption of strong foundationalism.

But this is ambiguous. Is the charge that inerrantists actually *are* strong foundationalists? Or is it that they do theology in the same manner in which a strong foundationalist like Descartes does philosophy, using the doctrine of inerrancy as a foundation? These are very different claims. If the charge is that inerrantists really *are* strong foundationalists, it follows that the inerrantist accepts the doctrine of inerrancy itself on strongly foundationalist

---

18. Grenz, *Renewing the Center*, 194–95.
19. Grenz, *Renewing the Center*, 194.
20. Boone, "Inferential, Coherential, and Foundational Warrant," 390–97.
21. Grenz, *Renewing the Center*, 195–98.
22. Grenz, *Renewing the Center*, 197.
23. Grenz, *Renewing the Center*, 197.

INERRANCY IS NOT A STRONG OR CLASSICAL FOUNDATIONALISM

grounds. However, on the latter charge, inerrantists may or may not be strong foundationalists, depending on why they accept the doctrine of biblical inerrancy. If the doctrine of inerrancy is accepted without regard to the standards of strong foundationalism, then the inerrantist is not a strong foundationalist at all. He is simply an inerrantist; inerrancy entails that the Bible is a solid foundation for theology, and it is not clear what is the point of making the comparison to strong foundationalism.

Grenz writes as if he has the latter idea in mind when he says these theologians "were confident that they could deduce from Scripture the great theological truths that lay within its pages."[24] The former, however, is suggested by Grenz's description of this theology as treating "the veracity" of the Bible as "unimpeachable when measured by the canons of human reason."[25] Instead of specifying on what strongly foundationalist grounds inerrancy was justified, Grenz returns to the latter alternative, saying that inerrancy treats the Bible as "an incontrovertible foundation."[26] If the canons of reason establish biblical inerrancy, then inerrancy rests on a foundation of some sort and cannot itself *be* such a foundation. If, however, the charge is that the inerrantist uses the Bible as a foundation in the manner of a foundationalist, this has nothing to do with inerrancy *being* a foundationalism. In this case there is a resemblance between the inerrantist's use of the Bible and Descartes's use of the proposition "I exist": Both serve as a solid basis for other knowledge. But the resemblance is superficial if the inerrantist thinks he has some evidence for inerrancy, and why we should care about the resemblance is a mystery.

Franke, in his contribution to *Five Views on Biblical Inerrancy*, makes some similar claims, albeit with kind words for inerrantists and some appreciation for the doctrine.[27] Franke writes,

> As a whole, the Chicago Statement is reflective of a particular form of epistemology known as classic or strong foundationalism. This approach to knowledge seeks to overcome the uncertainty generated by the tendency of fallible human beings to error, by discovering a universal and indubitable basis for human knowledge.[28]

---

24. Grenz, *Renewing the Center*, 198.
25. Grenz, *Renewing the Center*, 198.
26. Grenz, *Renewing the Center*, 198.
27. Franke, "Recasting Inerrancy," 259–87.
28. Franke, "Recasting Inerrancy," 261.

Citing Grenz, he correctly points to Enlightenment philosophy as the origins of this epistemology.[29] But why should we think that the CSBI reflects this Enlightenment perspective? Franke explains that according to it "Scripture is the true and sole basis for knowledge on all matters which it touches," and he adds that inerrantists display strong foundationalist presumptions about knowledge whenever they claim that any error in Scripture would render the whole of Scripture suspect.[30]

This is a little puzzling. To begin with, it is doubtful that any inerrantist ever thought the Bible is the *sole* source of knowledge on any matter it touches. The Bible tells us to expect to die (Heb 9:27), but inerrantists are well aware that this can also be learned from experience.

More importantly, what does Franke mean by claiming that inerrantists are thinking like strong foundationalists? He suggests they "view Scripture as a foundation for human knowledge."[31] He may mean that inerrantists regard the Bible's truthfulness as a properly basic belief like Descartes regards "I exist"—as having absolute certainty which is entirely underived from any other known beliefs.[32] But Franke does not cite any inerrantists claiming this, and indeed the CSBI and other sources justify inerrancy on various grounds, which precludes the Bible's being *this* sort of foundation.

Alternatively, Franke may simply mean that inerrantists *act as if* the Bible were absolutely certain by believing everything it says. But what sort of a charge against inerrancy is that? If inerrantists really believe that the Bible is always correct, should they *not* believe all things it teaches? Inerrantists are inerrantists, but how is that an objection to inerrancy? In any case, this does not make inerrancy a strong foundationalism unless it is *itself* accepted without any evidence.

Perhaps Franke only wants inerrantists to humbly recognize the possibility that they got it wrong—that maybe inerrancy is mistaken or their interpretation of the Bible on some point is wrong. Well and good. But epistemic humility is fully compatible with biblical inerrancy.[33]

Franke, noting that inerrantists now tend to style themselves as weak foundationalists, says, "In the framework of weak foundationalism, inerrancy could be mistaken and should be subject to critical scrutiny."[34] Is

---

29. Franke, "Recasting Inerrancy," 261.

30. Franke, "Recasting Inerrancy," 262.

31. Franke, "Recasting Inerrancy," 264.

32. Vanhoozer reads Franke as critiquing a largely Cartesian perspective ("Response to John R. Franke," 303).

33. Noted by Vanhoozer, "Response to John R. Franke," 305–6. See also the next chapter of this volume.

34. Franke, "Recasting Inerrancy," 263.

this not the attitude of the authors of the CSBI, who "invite response to this statement from any who see reason to amend its affirmations about Scripture by the light of Scripture"?[35] Franke asks, "What might the doctrine of inerrancy look like in a fallibilist perspective?"[36] I think it would look much like the CSBI. Or, contrary to his suspicion that CSBI inerrancy employs concepts foreign to church fathers,[37] a fallibilist inerrancy might look rather like Augustine![38]

Grenz and Franke join forces in *Beyond Foundationalism*, claiming that inerrantists have treated the Bible as an "invulnerable foundation."[39] This might be interpreted to mean simply that inerrantists have thought they could trust whatever the Bible says; this, once again, is merely what inerrancy means. Alternatively, it might mean that inerrantists have had 100% confidence in their theology, in which they might be said to have erred, although it is unclear how this weighs against their theology. (If I have 100% certainty that Tolkien is a better writer than Lewis, I may be overconfident, but that is no evidence that I am *mistaken*.) They also claim that *some*, but not all, inerrantists try to justify the doctrine "by appeal to rational argument,"[40] but at most this applies only to some inerrantists, not to inerrancy itself, and in any case the link to strong foundationalism remains unclear.

Brian McLaren, following Grenz and Franke, suggests that conservatives and liberals have the same roots in Enlightenment theology.[41] Yet the convergence of evangelical conservatism with foundationalism is in its conception of "an error-free Bible as the incontrovertible foundation of their theology."[42] He does not explain why we should not treat the Bible as an incontrovertible foundation if indeed we take it to be without error, nor why he thinks evangelicals who have thus taken it did so on strong foundationalist grounds.

Others have also found this critique a bit confusing. Peter Leithart notes that it is difficult fully to understand; he observes Franke has professed inerrancy in the past, that inerrancy might well be compatible with

---

35. The International Council on Biblical Inerrancy, The Chicago Statement on Biblical Inerrancy with Exposition (Chicago, 1978), Preface.
36. Franke, "Recasting Inerrancy," 263.
37. Franke, "Recasting Inerrancy," 260-61.
38. See the next chapter of this book.
39. Grenz and Franke, *Beyond Foundationalism*, 34.
40. Grenz and Franke, *Beyond Foundationalism*.
41. Brian McLaren, *A Generous Orthodoxy*, 10-11.
42. McLaren, *A Generous Orthodoxy*, 11.

some non-foundationalist epistemology, and that much depends on how these technical terms are defined.[43] Kevin Vanhoozer suggests that Franke errs in thinking inerrancy is necessarily linked to a theory of knowledge. Inerrancy is a theory in *theology* allowing us to treat the Bible as theologically foundational, but that does not mean that people who do so have any particular theory in epistemology.[44]

We should consider these charges more systematically. We may distinguish three.

First, there is the charge that, in seeking knowledge built on Scripture as a foundation, the structure of inerrantist thought resembles that of strong foundationalist thought. This is correct. It is also irrelevant. The very *meaning* of the doctrine of inerrancy entails that we can build on Scripture as a solid foundation for knowledge. Should we *not* act as if we believe our theology just because in doing so we might happen to resemble Descartes in some way? Whence comes this rule for doing theology? Perhaps the critic simply thinks that treating the Bible as a solid foundation for knowledge is *incorrect*. But this is no more than to say that *inerrancy* is incorrect. An argument against inerrancy and relying on this as a premise is fallaciously circular. As a mere counter-assertion, it is interesting but not an argument.

Second, there is the charge that inerrancy is part of a strongly foundationalist epistemology. If the idea here is that inerrancy *necessarily* is such, the charge is simply false. Inerrancy can only be part of a strong foundationalism if the doctrine is considered *either* to be a properly basic belief with no warrant derived from other beliefs at all, *or* to be derived from such beliefs. However, inerrancy may be supported with arguments, and these arguments may or may not conform to any particular epistemological outlook. If some inerrantist happens to accept the doctrine using a bad epistemology, perhaps that is his problem rather than inerrancy's. In any case, inerrancy is commonly supported in ways inconsistent with strong foundationalism—on which more anon.

Third, there is the charge that inerrancy is not epistemically humble—that it trusts too much in the human ability to gain certainty. This objection seems to miss the point that inerrancy looks to the *divine* aspect of the Bible, thinking only *God* can give us any infallible knowledge. One major reason inerrancy matters is that we humans *lack* the ability to reach certain knowledge of God. Moreover, the inerrantist has plenty of room for humility about what he thinks the Bible means. He can even admit that he might be wrong about inerrancy!

43. Leithart, "Foundationalism and Inerrancy."
44. Vanhoozer, "Response to John R. Franke," 304.

WHAT VIEW OF KNOWLEDGE DOES INERRANCY INVOLVE?

Several kinds of evidence are given for biblical inerrancy. The argument from the authority of Jesus Christ is significant. There is also a claim—not a giving of evidence *as such*—that the Holy Spirit tells us that the Bible is God's holy word. Sometimes there is an appeal to the effect of Scripture on our lives or to the Bible's consistency with currently available human knowledge. I will not thoroughly survey the voluminous scholarship in defense of inerrancy. Instead, I will consider the salient logical features of some significant justifications of inerrancy offered in the CSBI and by three of its signers—William E. Bell, J. I. Packer, and Kenneth Kantzer. We will see that inerrancy need not have anything to do with strong foundationalism. Moreover, by Plantinga's definition strong foundationalism limits the criterion for proper basicality to a belief's being incorrigible, self-evident, or evident to the senses, which would rule out the Holy Spirit's testimony as a source of warrant. Most importantly, these appeals from the CSBI tradition are to inferential, foundational, *and* coherential warrant on behalf of the doctrine, and this rules out most strong foundationalisms.

In what follows I shall look at the Christological argument for inerrancy, the appeal to the testimony of the Holy Spirit, and coherential warrant for inerrancy; then, finally, I shall explain more directly why inerrancy is not a strong foundationalism, although it is consistent with at least one form of it.

The Christological Argument: Inferential Warrant

An important argument for inerrancy is the Christological one. Roughly, it goes like this: What Jesus teaches we must accept; Jesus teaches that the Bible is the inspired Word of God; and so we must accept that the Bible is the inspired Word of God. A supplementary argument might be offered for Jesus's infallibility, or, as some do, we may simply point out that people who acknowledge Jesus as Lord must accept what he teaches. A supplementary argument that Jesus teaches that the Bible is the inspired Word of God must be made in two parts, one for each Testament. Roughly, the first part would present New Testament evidence that Jesus accepted a doctrine of Old Testament inerrancy (see his citations of the Old Testament as authoritative in John 5:39; 10:35; Luke 24:44; Matt 5:17–18; 7:12; 22:31; 23:2–3). The second part would present New Testament evidence that Jesus gave his authority to the apostles for the teaching and settling of doctrine and sent the Holy Spirit to make sure they got it right; passages such as Matt 16:19, Matt 18:18, and John 14:26 might be cited along with the record of the Holy Spirit's coming in Acts 1–2, and perhaps also an analysis of the origins of New Testament scripture in the authoritative apostolic testimony. (We might even posit a coextension of apostolic preaching, the gospel, oral tradition, and written Scripture—a coextension leading naturally to written canonization.)[45] Given that the apostles bore the authority of the risen Messiah, the holy status of the resulting writings would be taken as an extension of Jesus's authority.

William Bell's main argument for inerrancy is a fine example, and I shall look at it in some detail, showing that it says nothing about the structure of knowledge and is consistent with several views on the subject.[46] Then I shall more briefly consider Packer and Kantzer. Then I shall show that the Christological argument is in the CSBI itself. Then I shall review how this argument appeals to inferential warrant on behalf of inerrancy.

Despite having "no published works to speak of," Bell's "influence has been extensive and profound."[47] As a signer of the CSBI, he meticulously expounded inerrancy for his students. His lectures are available online.[48] His case for inerrancy is found in the "Doctrine of Scripture" lectures numbers 4–7; lectures 5–6 concern "The Christological Argument." Bell begins on historical and inductive grounds, making a secular case for the historical reliability of the Gospels, appealing to Louis Gottschalk's criteria for the historical reliability of ancient testimony. This, by itself, would not be a very strong case for the inerrancy of the Gospels. Such a methodology might be used to establish the historical reliability of non-inerrant texts from Herodotus, Josephus, or Aristotle. More generally, this sort of inductive evidence can only guarantee some finite degree of historical reliability. Inerrancy is a universal denial of *any* errors in the original biblical text, a claim of *total* reliability which cannot be guaranteed by such an argument.

Fortunately, Bell makes no such case. His goal is to establish on secular, historical standards a few claims that fit them—historical ones. He argues that the Gospels show that Jesus accepted the Hebrew Scriptures—our Old Testament—as the inerrant Word of God, and that he pre-authenticated the New Testament Scriptures, stamping them with his own authority. Thus, Bell argues, the Bible has inerrant authority because Jesus, with his own inerrant authority, treats it as such. Bell acknowledges that his argument is

---

45. A helpful book on this way of thinking is Kruger, *The Question of Canon*.

46. Bell's teaching on inerrancy and other theological topics is available at "William E. Bell," *Discipleship Library*.

47. Gilstrap, "Dispensationalism's Achilles' Heel: Part One," 1.

48. "William E. Bell," *Discipleship Library*.

INERRANCY IS NOT A STRONG OR CLASSICAL FOUNDATIONALISM   153

useless without Jesus's authority; he is arguing against those who acknowledge Jesus's authority but *not* the Bible's; "and for Christians," says Bell, "he is the Lord of glory," and we must not deny his teaching.

We must note some salient features of Bell's argument. First, note that biblical inerrancy is established by premises able to establish it. Only an infallible source of knowledge is sufficient to guarantee by its testimony that some source of knowledge is infallible. An argument from an infallible authority can guarantee any conclusion, given the truth of the premises.[49] If Christ be infallible, what he teaches is true, and he may teach us anything he likes.

Second, note that the argument is not circular, a danger Bell carefully avoids. The argument *would* be circular if it relied on inerrancy, but it only relies on the historical reliability of the Gospels and then proves their inerrancy on other grounds—Jesus's authority. Inerrancy is not in the premises of Bell's argument, as in the flawed argument *The Bible is inerrant, and it teaches that Jesus teaches inerrancy, and therefore inerrancy is true.* The historical reliability of the Gospels, if well established, is enough to establish that Jesus said something. If what he says happens to concern the same documents, no problem. An argument may establish whatever conclusion its premises support, and an infallible authority may tell us what he may.

Bell's conclusion of inerrancy actually does entail his premise of the Gospels' reliability, but this only goes to show that an argument's conclusion may occasionally have some support for its premise. Say I find evidence that Smith knows economics based on his understanding of the principle of comparative advantage and other insights in economics with which I am familiar. Once Smith's economic authority is established, it so happens that his testimony in favor of comparative advantage—an economic principle the truth of which was a premise in my reasoning to Smith's authority—also counts in its favor. Similarly, if Jesus is infallible, he can teach us what he wants, even about the same texts through which we know about *him*. The Gospels' historical reliability is a matter for the standards of history to establish. If they work for, say, Herodotus and if the Gospels satisfy the same standards well enough, then the historical premises of Bell's argument are established.

In short, Bell's argument is very well constructed; by relying on secular historical standards, it avoids circular reasoning. It depends on inductive evidence of a sort quite sufficient to get its own job done—to establish the historical facts about what Jesus said. Yet, and second, it also uses a premise

---

49. On this aspect of arguments from infallible authority, see the Howard-Snyders and Ryan Wasserman, *The Power of Logic*, chapter 10, section 2.

powerful enough to establish the inerrant authority of the Bible—the inerrant authority of Jesus Christ.

The premise that Christ really *has* this authority is the argument's vulnerability. Here is a third salient feature of Bell's argument: *There is no subargument for the crucial premise concerning Jesus's authority.* What are we to make of this premise? We might accept it as an article of pure unreasoning faith, or we might suggest that we know directly that Jesus Christ is Lord and Messiah, perhaps explaining things Plantinga's way by saying that we have a God-given faculty for knowing the truths of Christianity.[50] We might argue for Christ's authority on the basis of the authority of the church; this authority in turn, as Zeis suggests in his epistemology, might be recognized as a sort of (rational) leap of faith,[51] or explained in Plantingian fashion. Alternatively, we might find some other evidence for the authority of Jesus, perhaps by expanding Bell's argument from the historical reliability of the Bible and taking the resurrection and other miracles of Jesus as evidence for his authority. In this case, some leap would remain from the inductive evidence for these events to the total commitment to Christ's authority which the events warrant. (We might argue that this leap is rational much like a young man's leap from his inductive evidence that *Miss S. R. is the woman who should be my wife* to his total commitment to Miss S. R. in marriage. But see chapter 10 of this volume on these matters.)

If we take this last approach we would likely end up using some form of weak foundationalism. The fundamental premises of the study of history would be foundational. What these premises actually *are* would be a question for another study, but they would surely include the existence of the past, the reality of minds other than ourselves, and the fact that their testimony is a source of knowledge. This works well enough in a weak foundationalism. Taking such beliefs as properly basic automatically rules out strong foundationalism on Plantinga's definition.[52] Alternatively, we might follow Haack and Zeis and treat historical evidence as warranted along foundherentist lines. Or we might treat these properly basic beliefs as deriving no warrant from other beliefs and thus expand Bell's arguments along the lines of a *strong* foundationalism.

Thus, Bell's approach is consistent with foundherentism, weak foundationalism, and strong foundationalism (by my looser definition, although not by Plantinga's). In short, Bell's main argument—bracketing the whole

50. Plantinga, *Warranted Christian Belief*.

51. See Zeis, "A Foundherentist Conception," 154–55.

52. Plantinga makes this point with respect to memory beliefs in "Reason and Belief in God," 60.

question of how we know that Jesus is infallible—*implies nothing at all about the structure of knowledge*. More importantly for our purposes, Bell here uses inferential warrant, to the significance of which we will soon return.

Bell is not unique. Packer's little book *"Fundamentalism" and the Word of God* presents the case for biblical inerrancy in chapter 3, and his argument is much like Bell's.[53] Packer likewise does not present a case for the authority of Jesus, presumably because he is also addressing those who accept the authority of Christ but not Scripture: "If we accept Christ's claims, therefore, we commit ourselves to believe all that He taught—on His authority."[54] There is also Kantzer, who notes that Jesus "placed his imprimatur upon the Old Testament canon of the Jews."[55] Moreover, "The processes involved in the formation and reception of the New Testament duplicate those he approved in the Old Testament."[56] And Jesus commands that we recognize the authority of the Bible: "The real Jesus, the only Jesus for whom we have any evidence whatever, believed that the Bible was true and that it was the very word of God. He commanded his disciples to believe it and obey it."[57] The fundamental issue is whether we are willing to submit to Christ.[58]

The Christological argument is also in the CSBI, which comments on the importance of Christ as incarnate God, as mediator, as Messiah, and as "the central theme of Scripture."[59] It observes that "Christ testifies that Scripture cannot be broken"; Christ submitted to its authority, and requires the same of us.[60] By recognizing the Old Testament canon as authoritative and as defining his own mission, he testified to its authority; and the New Testament is "the apostolic witness to Himself which He undertook to inspire by His gift of the Holy Spirit."[61]

---

53. Packer, *"Fundamentalism" and the Word of God*, 54–64.
54. Packer, *"Fundamentalism" and the Word of God*, 59.
55. Kantzer, "Parameters of Biblical Inerrancy," 112.
56. Kantzer, "Parameters of Biblical Inerrancy," 112.
57. Kantzer, "Parameters of Biblical Inerrancy," 118.
58. Kantzer, "Parameters of Biblical Inerrancy," 118–19. Kantzer, much like Bell, states that those who doubt inerrancy should first answer the question of "the Lordship of Jesus Christ," which is a separate question; Kantzer, "Parameters," 125, n. 39.
59. The Chicago Statement on Biblical Inerrancy with Exposition, Exposition, Authority: Christ and the Bible. (Although some say that the Statement does not include the Exposition, I follow the Draft Committee's Preface in including it.)
60. Chicago Statement on Biblical Inerrancy with Exposition, Exposition, Authority: Christ and the Bible.
61. Chicago Statement on Biblical Inerrancy with Exposition, Exposition, Authority: Christ and the Bible.

There are other sources for the Christological argument, including David Kibble, John Wenham, and Alec Motyer.[62] However, we are not aiming at a scholarly survey so much as a study of the logic of the inerrantist position, which plainly has a notable tradition of appealing to the authority of Christ.

As we have seen, this argument by itself is compatible with several views on the structure of knowledge. More crucial for our purposes, the Christological argument employs inferential warrant on behalf of inerrancy. For, quite simply, it is an *argument*—from a premise concerning the authority of Christ and some premises (themselves having sub-arguments) about what Christ taught to the conclusion that what he taught is true. *Any* argument for *any* proposition is a use of inferential warrant—from premises to conclusion. The same points could just as easily be made regarding any justifications of inerrancy based on other arguments, such as arguments from the doctrine of the inspiration of Scripture[63] or Albert Mohler's "cumulative argument."[64]

The Testimony of the Holy Spirit: Foundational Warrant

The Christological argument, as noted, may be developed so as to point to foundational warrant in one way or another. More important for our purposes is the fact that *the doctrine of inerrancy itself* is said to have foundational warrant. We may note influential sources including Augustine, Calvin, and Plantinga; still more importantly, the CSBI is quite clear on this, along with Packer and Kantzer.

The CSBI's introduction states, "The Holy Spirit, Scripture's divine Author, both authenticates it to us by His inward witness and opens our minds to understand its meaning."[65] Again, in the Articles of Affirmation and Denial: "WE AFFIRM that the Holy Spirit bears witness to the Scriptures, assuring believers of the truthfulness of God's written Word."[66] We know of the Bible's truth through the Holy Spirit who informs us of it.

---

62. See Kibble, "The Jewish Understanding of the Old Testament," 145–55, especially the last two paragraphs; Wenham, *Christ and the Bible*, esp. 11–15; Cowan, "Is the Bible the Word of God?," 72–101; and Motyer, *Look to the Rock*, 21–22. Motyer is remarkably similar to Bell save that he apparently takes the last approach I suggested above for establishing the authority *of Christ* (*Look to the Rock*, 21).

63. A justification found in Chicago Statement on Biblical Inerrancy with Exposition, A Short Statement.

64. Mohler, "When the Bible Speaks, God Speaks," 36–43.

65. Chicago Statement on Biblical Inerrancy with Exposition, A Short Statement.

66. Chicago Statement on Biblical Inerrancy with Exposition, Articles of Affirmation and Denial, Article XVI.

The appeal to the testimony of the Holy Spirit parallels Plantinga's critique of strong foundationalism on the grounds that it improperly restricts the criteria for a belief with foundational warrant. By Plantinga's definition, any inerrantist source pointing to the Holy Spirit's testimony on inerrancy is inconsistent with strong foundationalism, for it posits as a source of foundational warrant the testimony of the Holy Spirit, not a noetic faculty recognized by strong foundationalism—neither self-evident nor evident to the five senses nor incorrigible. Plantinga himself goes over the rudiments of this idea.[67] The interplay of faith, the Holy Spirit's work, and the Bible produces warrant independent of inference—foundational warrant. He suggests one way this might work: "the Holy Spirit testifies in our hearts that this book is indeed from God," and goes on to explain several other ways the Holy Spirit might warrant our belief in biblical authority.[68]

The idea that God directly informs us of the truth of the Bible is very old. Augustine prays, "You told me with strong voice in the ear of Your servant's spirit, breaking through my deafness and crying: 'O man, what my Scripture says, I say . . . .'"[69] Similarly, Calvin says that the Bible "owes the full conviction with which we ought to receive it to the testimony of the Spirit."[70] Following and citing Calvin as well as the Westminster Confession and other sources, Packer emphatically concurs.[71] Kantzer also speaks of the Holy Spirit working in us to show that the Bible is the Word of God.[72]

We have already noted the inconsistency with strong foundationalism according to Plantinga's definition. Regarding strong foundationalism as I define it, we need only reiterate that the appeal to the testimony of the Holy Spirit is an appeal to foundational warrant for the doctrine of inerrancy itself, or else to the doctrine which immediately justifies it—that the Bible is the Word of God.

---

67. Plantinga, *Warranted Christian Belief*, 374.

68. Plantinga, *Warranted Christian Belief*, 380. Several of these involve inferential warrant for that belief, but all involve foundational warrant by the proper functioning of our spiritual noetic faculties; Plantinga notes that we need not choose just one. That knowledge of the Bible's authority might have inferential as well as foundational warrant is more evidence that Plantinga's epistemology is a weak foundationalism. For more on Plantinga as a weak foundationalist, see the chapters on Plantinga's epistemology in this book. Note that Plantinga is not explicit on biblical "inerrancy" here—only on biblical *authority*.

69. Augustine, *Confessions*, 13.29.44. Note the similarity to the final words of the Chicago Statement on Biblical Inerrancy with Exposition: "We affirm that what Scripture says, God says."

70. Calvin, *Institutes of the Christian Religion*, 1.7.5.

71. Packer, *"Fundamentalism" and the Word of God*, 118.

72. Kantzer, "Inerrancy and the Humanity and Divinity of the Bible," 157–58.

Coherential Warrant

Inerrantists also appeal to coherential warrant on behalf of inerrancy. This may be seen primarily in the claim that the Bible is consistent with other relevant areas of human knowledge. There is also a strong coherential aspect of the doctrine as articulated in the CSBI.

Bell is again a convenient illustration. After making the Christological argument he briefly reviews some other evidences for inerrancy.[73] For example, he notes the remarkable consistency of the teachings of so large a document composed over so long a period of time. He notes the considerable degree of confirmation from archaeology for claims made in the Bible. He also comments on the Bible's consistency with the observable facts of life concerning death and depravity and notes the positive effects the Bible has made in people's lives. Bell recognizes that "these are supplemental arguments" less binding than the authority of Christ. He follows it up with two more lectures on "Dealing with Biblical Difficulties,"[74] aimed to show how we can confirm that the Bible, at various points where it has been critiqued, is consistent with itself and with human knowledge generally. The general idea is that inerrancy so far appears consistent with itself and such other areas of knowledge and experience as are relevant to it. This is no positive proof, but it matters; in other words, it is coherential warrant.

Packer also delves into the coherential warrant for inerrancy.[75] Similarly, Greg Bahnsen, following Van Til, explains that the confirmation of Bible from history and science matters a great deal; even the believer who presupposes inerrancy seeks to confirm his theology inductively from other areas of human knowledge.[76] More generally, find any inerrantist who thinks it *matters* whether the tendency of human knowledge from science, psychology, archaeology, or whatever else is to cohere with Scripture, and you will find an inerrantist appealing to coherential warrant; and any such case is incompatible with most forms of strong foundationalism.

Finally, we can find in the inerrantist tradition an interesting coherential notion in the claim that the authority of Christ and of the Bible mutually confirm each other. In the same passage inferring the authority of Scripture from that of Christ, the CSBI tells us that the inference goes the other way as well. The Bible testifies to the authority of Christ, and so the

---

73. Bell, "Doctrine of Scripture," lecture 7.
74. Bell, "Doctrine of Scripture," lectures 8–9.
75. Packer, "Problem Areas," 205–13.
76. Bahnsen, "Inductivism, Inerrancy, and Presuppositionalism," 292–93.

CSBI says, "the authority of Christ and that of Scripture are one."[77] The inference is symmetrical: "By authenticating each other's authority, Christ and Scripture coalesce into a single fount of authority."[78] This is an aspect of coherentism—the mutual confirmation of beliefs. It is not, strictly speaking, what I am calling coherential warrant, although it is not typical of strong foundationalism. (This bi-directionality of warrant is inconsistent with *all* foundationalisms as defined by Haack.)

Of course, if this were all the CSBI could say on behalf of inerrancy, it would be a poorly defended doctrine indeed. It would rest on a sample of purified circular reasoning, which also turns out to be the problem with pure coherentism.[79] Yet, as we have seen, the CSBI appeals to foundational warrant. So it is not touting circular reasoning. The mutual confirmation of these authorities is a matter of spreading warrant around, not conjuring it out of nowhere. To paraphrase what Barack Obama said to Joe the Plumber, when you spread the warrant around, it's good for every belief.[80] But, of course, before it can be spread around it has to *come from* somewhere, and it comes from foundational warrant, such as that imparted by the Holy Spirit's testimony for the doctrine or in the form of other evidence for the authority of Christ or Scripture such as inerrantists may provide.

Let us review these facts and tie them all together.

Inerrancy Is Not a Strong Foundationalism

Strong foundationalism is a theory on the structure of knowledge, namely that knowledge has a foundation in beliefs warranted by foundational warrant and not needing additional warrant of the other varieties. Typically, such a theory is false because it ignores the fact that a belief, even a basic belief, may have not only foundational warrant but also inferential or coherential warrant, or both. If inerrancy is a strong foundationalism, then it must be the case either that it is warranted (or is said by its proponents to be warranted) by foundational warrant alone, or else that it is based (or is said by its proponents to be based) on beliefs that are. Despite what some critics allege, neither of these is the case.

77. Chicago Statement on Biblical Inerrancy with Exposition, Exposition, Authority: Christ and the Bible.

78. Chicago Statement on Biblical Inerrancy with Exposition, Exposition, Authority: Christ and the Bible.

79. See the explanation in Boone, "Inferential, Coherential, and Foundational Warrant," 388–90.

80. For a proper account of the mutual support of beliefs, I suggest McGrew, "How Foundationalists Do Crossword Puzzles," 333–50.

We have noted a number of difficulties in treating inerrancy as a strong foundationalism. Employing Plantinga's definition, strong foundationalism only recognizes as having foundational warrant those beliefs which are self-evident, incorrigible, or evident to the senses; and yet inerrantists have often claimed that the Holy Spirit is a source of warrant for inerrancy. Another, more universal difficulty is that inerrancy is a piece of theology, and *not* a theory on the structure of knowledge.

What I regard as the most crucial difficulty is that, given strong foundationalism, a theory possessing foundational warrant cannot or at least need not possess the other varieties. However, as we have seen, notable sources on inerrancy plainly treat that doctrine as being warranted foundationally but also inferentially, coherentially, or both. Bell treats inerrancy as warranted *inferentially* and *coherentially*. Kantzer and the CSBI treat it as warranted *inferentially* and *foundationally*. Packer treats it as warranted in *all three ways*. This precludes inerrancy being a basic belief in a strongly foundationalist epistemology. Nor must inerrancy be based on beliefs warranted only foundationally. One may base inerrancy on the Messiah's testimony concerning Scripture and not even explain the basis of our knowledge of *his* authority. Thus Bell, Packer, and Kantzer, for whom beginning with the authority of Christ is enough.

Now I do not claim that *no* inerrantist has ever been a strong foundationalist. Rather, I say that nothing in the doctrine entails strong foundationalism, and that the CSBI and some of its signers do not tie inerrancy to strong foundationalism, and indeed have theology inconsistent with most strong foundationalisms.

What *would* a strongly foundationalist inerrancy look like? I can think of three forms it might take, two of which are not particularly good epistemologies.

First, the Bible might be treated as the sole foundation of knowledge, whose truth is beyond reasonable doubt and is not warranted by any external evidence. The warrant for inerrancy would be considered *purely* foundational; presumably the explanation for how this works would claim that the Holy Spirit so warrants inerrancy that on this basis alone we know it to be true with such certainty that doubting it on the basis of any conceivable evidence is about as difficult as my finding evidence that I do not exist! (Bear in mind that an inerrantist with such a strong view of the testimony of the Holy Spirit to the authority of the Bible would have to think *not* that the Bible is inconsistent with human knowledge generally so much as that such consistency is not very important.) I cannot confirm whether any inerrantist has held this view, although at least one source is suggestive of such a theory.[81]

Second, the inerrantist might claim that the authority of the Bible rests solely on the authority of Christ (not at all on the testimony of the Holy Spirit); that Christ's authority is known from his miracles and in particular the resurrection; that these are historical events known by the usual methods of gaining historical knowledge, and that the whole thing rests on certain commonsense beliefs, such as that testimony is a source of knowledge. The inerrantist furthermore would need to consider this whole chain of evidence to be so strong that corroboration from human knowledge generally is not only unnecessary but downright irrelevant.

To be fair to Grenz, Franke, and others, it may well be that inerrantists have sometimes fallen into strong foundationalism or strayed near it, perhaps in this very manner. Indeed, luminaries no less than B. B. Warfield and Carl Henry may have had something like a strong foundationalist inerrancy if one scholar's reading of them is correct,[82] and, to read Bahnsen at least, it seems that Daniel Fuller and Clark Pinnock (in an early stage) may have aimed to establish the truth of inerrancy on an inductive model of strong foundationalism.[83] More generally, I do not dispute that evangelical inerrantists have been known to stray into unbiblical or unchristian modes of Enlightenment thinking, as Robert Kurka concedes.[84]

A third account merging inerrantist theology with strong foundationalism is more promising. I think McGrew's account suggests the best convergence with inerrancy. Briefly, here is how I think it might account for the testimony of the Holy Spirit as well as the Christological argument. The latter would be established in ways already suggested, but elaborated in terms of McGrew's strong foundationalism. From the certain foundation of our knowledge of our own beliefs, we reason inductively to knowledge of the world outside the mind; from there we can justify history and, from history, the whole evidence chain from miracles via Christ's authority to the authority of the Bible. As for the Holy Spirit, we could follow Plantinga in explaining his testimony as a source of foundational warrant, but with

---

81. Young, "The Relationship Between Biblical Inerrancy and Biblical Authority," 391–409.

82. Jeffrey Steven Oldfield argues that Warfield and Henry are foundationalists in "The Word Became Text and Dwells among Us?," 84–102. An evaluation of Oldfield's interpretation is well outside the scope of this investigation.

83. Bahnsen. An evaluation of this interpretation of Fuller and early Pinnock is, likewise, outside the scope of this investigation.

84. Kurka, "*Before* 'Foundationalism,'" 147–48. This included at times "A quest for unshakeable foundations." Kurka, "*Before* 'Foundationalism,'" 148.

a twist fitting McGrew's epistemology. Roughly, I have certain knowledge that it seems to me, on a daily basis when I read from the Bible, that I am encountering the holy Word of God; I reason, using an argument modeled after the one in chapter 7 of McGrew's book, that this is probably a perception matching reality—what causes my daily perceptions of the Word of God *is* the *actual* Word of God. We can then appeal to the Holy Spirit's inward testimony about the Bible as a way of explaining how that perception is reliable. Thus, inerrancy is warranted by the testimony of the Holy Spirit *and* by Christ's authority, but all this warrant begins with absolutely certain beliefs about my own thoughts.[85]

So I do not claim that inerrancy has never been or cannot be linked to a strong foundationalism. Rather, I have shown that inerrancy is not by its nature a strong foundationalism, and that some notable sources in the CSBI tradition have promoted the doctrine in ways incompatible with most forms of strong foundationalism and employing the very sort of eclectic account of the sources of warrant for ignoring which strong foundationalism has often been criticized. The ongoing discussion of inerrancy and epistemology would benefit from keeping in mind the reasoning offered by these theologians and these considerations of the structure of knowledge.

There are other lessons to learn from considering inerrancy and philosophy, to which we will turn in the next chapter.

WORKS CITED

Augustine. *Confessions.* Translated by F. J. Sheed. Introduction by Peter Brown. 2nd ed. edited and notes by Michael P. Foley. Indianapolis: Hackett, 2006.

Bahnsen, Greg. "Inductivism, Inerrancy, and Presuppositionalism." *Journal of the Evangelical Theological Society* 20.4 (1977) 289–305.

Beilby, James. *Epistemology as Theology: An Evaluation of Alvin Plantinga's Religious Epistemology.* London: Routledge, 2006.

Bell, William E. "William E. Bell." http://www.discipleshiplibrary.com/dr_bell.php; accessed April 18, 2018.

BonJour, Laurence. "Can Empirical Knowledge Have a Foundation?" *American Philosophical Quarterly* 15.1 (1978) 1–13.

———. *The Structure of Empirical Knowledge.* Cambridge: Harvard University Press, 1985.

Boone, Mark J. "Inferential, Coherential, and Foundational Warrant: An Eclectic Account of the Sources of Warrant." *Logos & Episteme* 5 (2014) 377–98.

---

85. I think McGrew's account, at a minimum, succeeds in describing a possible, and valuable, source of warrant in absolutely certain beliefs. I do have one or two concerns with his account, but that shall have to wait for a closer engagement with his excellent work in my next book.

Calvin, John. *Institutes of the Christian Religion*. Translated by Henry Beveridge. Grand Rapids: Eerdmans, 1994.
Cowan, Steven B. "Is the Bible the Word of God?" In *In Defense of the Bible: A Comprehensive Apologetic for the Authority of Scripture*, edited by Stephen B. Cowan and Terry L. Wilder, 72–101. Nashville: B&H Academic, 2013.
Haack, Susan. "Double-Aspect Foundherentism: A New Theory of Empirical Justification." *Philosophy and Phenomenological Research* 53.1 (1993) 113–28.
———. "Précis of *Evidence and Inquiry: Towards Reconstruction in Epistemology*." *Synthese* 112.1 (1997) 7–11.
———. "Reply to BonJour." *Synthese* 112.1 (1997) 25–35.
Hume, David. *Enquiry Concerning Human Understanding*.
The International Council on Biblical Inerrancy. The Chicago Statement on Biblical Inerrancy. Chicago, 1978.
Franke, John R. "Response to Michael F. Bird." In *Five Views on Biblical Inerrancy*, edited by J. Merrick and Stephen M. Garrett, 77–82. Grand Rapids: Zondervan, 2013. Kindle.
Fumerton, Richard. "Classical Foundationalism." In *Resurrecting Old-Fashioned Foundationalism*, edited by Michael DePaul, 3–20. New York: Rowman and Littlefield, 2000.
Gilstrap, Michael R. "Dispensationalism's Achilles' Heel: Part One." In *Dispensationalism in Transition* 2.2 (February 1989); available at https://www.garynorth.com/freebooks/docs/a_pdfs/newslet/dt/8902.pdf.
Grenz, Stanley. *Renewing the Center: Evangelical Theology in a Post-Theological Era*. Grand Rapids: Baker, 2000.
Grenz, Stanley J., and John R. Franke. *Beyond Foundationalism: Shaping Theology in a Postmodern Context*. Louisville, KY: Westminster John Knox, 2001.
Howard-Snyder, Frances, Daniel Howard-Snyder, and Ryan Wasserman. *The Power of Logic*. 4th ed. New York: McGraw-Hill, 2008.
Kantzer, Kenneth. "Inerrancy and the Humanity and Divinity of the Bible." In *The Proceedings of the Conference on Biblical Inerrancy 1987*, 153–63. Nashville: Broadman, 1987.
———. "Parameters of Biblical Inerrancy." In *The Proceedings of the Conference on Biblical Inerrancy 1987*, 111–25. Nashville: Broadman, 1987.
Kibble, David G. "The Jewish Understanding of the Old Testament as the Word of God." *The Evangelical Quarterly* 51.3 (1979) 145–55.
Kruger, Michael J. *The Question of Canon: Challenging the Status Quo in the New Testament Debate*. Downers Grove, IL: InterVarsity, 2013.
Kurka, Robert C. "*Before* 'Foundationalism': A More Biblical Alternative to the Grenz-Franke Proposal for Doing Theology." *Journal of the Evangelical Theological Society* 50.1 (2007) 145–65.
Leithart, Peter. "Foundationalism and Inerrancy." *Patheos.com*. December 29, 2005. http://www.patheos.com/blogs/leithart/2005/12/foundationalism-and-inerrancy/; accessed February 7, 2018.
McGrew, Timothy. *The Foundations of Knowledge*. Lanham, MD: Rowman & Littlefield, 1995.
———. "How Foundationalists Do Crossword Puzzles." *Philosophical Studies* 96 (1999) 333–50.

McLaren, Brian. *A Generous Orthodoxy: Why I Am A Missional, Evangelical, Post/Protestant, Liberal/Conservative, Mystical/Poetic, Biblical, Charismatic/Contemplative, Fundamentalist/Calvinist, Anabaptist/Anglican, Methodist, Catholic, Green, Incarnational, Depressed-Yet-Hopeful, Emergent, Unfinished Christian*. Grand Rapids: Zondervan, 2006.

Mohler, Albert J. "Response to John R. Franke." In *Five Views on Biblical Inerrancy*, edited by J. Merrick and Stephen M. Garrett, 288–91. Grand Rapids: Zondervan, 2013. Kindle.

———. "When the Bible Speaks, God Speaks: The Classical Doctrine of Biblical Inerrancy." In *Five Views on Biblical Inerrancy*, edited by J. Merrick and Stephen M. Garrett, 29–82. Grand Rapids: Zondervan, 2013. Kindle.

Motyer, Alec. *Look to the Rock: An Old Testament Background to Our Understanding of Christ*. Grand Rapids: Kregel, 1996.

Oldfield, Jeffrey Steven. "The Word Became Text and Dwells among Us?: An Examination of the Doctrine of Inerrancy." PhD thesis, University of St. Andrews, 2008.

Packer, J. I. *"Fundamentalism" and the Word of God: Some Evangelical Principles*. Grand Rapids: Eerdmans, 1958.

———. Packer, J. I. "Problem Areas Related to Biblical Inerrancy." In *The Proceedings of the Conference on Biblical Inerrancy 1987*, 205–13. Nashville: Broadman, 1987.

Plantinga, Alvin. "Is Belief in God Properly Basic?" *Noûs* 15.1 (1981) 41–51

———. "Reason and Belief in God." In *Faith and Rationality: Reason and Belief in God*, edited by Alvin Plantinga and Nicholas Wolterstorff, 16–93. Notre Dame, IN: University of Notre Dame Press, 1991.

———. *Warrant and Proper Function*. New York: Oxford University Press, 1993.

———. *Warranted Christian Belief*. New York: Oxford University Press, 2000.

Poston, Ted. "Foundationalism." *Internet Encyclopedia of Philosophy*; https://www.iep.utm.edu/found-ep/; accessed September 12, 2018.

Vanhoozer, Kevin J. "Response to John R. Franke." In *Five Views on Biblical Inerrancy*, edited by J. Merrick and Stephen M. Garrett, 302–8. Grand Rapids: Zondervan, 2013. Kindle.

Young, J. Terry. "The Relationship between Biblical Inerrancy and Biblical Authority." In *The Proceedings of the Conference on Biblical Inerrancy 1987*, 391–409. Nashville: Broadman, 1987.

Wenham, John. *Christ and the Bible*. 3rd ed. Reprint, Eugene, OR: Wipf and Stock, 2009.

Zeis, John. "A Foundherentist Conception of the Justification of Religious Belief." *International Journal for Philosophy of Religion* 58 (2005) 133–60.

9

Ancient-Future Hermeneutics
Postmodernism, Biblical Inerrancy, and the Rule of Faith

IN RECENT DECADES MANY theologians and philosophers have turned to a study of hermeneutics.[1] This has proved to be a fruitful development. Ideas from the postmodern tradition have been particularly effective stimuli to thought and discussion, and some thinkers, such as Kevin Vanhoozer,[2] have done very good work integrating postmodern insights with traditional Christianity.

This chapter explores one area of possible integration that has not yet received sufficient attention, if indeed it has been attempted at all, by contemporary theologians. At first glance, it may seem that few traditions could be more antithetical than postmodern theology and biblical inerrancy. Yet, I contend, inerrancy and postmodern theology are not (or not entirely) antithetical. To the contrary, central components of these traditions are consistent and can be integrated. Moreover, the integration of these very insights has already been accomplished in the writings of Augustine!

What insights? Primarily these: The authority of the human authors of the Christian Scriptures is such that whatever is included in their original intent in these Scriptures is true. This doctrine calls the reader of Scripture

---

1. The title "Ancient-Future Hermeneutics" is influenced by Robert E. Webber, especially his *Ancient-Future Faith: Rethinking Evangelicalism for a Postmodern World*. Since its initial publication, the biggest change to this chapter is a slight extension of the explanation of textual realism.

2. Vanhoozer, *Is There a Meaning in This Text?*.

who does not have the original meaning at arm's length to a posture of epistemic humility—an epistemically humble approach to the reading of Scripture. However, the significance of Scripture surpasses that which was intended by its human authors, meaning no less than what the divine Author of Scripture intends. This calls for an epistemically humble approach to human authorship.

This hermeneutical perspective consists mainly of two broad claims about the original intent of the human authors and about biblical meaning: that the former is without error, and that the latter transcends the former. The integration of these claims is part of the rule of faith in Augustine's theology. Yet this ancient theology still lives. The postmodern turn in philosophy serves as a poignant reminder of epistemic humility, urges us to not take a purely rationalistic approach to the biblical text, and reminds us that the biblical text is more than its human authorship. From an Augustinian perspective, the doctrine of inerrancy in the postmodern era maintains, as it always did, its guardianship of the rule of faith—of the essentials of Christian orthodoxy and the rule to love God and neighbor.

In this paper I shall develop these ideas through interaction with texts both recent and ancient. I shall begin with postmodernism. Following that I shall look at inerrancy. Then I shall show how postmodern insights may be applied to the Bible in ways consistent with inerrancy. This will lead us back to the hermeneutics of Augustine.

POSTMODERNISM

The postmodern era is characterized by a rediscovery of epistemic humility, and postmodern theology is no exception. In this section I shall first look at Jean-François Lyotard's definition of postmodernism and discuss its relationship to Christianity. Then I shall turn to Martin Heidegger's critique of "onto-theology." Finally, I shall examine Jean-Luc Marion' critique of intellectual idolatry in *God without Being*.

What is more or less the official definition of postmodernism is found in Lyotard's *The Postmodern Condition*: "incredulity toward metanarratives."[3] So what is a metanarrative? Lyotard gives the following examples: "the dialectics of Spirit, the hermeneutics of meaning, the emancipation of the rational or working subject, or the creation of wealth."[4] Now these are the narratives of modernism, not of Christianity, which predates modernism; accordingly, Merold Westphal lists in the introduction to his *Overcoming*

---

3. Lyotard, Introduction, xxiv.
4. Lyotard, Introduction, xxiii.

Onto-theology three senses of *metanarrative* that do not describe the Christian "*mega*narrative," and just one sense in which it does.[5] Modernism, the main target of postmodern skepticism, is "a story of progress from opinion and superstition to scientific truth and on to universal peace and happiness."[6] Two problems with the metanarratives of modernism immediately present themselves. For the first, Bruce Ellis Benson has this to say: "One characteristic of all *grand reçits* is that they are encompassing enough to explain everything."[7] But surely finite knowers will never possess an explanation of *everything*, and historic Christianity has certainly never said such a thing. As Westphal says: "The truth is that there is Truth, but in our finitude and fallenness we do not have access to it. We'll have to make do with the truths available to us; but that does not mean either that we should deny the reality of Truth or that we should abandon the distinction between truth and falsity."[8] Westphal also points out the second problem with the metanarratives of modernism: "One of the most important assumptions of philosophical modernity . . . is the autonomy of the human knower."[9] Again, historic Christianity dissents: Scripture has complete authority over the individual Christian, and the Creeds and church history also have their own degrees of epistemic authority.

One component of the postmodern tradition's skepticism toward metanarratives has been particularly formative of postmodern thought on religion, and that is Martin Heidegger's critique of what he labeled "onto-theology." The etymology of the term is obvious; it is plain from its Greek ancestors *ontos*, *theos*, and *logos* that it has something to do with the study of God and metaphysics. That to which Heidegger referred when he coined the term is no less than an attempt to fit God within our metaphysical categories. Ontology, he explains, is the study of beings, while theology is the study of the Being of beings, that which gives existence to beings; metaphysics has historically been the study of both beings and Being.[10] In Heidegger's words, "this means: metaphysics is onto-theo-logy."[11] Metaphysics has carried out its project by beginning with beings; later, when it needs something to solve the problem of the metaphysical ground of beings, it ushers God into the equation as Being. So that Being can be the cause of all beings, God

---

5. Westphal, *Overcoming Onto-theology*, xii–xv; hereafter *OO*.
6. Westphal, *OO*, xii.
7. Benson, *Graven Ideologies*, 29.
8. Westphal, *OO*, 87.
9. Westphal, "Blind Spots."
10. Heidegger, "The Onto-theo-logical Constitution of Metaphysics," 54.
11. Heidegger, "The Onto-theo-logical Constitution of Metaphysics," 54.

is treated as the *causa sui*, the cause of itself. This is the only use metaphysics has for God: "The Being of beings is represented fundamentally, in the sense of the ground, only as *causa sui*."[12]

Besides the logical problems involved with anything being the cause of itself, this onto-theological God is merely a tool of metaphysics. This God is a concept used to serve a purpose, a God created by metaphysical inquiry and subservient to its ends. Perhaps still worse, one cannot truly worship this intellectual God; in Heidegger's memorable words, "This is the right name for the god of philosophy. Man can neither pray nor sacrifice to this god. Before the *causa sui*, man can neither fall to his knees in awe nor can he play music and dance before this god."[13]

Thus Heidegger. Let us turn to Marion to see how he applies postmodern thought to religion. What is the difference between an icon and an idol? Marion answers this question by calling our attention to the *intention* with which we approach a religious object. The idol is that at which, when we look at it, our gaze stops. In Marion's words, "In the idol, the gaze is buried."[14] The idol is that which a human approaches with the intention of seeing a full disclosure of the divine. The icon, however, is the same object looked at with a different intention. We look at an icon in order that it may draw our gaze to see the divine *beyond* it. The gaze that looks at the icon is a gaze that *pierces* the visible.[15] The idol is that at which I gaze when I hope to see God fully disclosed to me, but the icon is that at which I gaze when I hope to see God while at the same time remembering that I cannot see *all* of God.

Because we look at an idol with the intention of seeing the divine, the idol "consigns the divine" to fit within "the measure of a human gaze."[16] Such is the general difference between an icon and an idol; but Marion is critiquing intellectual idolatry specifically. The intellectual idol reduces the divine to the limits of our comprehension. The intellectually idolatrous gaze replaces the divine with a concept that fits inside the human understanding. But the intellectual *icon* is a concept for God that does not purport to be a full disclosure of the divine. Thus David Tracy in the Foreword to *God without Being*: "For Marion, reason, although crucial . . . , is, on its own, not an icon but an 'idol.'"[17] To try to fit God within the limits of human reason

---

12. Heidegger, "The Onto-theo-logical Constitution of Metaphysics," 60.
13. Heidegger, "The Onto-theo-logical Constitution of Metaphysics," 72.
14. Marion, *God without Being*, 13; hereafter *GWB*.
15. Marion, *GWB*, 11.
16. Marion, *GWB*, 14.
17. Tracy, Foreword, xi.

is to make an idol out of reason. Our concepts of God show us a shadow of God, not God in his fullness.

INERRANCY

In light of these lessons on epistemic humility, I wish to look at the doctrine of biblical inerrancy, taking as my primary text The Chicago Statement on Biblical Inerrancy. First I shall give a rudimentary definition and explanation of inerrancy. Then I shall develop this account of inerrancy by responding to three objections and elucidating the doctrine's presumption of a view I will call textual realism. This assumption, I argue, is a rational assumption; moreover, I consider both it and inerrancy to be consistent with major hermeneutical claims from the likes of Vanhoozer and Hans Frei. Textual realism is also an assumption which points us to epistemic humility. Epistemic humility is necessary not despite but rather *because of* textual realism. We need an epistemically humble approach (on the part of the reader) to authorial intent. Epistemic humility leads us back to postmodern philosophy, and so in the following section I shall examine inerrancy's relation to postmodern thought.

Inerrancy is simply the doctrine that the intent of the human authors of Scripture, whatever that intent is, is not open to the possibility of error. Since inerrancy is about the author's intent, the scope of the doctrine is less than is sometimes thought. For example, the Chicago Statement explicitly limits the doctrine to the autographs: "We affirm that inspiration, strictly speaking, applies only to the autographic text of Scripture . . . ."[18] Both surviving manuscripts and biblical translations are open to the possibility of error; indeed, errors frequently occur in transmission and translation.

Nor does inerrancy amount to a thesis supporting the univocity of theological language. Whatever a biblical author is trying to communicate to his readers is inerrant, but he may choose to communicate it in literal or non-literal language. It is a misunderstanding of inerrancy to think that it commits one to "letterism or wooden literalism."[19] When interpreting Scripture, all the usual hermeneutical rules apply: The original language, historical context, literary context, and literary genre all must be taken into account. Again, the Chicago Statement is explicit: "So history must be

---

18. The International Council on Biblical Inerrancy, The Chicago Statement on Biblical Inerrancy; hereafter referred to simply as Chicago Statement on Biblical Inerrancy in notes; the term Chicago Statement in text should be taken as referring to the same document, not to the Chicago Statement on Biblical Hermeneutics.

19. Ramm, *Protestant Biblical Interpretation*, 126.

treated as history, poetry as poetry, hyperbole and metaphor as hyperbole and metaphor, generalization and approximation as what they are, and so forth."[20]

Let's look at some objections to inerrancy, beginning with two typical and simple objections and then proceeding to a more sophisticated and postmodern one.[21] One of the most common objections is the claim that the doctrine does us no good since we don't have that to which inerrancy is ascribed, namely the autographs. This objection represents a misunderstanding of the doctrine. The Chicago Statement is correct when it says that, "strictly speaking,"[22] inerrancy applies to the autographs; this is because, strictly speaking, the original meaning of *any* ancient text is to be found in that text's autographs! It is not a question of whether we have the original *texts* of Scripture, but of whether we have the original *meaning* of Scripture. We can have at least as much confidence in the accessibility of the original biblical texts as for other ancient texts. We lack the autographs for Plato's *Republic*, but we are able to piece together a close resemblance of the original text from surviving manuscripts; the biblical autographs can be similarly reconstructed. In short, lacking the autographs does not prevent us from accessing the original meaning of Scripture, or from making claims about it.

A second typical objection to inerrancy is that it makes too many distinctions and qualifications to be a meaningful doctrine. But this objection is either severely wrongheaded, or else is rooted in a misunderstanding of inerrancy. Inerrancy presumes a degree of realism in regards to ancient texts. What I propose to call *textual realism* is the conjunction of three commonsense principles: that there is a text, that it has an original meaning, and that that original meaning is to some degree accessible to the contemporary reader. In presupposing textual realism, inerrancy merely adopts the same attitude towards ancient texts with which the historian approaches Herodotus, the scholar of literature *Gilgamesh*, and the philosopher the *Nichomachean Ethics* of Aristotle. Most of the distinctions and qualifications the objector has in mind describe how to reach (or not reach) the original meaning of the text. The facts remain that there is an original meaning to each biblical text and that this meaning is contained in the author's intent in the autographs, *as is the case with any ancient text.*

We read a line from Aristotle, for example that happiness requires virtue. We understand that Aristotle said it; if we are informed and attentive,

---

20. Chicago Statement on Biblical Inerrancy, Section III, Letter C.

21. Although I have heard these typical objections on several occasions, I first became familiar with them through an essay by Denison, "Inerrancy: Definitions and Qualifications."

22. Chicago Statement on Biblical Inerrancy, Section II, Letter X.

we also understand that our knowledge of what he said is filtered through his students, textual transmission, translation, and our own minds; we know in part; and yet . . . we *still* understand that Aristotle said that virtue is necessary for happiness. Tradition and scholarship have done their work bringing the proposition to us, and our own minds have done their work understanding it; and thus we know, knowing in part. It's the same with the Bible, with relevant differences (such as the Bible's much better history of textual transmission).

Rather than transgress this commonsense textual realism by making its various qualifications, inerrancy is simply elucidating textual realism through these qualifications. Inerrancy is merely a claim about the original meaning of the biblical text—the claim that, due to its divine inspiration, it is never inaccurate. Any difficulties involved with access to original meaning simply fail as objections to this particular—as well as to practically any other—claim about original meaning. If they succeeded, then the same difficulties would prevent a philosopher from claiming that Aristotle's ethical theory is right or wrong; they would prevent a historian from assessing Herodotus's historical claims as reliable; and they would prevent a reader of *Gilgamesh* from saying that the story told by its author is a beautiful story.

Now there is a different sort of objection to inerrancy, more sophisticated but also more dangerous. I refer to the objection that textual realism is simply mistaken—a common enough view in contexts where postmodern thought reigns. Here there is a turn to the *reader* and away from the *author* for meaning. This objection, of course, cannot sensibly be applied to the biblical text *uniquely*, for the correctness of the objection would render impossible not only an evangelical's affirmation of inerrancy, but also a philosopher's disagreement with Aristotle's ethical theory, a historian's agreement with Herodotus, and so forth. (It would even render impossible the objector's own objection—assuming he bothered to write in a text.)[23]

John R. Franke, for example, suggests that "language is a socially constructed human product" and that, as a result, "our words and linguistic conventions do not have timeless and fixed meanings that are independent from their particular usages in human communities and traditions."[24] He intends this not (or not directly) as a remark about the Bible, but rather as an objection to the Chicago Statement, which he says cannot be translated out of its own particular north American, late-twentieth century context. Franke's remark is either incorrect, or else fails as an objection to the

---

23. A matter I consider in more detail in Mark J. Boone, "Is There Life in This Author?"

24. Franke, "Response to Michael F. Bird."

Chicago Statement. If Franke means to deny the possibility of meaningful communication through language, then he cannot communicate his denial using language, as Norman Geisler notes.[25] But if Franke only means that claims made in one cultural and temporal context do not mean quite the same thing in another context, his remark is precisely correct; for this is why we need things such as historical literacy and good translations. Yet the objection is also entirely irrelevant. For, if it *is* relevant, then a modified form of Geisler's response will apply: Franke's objection to the Chicago Statement will be no less invalid than the Chicago Statement itself after enough years have passed, and it is *already* invalid in, for example, sub-Saharan Africa. Moreover, the Chicago Statement's central inerrantist claim is only that the original intent of the human author of the Bible is always true. For this claim to translate across time and cultures, it is merely necessary that the notions of authorship and truth be able to translate across time and cultures. And of course they can; for a philosopher can believe that Confucius's or Aristotle's claims are true, a historian can believe that Herodotus's claims are true, and so on.

But there is more to say about textual realism. Kevin Vanhoozer has dealt with the rejection of textual realism in *Is There a Meaning in This Text?*, and a thorough treatment of the topic is not necessary here. A brief word on the rationality of accepting textual realism will suffice, for textual realism is indeed a *rational* view. Vanhoozer delightfully links textual realism to Alvin Plantinga's epistemology, which is rooted in the commonsense tradition of philosophers such as Thomas Reid.[26] This is very right and proper; I am right to believe in textual realism in the same way I am right to believe that other minds exist, that a world outside my mind exists, that my five senses allow me to access that world, and so on. If someone objects to any of these beliefs, I can reasonably infer that the objection is mistaken; if a good argument is given, I can reasonably infer that there is probably something wrong with the premises.

Now a *thorough* and *complete* defense of textual realism would entail a systematic dismantling of objections, a presentation of arguments for textual realism, and an account of the quality that makes my belief in it rational—the sort of account Plantinga eventually gave in his Warrant Trilogy.[27] Nevertheless, even for a person who has *not* made such a defense or studied one made by others, it is best to accept the commonsense notion that there

---

25. Geisler, "A Review," 80.

26. Vanhoozer, *Is There a Meaning In This Text?*, 283–91.

27. Plantinga, *Warrant: The Current Debate*; Plantinga, *Warrant and Proper Function*; Plantinga, *Warranted Christian Belief*.

is a text having an original meaning which is to some degree accessible to the reader. Like the belief that other minds exist, the eminently sensible belief in textual realism has a stronger presumption in its favor than the premises of any objection are likely ever to have. The fact that *you* are reading a paragraph by *me* and understanding some (hopefully *all*) of what I say testifies to this. You are able to claim that what I am saying is correct, incorrect, reasonable, etc., on the basis of whatever relevant evidence you have available. Likewise, it is possible for an inerrantist to claim that the original meaning of a biblical author is entirely correct on the basis of whatever evidence he has available for the Bible's authority.

Now it may at first seem that the textual realism of Vanhoozer is inconsistent with biblical inerrancy, but this is not so. Vanhoozer argues for a particular account of what biblical meaning is—that meaning is an action on the part of the author, an action demanding a response from the reader. Inerrancy is merely a claim about the accuracy of the original meaning of the biblical text, not a claim about what that meaning *is*. So far as I can tell, Vanhoozer's analysis is entirely consistent with the Chicago Statement; moreover, insofar as it simultaneously supports biblical authority and considers biblical meaning *as it is meant by the authors* of the Bible, it implicitly supports the Chicago Statement's central thesis.

Similarly, Hans Frei's *The Eclipse of Biblical Narrative* may at first appear to be inconsistent with inerrancy. (In fact, this volume was first recommended to me by someone who thought it might cure me of my commitment to inerrancy!) But Frei's *Eclipse* merely resists the theory that biblical meaning is found in its reference to external fact, arguing that the meaning of the biblical text is found internally—in the biblical narrative.[28] But if this is about some narrative *beyond* what the authors intend, the claim that there is an important meaning beyond their intention is consistent with the Chicago Statement's thesis. And if the authors intend this narrative *themselves*, that is certainly no problem for inerrancy. Insofar as it both supports the authority of the Bible and simultaneously calls our attention *to the narrative intent of the authors of Scripture*, it is implicitly supportive of the thesis of the Chicago Statement. Inerrancy does not require that we consider Scripture to be a vast theological treatise consisting simply of one straightforward true proposition after another. The Chicago Statement says, "history must be treated as history, poetry as poetry, hyperbole and metaphor as hyperbole and metaphor," etc. Let us also add, with Vanhoozer and Frei in mind: Action is to be taken as action, speech act as speech act, and narrative as narrative. There may remain important differences on the

---

28. Frei, *Eclipse of Biblical Narrative*

intent of the authors, but what matters most is whether that intent, whatever precisely it is, actually has authority.

For precisely this reason, however, textual realism is one of the reasons I said at the beginning that inerrancy calls for humility on the part of the reader of Scripture. The intent of the biblical authors is not always at arm's length for us. We easily misinterpret, especially under the influence of literary norms affecting our own post-Enlightenment culture and differing from those of the biblical cultures. We read different poetry; we write letters according to different norms; our ways of doing philosophy are different; our standards for keeping historical records demand a higher degree of precision; and Hebrew is as much Greek to most of us as is biblical Greek. We must be humble because sometimes we cannot know what the authors of Scripture are saying as easily as we would like to.

An even more significant reason for humility is that sometimes when we do know what they are saying we cannot fully understand it. As the truth accommodated to our human understanding we might say that it lacks *correctness* in the most robust sense; but it is not *in*correct.[29] As inerrantist Kenneth Kantzer said, Scripture is "divinely revealed misinformation about God." It takes humility to believe what we don't understand, and at times biblical authority requires such humility of us. Unlike the God of onto-theology, the God who inspires Scripture is a God before whom we can kneel in humble worship.

EPISTEMIC HUMILITY AND THE BIBLE

This calls for revisiting the postmodern philosophers, who are surprisingly consistent with the inerrantist tradition. Postmodern philosophers have not neglected to apply their insights to the Bible, and both they *and* the contemporary inerrantist tradition explain that we must approach the Bible with epistemic humility. We must be humble as readers. We also need an epistemically humble approach to authorship, an approach which is consistent with inerrancy and at which the contemporary inerrantist tradition occasionally hints.

Marion and Westphal are powerful figures in postmodern philosophy of religion, but it is best to begin with Jacques Derrida and to review

---

29. Franke correctly notes that "As finite creatures, we are not able to grasp the truth as God, who is truth, knows that truth to be." Franke, "Recasting Inerrancy," Section Three. As he says, "all human knowledge of God" has an "accommodated character;" Section Two. But this does not entail that biblical knowledge is not real knowledge or is in *error*.

postmodern theology's usual alternative of doing without inerrancy. Derridas has said, "*There is nothing outside of the text*,"[30] meaning that there is no such thing as a construal of reality which is exhaustive, correct in every detail, and accessible to any attentive knower. Every construal of reality is subject to interpretation; more precisely, every construal of reality *is* an interpretation of reality.

Unsurprisingly, there is a strong tradition among postmodern theologians of doing without inerrancy. This seems a natural application of postmodernism and is common, for example, in the emerging church. Inerrancy may be rejected outright, or the theologian may suggest that it is a mistake even to ask whether inerrancy is correct. Or the doctrine may simply be set aside and ignored in favor of other hermeneutical principles. Such principles may include the notion of the Bible as a narrative, the notion that the Bible's authority is found in its guidance of the life of the church rather than in its propositional accuracy, or the notion that the Bible's interpretation is the work of the Christian community rather than the work of scholars who have gained an expertise in the thoughts of long-dead writers.

If I am not mistaken, one or more of these non-inerrantist approaches is taken by such theologians as Stanley Grenz,[31] Brian McLaren,[32] and Ray Anderson.[33] However, I think we can do better, and I am *certain* we can do otherwise. To be precise, we can do something more like what Augustine does, mingling inerrancy with some lessons of postmodernism—and perhaps incorporating some of the afore-mentioned hermeneutical principles favored by the non-inerrantist postmodern theologians. Accordingly, in what follows I will explore the consistency of some postmodern insights with biblical inerrancy before exploring how such doctrines were harmonized in the theology of Augustine.

The inerrantist can incorporate Derrida's insight, and Marion and some other Christian philosophers show how.[34] The biblical text is neither exhaustive, nor fully accessible to all readers; moreover, while not *in*correct, it is not *correct* in the robust sense denied by Kantzer. In short, it is not the systematic construal of reality sought by Enlightenment philosophers. It is a divinely inspired interpretation of reality—but still an interpretation.

30. Derrida, *Of Grammatology*, 158.
31. Grenz, *Renewing the Center*.
32. MacLaren, *A Generous Orthodoxy* and *A New Kind of Christianity*.
33. Anderson, *An Emergent Theology*.
34. These include Westphal and Benson, especially chapters 4–6 of *Graven Ideologies*. Also helpful is Smith, *Who's Afraid of Postmodernism?*, chapter 2.

More than this, inerrancy suggests an epistemically humble approach to human authorship. Inerrancy is rooted in the doctrine of the divine inspiration of Scripture.[35] God is the reason that the biblical authors were protected from error, and God has a better knowledge of the text than even they did. The Chicago Statement on Biblical Hermeneutics is explicit on this: "We deny that the writers of Scripture always understood the full implications of their own words."[36] To limit the divine Author of Scripture to what its human authors understood is an idolatry of human authorship. Furthermore, while the text is inerrant, what God does *through* the text is also important, and this is often more than the human author understood. Inerrantists are explicit that, as Bernard Ramm says, "Interpretation is one, application is many."[37]

Marion goes much further in this vein, explicitly affirming that the meaning of the text is much more than its human authors intended, reminding us that the human component of Scripture is under the authority of Christ. Intellectual idolatry is banished from our reading of Scripture when we acknowledge that its human authorship is under the authority of Christ, and that therefore a human interpreter should submit to the guidance of Christ. The meaning of Scripture is not limited to that intended by its human authors, for God may bring to us any number of meanings of the text that are not contained within the author's intent: "The text escapes the ownership of its literary producers in order to be inspired, so to speak, by the Word" (Christ).[38] Under the authority of God's use of the text, the text "offers, potentially, an infinite reserve of meaning" and "demands an infinity of interpretations, which, each one, leads a fragment of the text back to the Word," which is the full meaning of Scripture, which is Christ.[39] (In similar fashion, Franke suggests that the full meaning of Scripture is determined by the Holy Spirit, explicitly tying his theology to the hermeneutics of postmodern philosopher Paul Ricoeur.)[40]

Thus Marion on epistemic humility with regard to the biblical text. Similarly, Westphal calls for rejecting the "traditional (modern) approach" according to which a text "contains all and only what the creator consciously

---

35. Chicago Statement on Biblical Inerrancy, Section III, Letter A.

36. The International Council on Biblical Inerrancy, The Chicago Statement on Biblical Hermeneutics, Article XVIII.

37. Ramm, *Protestant Biblical Interpretation*, 113. See also Chicago Statement on Biblical Inerrancy, Section III, Letter C.

38. Marion, *GWB*, 156.

39. Marion, *GWB*, 156.

40. Frank, "Recasting Inerrancy," Section Four.

intended."⁴¹ He explicitly applies this insight to the biblical text, and favorably quotes Kantzer: The Bible, as "divinely revealed misinformation about God," must be interpreted with humility.⁴²

At this point one may well respond:

> Well, what is the use of inerrancy? Why bother talking about such authority? Why can't I just read the Bible and trust God to show me what it means, since you've already admitted that God knows what it means better than the human authors? Their authority does us no good when it's so hard to know what they meant and when God can tell us more than what they meant. Besides, inerrancy makes it too easy for us to set up our own interpretations as the right ones; we'll start fighting each other over who has the original meaning and, before you know it, we'll be so busy arguing that we'll forget to love our neighbors!

These are good questions, and the answers are just as good: Inerrancy is just as useful as the original meaning of Scripture is available to us. Sometimes the original meaning of a biblical text is more or less remote, perhaps at times very obscure. But the original meaning is often more or less clear, tending at times towards complete lucidity. These moments may be rarer than we would sometimes like, but at the very least they occur often enough to give us the basic truths of the faith and the command to love God and our neighbor. Indeed, the love of God and neighbor, so important to this imagined (but typical) detractor from inerrancy, is meant to be expressed in a community grounded in the authority of Scripture. This is why the authority of the human authors of Scripture was so important to the church fathers, and especially to Augustine, and it is to him that we now turn. As we shall see, for Augustine the doctrine of authorial authority was never separate from the doctrine that textual meaning is not limited to authorial intent.

THE RULE OF FAITH

There is a curious misconception that, if the human author's intent is not open to the possibility of error, then the Bible cannot mean anything else.⁴³

---

41. Westphal, "Blind Spots.
42. Westphal, *OO*, 79. (He does not mention Kantzer by name here.)
43. Franke: "the meaning of Scripture as the Word of God is pluriform and inexhaustible;" "Recasting Inerrancy," Section Five. This, he takes it, is contrary to Chicago Statement inerrancy; however, the plurality of biblical meanings has no bearing on the possibility of error in the particular subset of biblical meanings that is authorial intent.

Another common misconception is precisely the reverse: If not all biblical meaning is intended by its human authors, then their intent is open to the possibility of error. But, as it happens, these doctrines are logically compatible. Moreover, each is an essential part of the hermeneutical vision of Augustine. In this section I shall first briefly look at his claim that authorial intent in the Bible is without error and that biblical meaning is not fully contained within the intent of its human authors. Then I shall look at the relation of these two types of meaning, for Augustine took authorial intent to be the necessary guide that leads us to that meaning which transcends it. Finally, I shall contrast the view I am developing with that of Vanhoozer's "Augustinian inerrancy" and distinguish my view from some likely misunderstandings of it.

We need to see that the Fathers, like contemporary inerrantists, hold a high view of biblical authority, and that this high view extends to the intent of the human authors of Scripture, which they consider to not be open to the possibility of error. Augustine, for example, affirms that Scripture is indeed the Word of God, saying that God might say to him, "O man, true it is that what my Scripture says I myself say."[44] Furthermore, "we dare not assert that" Moses "spoke anything we know or think to be false."[45] Believing that an author of Scripture is in error is simply not an option.

Of course, the Chicago Statement and the evangelical tradition it represents tend to read the Bible more literally, and deny the possibility of science correcting Scripture;[46] yet Augustine is well-known for promoting non-literal readings of Scripture, and for allowing science (or the pre-science current in his day) to interpret Scripture! But there is an agreement here on the authority of authorial intent—an authority higher than science. If there is any divergence, it is not over the authoritative character of authorial intent but over just what that intent *is*, or perhaps over how we can *learn* what it is.

In Augustine the meaning of Scripture is not limited to authorial intent. Augustine continues: "Therefore, while every man tries to understand in Holy Scripture what the author understood therein, what wrong is there if anyone understand what you . . . reveal to him as true, even if the author he reads did not understand this . . . ?" The text is open to multiple true meanings. Other fathers concur; according to John O'Keefe and R. R. Reno, with the "early Christian readers" it was no different: "They thought the

---

44. Augustine, *Confessions*, 13.29, page 364.
45. Augustine, *Confessions*, 12.18, page 320.
46. Article XII of the Chicago Statement on Biblical Inerrancy, for example.

Scriptures infinitely rich" in meaning.[47] This point helps to close the conceptual gap between the contemporary mind and the ancient mind.

Finally, we turn to the relation between authorial intent and textual meaning in the eyes of Augustine, according to whom original authorial intent is precisely what leads us to the full significance of the biblical text. The broader meaning of the text transcends the author's intent; but authorial intent is also the path to that broader meaning. I shall elaborate by making four observations.

In the first place, the intent of the human authors of Scripture is at least clear enough to tell us about *the essential truths of the faith*: The Trinity, the incarnation, the drama of the creation-fall-incarnation-redemption narrative, etc. Thus Augustine tells us that the clearly understood authorial intent is enough to tell us to love God and our neighbor: "what all that has been said amounts to . . . is that *the fulfillment and the end of the law* and of all the divine scriptures *is love* . . . ."[48] Now this is in Book I, chapter 35 of his *Teaching Christianity*, and it is a summary of what has preceded. In what has preceded he has given us a full course of Christian theology, including Trinitarianism (chapter 5), God's unchangeableness (chapters 8-9), the incarnation (chapters 11-14), the resurrection and ascension (chapter 15), ecclesiology (chapters 16-18), and eschatology (chapters 19-21). It is worth noting, once more, that Augustine is not alone among fathers in thinking that the intent of the human authors of Scripture gives us the basics of Christian doctrine. O'Keefe and Reno explain:

> According to Irenaeus, proper interpretation depends on fidelity to the apostolic witness, preserved in the canonical books and taught by the authority of those bishops who are successors to the apostles. Irenaeus calls this witness the "rule of truth" or "rule of faith." This rule, which over the course of the early centuries of Christianity solidified into creeds, is an interpretive control that directs and orients the exegete as he employs various interpretive techniques.[49]

In the second place, authorial intent is a *check on error* when we are exploring the potentially infinite meaning of a text. When faced with an ambiguous passage in Scripture, we are forbidden to assert that it means anything which would be contrary to the sense of a clearer passage. As Augustine says, "faith will start tottering if the authority of scripture is undermined" by interpretations that are "impossible to square with the author's

---

47. O'Keefe and Reno, *Sanctified Vision*, 67.
48. Augustine, *Teaching Christianity*, 1.35.39, page 123.
49. O'Keefe and Reno, *Sanctified Vision*, 23.

meaning."[50] Though the fields of biblical meaning be infinite, we need not fear getting lost as we explore them, for we can at least be sure we are not going the wrong way. For this reason, Augustine claims that even a mistaken interpretation of a biblical text that is nonetheless consistent with the rule of faith tends to do us good.[51]

In the third place, authorial intent provides a *goal for interpretation*; when we interpret an ambiguous biblical text, we should aim to arrive at meanings that more fully express what is clear in Scripture. When the text is ambiguous, the rule of thumb is to go with whatever meaning would express the truths of the faith and the love of God and neighbor. Augustine says, "you should refer it to the rule of faith, which you have received from the plainer passages of scripture and from the authority of the Church . . . ."[52] By interpreting ambiguous passages we are working to better express both the truths of the faith and the command to love.

In the fourth place, the clear content of Scripture grounds a *community of interpretation* in which we live out what we know Scripture says and work together to learn what we don't know about Scripture. One passage beautifully depicting this is chapter 36 of Book I of *Teaching Christianity*, where Augustine explains how an interpretation errant yet supporting the love of God and neighbor does some good; yet one having such an interpretation should be corrected by those having a better knowledge of Scripture. The very purpose of *Teaching Christianity*, a textbook for preachers, further confirms this notion of a communal reading of Scripture. Again, although my emphasis is on Augustine, O'Keefe and Reno show how this attitude is not limited to Augustine: "scriptural interpretation was an ongoing research project under the guidance of a body of doctrine that they called the rule of truth or the rule of faith."[53] "A community of inquiry"[54] was needed to conduct this research project.

It is in the context of such a community that authorial intent and the broader sense of the text come together. As Augustine says, we read Scripture to know what its authors say and, by means of that, to know what God is saying to us.[55] What they say gives us the truths of the faith; it also gives us the command to love God and our neighbor. We practice love in the context of a community that guides interpretation according to these truths

50. Augustine, *Teaching Christianity*, 1.37.41.
51. Augustine, *Teaching Christianity*, 1.36.41.
52. Augustine, *Teaching Christianity*, 3.2.2, page 169.
53. O'Keefe and Reno, *Sanctified Vision*, 118.
54. O'Keefe and Reno, *Sanctified Vision*, 118.
55. Augustine, *Teaching Christianity*, 2.5.6, page 131.

of the faith. But, as Augustine says, without "the authority of Scripture" faith itself "will start tottering," and without the faith "charity itself also begins to sicken."[56]

This, I suggest, is more truly an Augustinian inerrancy that what Vanhoozer has called such in his contribution to the volume *Five Views on Biblical Inerrancy*.[57] Vanhoozer does tell us that his view is not actually Augustine's.[58] Rather, it is Augustinian in various respects. For one, like Augustine it affirms "the entire truthfulness of the Bible in the strongest of terms."[59] Also, it is, like Augustine, *literate*, attentive to "the nature and interpretation of language."[60] It is, again like Augustine, *well-versed* in that it "[calls] attention to Scripture as composed of various kinds of discourse."[61] In a third similarity to Augustine, it "gives priority to the Bible's own teaching about God, language, and truth."[62] This is all well and very good; I affirm it, and join Albert Mohler in recognizing that Vanhoozer's is a serious commitment to inerrancy.[63] I offer no objection to the very important analyses of the nature of the biblical text or of the biblical teaching on the nature of truth contained in Vanhoozer's essay.[64] Yet his inerrancy lacks two features of a thorough Augustinian inerrancy, for such would include an account of the meaning that was intended by the divine Author of Scripture yet not by its human authors, and an account of the connection between those two varieties of meaning. A truly Augustinian inerrancy would allow for the clear affirmations of the authors of Scripture to govern our explorations of meanings of which they were *not* aware.

At this point it would be appropriate to address two possible misunderstandings. In the past few paragraphs I have been looking at several different sources of meaning or authority including the original meaning

56. Augustine, *Teaching Christianity*, 2.37.41, page 124.
57. Vanhoozer, "Augustinian Inerrancy."
58. Vanhoozer, "Response to R. Albert Mohler Jr."
59. Vanhoozer, "Response to R. Albert Mohler Jr."
60. Vanhoozer, "Augustinian Inerrancy," Section 4.
61. Vanhoozer, "Augustinian Inerrancy," Section 4.
62. Vanhoozer, "Augustinian Inerrancy," Section 2.

63. Mohler, "Response to Kevin J. Vanhoozer." I thus dissent from Geisler's labeling of Vanhoozer as a "non-inerrantist"; Geisler, "A Review of *Five Views of Biblical Inerrancy*," 69.

64. This is not to say that I would not dispute some of the specifics. Moreover, I strongly concur with Geisler's warnings against reducing biblical meaning to authorial purpose; Geisler, "A Review of *Five Views of Biblical Inerrancy*," 70. I think Vanhoozer's view of the nature of biblical meaning is consistent with Chicago Statement inerrancy, and I think he, like Frei, has well described a large swath of biblical meaning. But I rather doubt he has captured *all* of it.

of the Bible, the rule of faith, and the testimony of the church. How are these authorities related, and what did Augustine (and other fathers) think of the relation? Does biblical authority establish the other authorities, or vice versa? Or are these authorities mutually interdependent? These are interesting and important questions, but as it happens they are outside the scope of this paper; I am not staking out a position on any of them (though I myself am a child of the Reformation and the doctrine of *sola Scriptura*). Here I have been concerned only with other questions: whether the inerrancy of original meaning is compatible with meaning which goes beyond the original, what is the relationship between these two kinds of meaning, and what some noteworthy theologians and philosophers have thought of these matters.

Finally, I am not endorsing Augustine's famed allegorical technique for reading Scripture.[65] While I think his overall hermeneutic provides strong safeguards against grievous error, I think a better way of finding biblical meaning outside the original intent of the human authors would focus more sharply on Old Testament pictures of the gospel. Old Testament pictures and predictions of the Messiah frequently had more meaning than the Old Testament authors could fully know. And, in keeping with Augustine's own advice to let known authorial intent guide our exploration of other meanings of Scripture, we should look to the explicit teaching of New Testament writers to make these richer Old Testament readings clear.

CONCLUSION

I have examined some of the hermeneutical principles of two recent movements in Christian theology. According to the doctrine of biblical inerrancy as it has been recently developed by evangelicals, Scripture has an original meaning, and that meaning is protected from error by divine inspiration. According to some thinkers in postmodern theology, Scripture calls for epistemic humility, we should not approach the biblical text through the paradigms of Enlightenment rationality, and the meaning of Scripture transcends its original meaning. These notions are not only consistent but are both found in the writings of Augustine. Perhaps there is room for friendship between postmodern Christians and inerrantists, for they share a common heritage in Augustine, in whom some of their most cherished doctrines are both honored and harmonized.

---

65. I have recently considered this topic more adequately in Boone, "How Does the Bible Refer to Christ?," 743–858.

I said at the beginning that there are insights treasured by the traditions of inerrancy and postmodern theology, insights which are consistent and can be and *have been* integrated. If my analysis is correct, then it contains no original thoughts, but only thoughts expressed differently in different ages. Had these thoughts had not been expressed since ancient times, my analysis would be very useful indeed. Perhaps, however, some degree of integration of them has already been accomplished by contemporary theologians; if so, then so much the better. Consider, for example, Vanhoozer's warning against the interpretive sins of pride and sloth.[66] Respect for the biblical author guards against sloth by helping us know there *is* a meaning, and against pride by reminding us that *we* do not control it. Humility and the importance of the original meaning—precisely the insights of the theological traditions I have explored. Nevertheless, to whatever degree integration has been accomplished by contemporary theologians, it is not sufficiently recognized that the traditions of contemporary postmodern theology and contemporary inerrancy are sources of these insights. We should recognize these insights where they appear: first in fathers like Augustine and now in postmodern theology and in biblical inerrancy—theologies which may be fit for the future, all the more so because so much of them is also ancient.

We will consider other ancient-future insights on faith and reason in the next chapter.

WORKS CITED

Anderson, Ray. *An Emergent Theology for Emerging Churches*. Downers Grove, IL: InterVarsity, 2006.

Augustine. *Confessions*. Translated by John K. Ryan. New York: Image, 1960.

———. *Teaching Christianity*. Translated by Edmund Hill; edited by John E. Rotelle; volume I.11, *The Works of Saint Augustine: Translations for the 21st Century*. Hyde Park, NY: New City, 1996.

Benson, Bruce Ellis. *Graven Ideologies*. Downers Grove, IL: InterVarsity, 2002.

Boone, Mark J. "How Does the Bible Refer to Christ? Interacting with Augustine the Allegorist." *The Heythrop Journal*: 64.6 (2023) 743–858.

———. "Is There Life in This Author? The Living Author and the Business and Importance of the Humanities in South Asia." In *Transcultural Humanities in South Asia: Critical Essays on Literature and Culture*; edited by Waseem Anwar and Nosheen Yousaf, 83–94. London: Taylor & Francis, 2022.

Denison, James. "Inerrancy: Definitions and Qualifications." Texas Baptists Committed. May 2000 [reprinted from TBC's July 1994 newsletter]; available from http://www.txbc.org/2000Journals/May2000/May00inerrancydefi.htm (accessed September 13, 2023.

---

66. Vanhoozer, *Is There a Meaning In This Text?*, 462–63.

Derrida, Jacques. *Of Grammatology*. Translated by Gayatri Chakravorty Spivak. Baltimore: Johns Hopkins University Press, 1974.

Franke, John R. "Recasting Inerrancy: The Bible as Witness to Missional Plurality." In *Five Views on Biblical Inerrancy*, edited by J. Merrick and Stephen M. Garrett, 259–87. Grand Rapids: Zondervan, 2013. Kindle.

———. "Response to Michael F. Bird." In *Five Views on Biblical Inerrancy*, edited by J. Merrick and Stephen M. Garrett, 192–97. Grand Rapids: Zondervan, 2013. Kindle.

Frei, Hans W. *The Eclipse of Biblical Narrative*. New Haven, CT: Yale University Press, 1974.

Geisler, Norman L. "A Review of *Five Views of Biblical Inerrancy*." *The Master's Seminary Journal* 25.1 (2014) 65–96.

Grenz, Stanley. *Renewing the Center: Evangelical Theology in a Post-Theological Era*. Grand Rapids: Baker, 2000.

Heidegger, Martin. "The Onto-theo-logical Constitution of Metaphysics." In *Identity and Difference*, translated by Joan Stambaugh, 42–76. New York: Harper & Row, 1969.

The International Council on Biblical Inerrancy. The Chicago Statement on Biblical Hermeneutics. Chicago, 1982.

———. The Chicago Statement on Biblical Inerrancy. Chicago, 1978.

Lyotard, Jean-François. Introduction to *The Postmodern Condition: A Report on Knowledge*. Translated by Geoff Bennington and Brian Massumi. Minneapolis: University of Minnesota Press, 1984.

MacLaren, Brian. *A Generous Orthodoxy: Why I Am a Missional, Evangelical, Post/Protestant, Liberal/Conservative, Mystical/Poetic, Biblical, Charismatic/Contemplative, Fundamentalist/Calvinist, Anabaptist/Anglican, Methodist, Catholic, Green, Incarnational, Depressed-yet-Hopeful, Emergent, Unfinished CHRISTIAN*. Grand Rapids: Zondervan, 2004.

———. *A New Kind of Christianity: Ten Questions that Are Transforming the Faith*. New York: HarperCollins, 2010.

Marion, Jean-Luc. *God without Being*. Translated by Thomas A. Carlson. Chicago: University of Chicago Press, 1991.

Mohler, Albert J. "Response to Kevin J. Vanhoozer." In *Five Views on Biblical Inerrancy*, edited by J. Merrick and Stephen M. Garrett, 236–41. Grand Rapids: Zondervan, 2013. Kindle.

O'Keefe, John J., and R. R. Reno. *Sanctified Vision: An Introduction to Early Christian Interpretation of the Bible*. Baltimore: Johns Hopkins University Press, 2005.

Plantinga, Alvin. *Warrant and Proper Function*. New York: Oxford University Press, 1993.

———. *Warrant: The Current Debate*. New York: Oxford University Press, 1993.

———. *Warranted Christian Belief*. New York: Oxford University Press, 2000.

Ramm, Bernard. *Protestant Biblical Interpretation*. Grand Rapids: Baker, 1970.

Smith, James K. A. *Who's Afraid of Postmodernism? Taking Derrida, Lyotard, and Foucault to Church*. Grand Rapids: Baker, 2006.

Tracy, David. Foreword to *God without Being* by Jean-Luc Marion; translated by Thomas A. Carlson. Chicago: University of Chicago Press, 1991.

Vanhoozer, Kevin J. "Augustinian Inerrancy: Literary Meaning, Literal Truth, and Literate Interpretation in the Economy of Biblical Discourse." In *Five Views on

Biblical Inerrancy, edited by J. Merrick and Stephen M. Garrett, 199–235. Grand Rapids: Zondervan, 2013. Kindle.

———. *Is There a Meaning in This Text?: The Bible, the Reader, and the Morality of Literary Knowledge*. Grand Rapids: Zondervan, 1998.

———. "Response to R. Albert Mohler Jr." In *Five Views on Biblical Inerrancy*, edited by J. Merrick and Stephen M. Garrett, 71–76. Grand Rapids: Zondervan, 2013. Kindle.

Webber, Robert E. *Ancient-Future Faith: Rethinking Evangelicalism for a Postmodern World*. Grand Rapids: Baker, 1999.

Westphal, Merold. "Blind Spots: Christianity and Postmodern Philosophy." *Christian Century*, June 14, 2003. Available at https://www.christiancentury.org/article/2003-06/blind-spots (accessed September 13, 2023).

———. *Overcoming Onto-theology: Toward a Postmodern Christian Faith*. New York: Fordham University Press, 2001

10

Two Ways Faith Goes beyond Reason

WE ALL KNOW FAITH and reason are not exactly the same thing.[1] What exactly is the difference, and how are they related? A good orthodox Christian answer is that faith transcends reason, and for at least two reasons. First, the doctrines of orthodox Christian theology are beyond comprehension. Second, faith requires a total commitment when reason can provide only partial evidence. We cannot act meaningfully if we act only halfway. If evidence produces a 95% probability that a particular conclusion is true, sometimes 100% is still the only way to act on it; commitment to Christ must lead all the way (perhaps unto death).

After a look at some definitions, some distinctions, and an illustration, I will consider what Immanuel Kant, Augustine of Hippo, William James, and Søren Kierkegaard have said about how faith goes beyond reason.[2] Kant thinks faith goes beyond reason as a matter of necessity given the nature of human knowledge. Augustine thinks faith goes beyond reason, but this is not a permanent thing; with sufficient mental training and contemplation, we may hope to achieve knowledge of God. James concurs, but he looks to future experience rather than contemplation. Finally, Kierkegaard thinks Christian faith must always by nature go beyond reason; neither philosophical contemplation nor any experience in this life will change this;

---

1. The biggest change to this chapter since its initial publication is an examination of James 1:6.

2. For a more detailed analysis of a different but overlapping set of thinkers, see Evans, *Faith beyond Reason*. For a more detailed look at Augustine and James on faith and reason, see the relevant chapter in this book.

faith cannot be fully understood by reason and requires a commitment beyond what the evidence alone guarantees.

FAITH, REASON, TRANSCENDENCE, AND COMMITMENT

"Faith" means trust. This is true of the English term and also its precursors, *pistis* in Greek and *fides* in Latin. *Fides* links the related concepts of religious belief, trust, and economic credit. Religious faith may be taken merely as trust that such belief is true although it would be more appropriate to take it as trust in the *source* of those beliefs—biblically speaking, trust in the authority of Scripture (Acts 17:11), trust in Jesus the Messiah to deal with our sins (Matt 1:21; Acts 16:30–31), or trust in God to keep his promises (2 Cor 5:5–7). Credit in the fiscal or economic sense is also trust: The hotel trusts the credit card corporation to pay it for my stay, the credit card corporation trusts me to pay them in turn, and so on.

Trust may even be understood as action without explicit reference to belief. Suppose that I am on a small volcanic island and that the volcano is erupting! I could wait it out, hoping the lava does not get to me. I might try swimming, hoping to make it to safer shores before exhaustion—or a shark—claims me. Instead, I decide to rely on the rickety old airplane that happens to be on the island, hoping that both it and its drunken charter pilot will do their jobs properly. As I, trembling with fear, fasten my seat belt, I reflect on the fact that I am putting my faith in this old aircraft and yet am not quite sure I actually believe that it will not crash.[3] Biblically speaking, I know that I am a sinner (Rom 3:23). In desperate need of help, I trust Jesus to take care of my sin problem rather than try to save myself (Acts 4:12). I know that the requirement for faith involves following Jesus (Matt 16:24), but I am not sure I am never allowed to doubt, although it does seem that not doubting is at least preferable.

A brief look at the New Testament passages that seem to say that we should never doubt would be in order. Although Mark 11:23 may appear to speak of belief without any doubt, the Greek *diakrino* can also be translated as "waver" and may refer to wavering in our commitment to Christ, not to the entertaining of doubts.[4] Similarly, in Jas 1:5–6 we are advised to

---

3. Daniel Howard-Snyder is helpful on the active aspect of faith. See Howard-Snyder, "Propositional Faith," 357–72.

4. See, for a detailed look on how *diakrino* is used in the New Testament, DeGraaf, "Some Doubts about Doubt," 733–55. *Diakrino* often means "divided loyalty or disunity" (733), and in Mark 11:23 it involves "a call to wholeheartedness" (746).

pray for wisdom without doing any of whatever this verb denotes in this context. The phrase *mehden diakrinomenos* can be reasonably translated "doubting nothing," in which case Jas 1:6 would begin, "But let him ask in faith, doubting nothing." Alternatively, we could understand *diakrinomenos* in the sense of wavering—something along the lines of "But let him ask in faith, wavering not at all." This fits the rest of the verse, which states, "for the one doubting (*diakrinomenos*) has become like a wave of the sea being blown by the wind and being tossed by the wind." This certainly fits the rest of James well enough, with its emphasis on faithfulness. And, in fact, *pistis* could be translated "faithfulness" as easily as "faith," denoting a penitent, Christ-following *way of life* more than a *state of belief*—"But let him ask in faithfulness, wavering not at all." However, I have to admit that I cannot quite justify this as a translation of Jas 1:6, for *mehden* is an adjective in the accusative case, serving as direct object of *diakrinonemos*. This means that there is nothing we should be *diakrino*-ing. We can doubt nothing, but I am not sure what it means to waver nothing; accordingly, the necessary literal translation would seem to be "doubting nothing," although with a strong sense of doubt as a faltering in our commitment to Christ.[5] Perhaps biblical faith *with wavering* is right out, while biblical faith *with doubting* is welcome, but is only a starting-point, a thing we need to grow past.[6] Not doubting does appear to be at least a desideratum for biblical faith—"I believe; help my unbelief!" (Mark 9:24 ESV).

So we should beware of thinking of faith simply in terms of belief; still less should we think of faith simply in terms of irrational belief or belief without evidence. Trust is the main point of faith. Trust may be rational or irrational, evidenced or not, within or without the bounds of reason. It typically involves belief and, biblically speaking, *always* requires obedience.[7]

Now let us consider our second key term, "reason." First, the most broad sense would be something along the lines of proper thinking, the correct operating of our minds, or being in our right minds. More specifically, and second, "reason" may refer to one or more of the things we do when our minds are operating properly. For example, belief based on evidence is a paradigmatic function of reason, a normal and important way of using our minds to know the truth. After all, reason involves logic—the weighing of evidence to see how well it supports a particular conclusion. A third sense of "reason" is full comprehension or complete understanding, the ability to

---

5. DeGraaf considers *diakrino* here to involve "divided motives and divisive attitudes;" DeGraaf, "Some Doubts about Doubt," 742.

6. "Doubt is not faith's enemy; rather, the enemies of faith are misevaluation, indifference or hostility, and faintheartedness;" Howard-Snyder, "Propositional Faith," 370.

7. A helpful related analysis may be found in Evans, *Faith beyond Reason*, chapter 1.

wrap our brains around a matter and fully grasp it, to know it for ourselves and not by relying on any authoritative testimony.

Now in what senses of the term "reason" does faith go beyond it? Not the broadest sense. At least according to orthodox Christianity, Christian faith is believing and following the truth, especially the truth about God and us. There could be no more proper operation of the mind than this. Indeed, some truths about himself God has made known by natural means (Rom 1:18–20). Others he has made known by means of prophecy, miracles, and scripture. (See, for example, John 20:30–31; 21:24; Acts 17:31; Heb 1:1–2; 2 Pet 1:19–21.)

Even in the second sense of the term it is difficult to say that faith transcends reason. At any rate, insofar as testimony is a legitimate source of evidence, it is bad theology to say that faith transcends reason in the sense of belief based on evidence. God can be trusted to keep his promises (Josh 23:14–15; Heb 6:18; 2 Cor 1:20). Jesus can be trusted (John 14:1). The Bible can be trusted (2 Tim 3:15–16). The apostolic witness (Gal 1:11–12) and the prophetic witness (2 Pet 1:16–21) can be trusted. Christian faith based in these trustworthy sources is faith based on good testimonial evidence.

It is in our third sense of the term that faith can best be said to go beyond reason. Certain Christian doctrines are rightly said to be mysteries: Their full comprehension is beyond us. We should not expect anytime soon fully to grasp either the infinite goodness of God or the doctrines of the incarnation and the Trinity. Nor to know firsthand the glories of the eschaton in this life, for what we do know of this we know by faith rather than sight—by trusting in the apostolic testimony and in God's promises accompanied by the down-payment of the Holy Spirit (2 Cor 5:1–5). Although the New Testament does teach that we know the gospel and, more generally, the truths of Christianity, this knowledge is largely secondhand and based on trust. It is not knowledge borne of full comprehension.

How best to characterize this relationship between faith and reason? As transcendence. This faith is not contrary to reason. *Un*reasonable faith is not biblical, no matter how often people may refer to the alleged absurdity of faith. Nor should faith be understood as simply separate from reason and having nothing to do with it. Then there would be no relevance of the evidence for faith such as we have recently considered. Entire scholarly traditions, theology and apologetics, would be contradictions in terms. From Augustine to C. S. Lewis, from Aquinas to Luther, from William Lane Craig to Alvin Plantinga, both enterprises would be based on a delusion if, indeed, reason is not even relevant to faith.

So faith, Christianly conceived, is neither in conflict with reason nor totally cut off from it. Nor is it fully within the jurisdiction of reason defined as full comprehension. Were that the case, Christianity would be a matter of reason alone and would not require trust. Faith, Christianly conceived, transcends reason. It is something to which reason is relevant, yet which is outside of the jurisdiction of reason. In this unconventional Venn diagram,[8] it occupies the outermost circle alone. All unreasonable things are within the jurisdiction of reason, but not vice versa; all things within the jurisdiction of reason are things to which reason is relevant, but not vice versa. That is one important sense in which faith may be said to go beyond reason. Let's look at another.

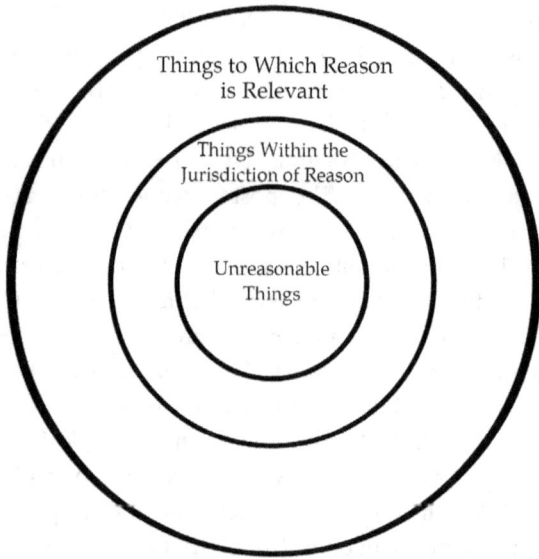

Say a young man (call him Mark if you like) is in love with a young lady (you could call her Shonda). He is seriously thinking about putting a ring on her finger. Suppose he were to sit down with a pen and paper to analyze his situation and were to estimate the probability that this course of action will lead to years of marital bliss (stipulating that he is the kind of nerd who might actually do this). He is not going to end up with a result of 100%. There is always the tiny, tiny chance that she is secretly a witch, an alien, or a robot. More likely, perhaps personality differences that have already become evident hint at years of communication problems and marital fights. Optimistically, the young man would be pretty lucky to be able to estimate a probability of around 95%.

But what young lady wants 95% of a ring?

---

8. In a standard Venn diagram in a logic course, all three circles bisect each other.

The fact of the matter is simple: His action ought to be either 100% or 0%.

Of course, his conclusion may be a 100% matter. Given pretty good odds that they are meant to be together, it is reasonable to say that there is only one right course of action. What right action avoids all possible risk of a bad outcome? And that is another way of making the main point: Even an action which is *certainly* right may be based on *uncertain* evidence. In any case, the action must be either done or not: He must give his lady friend a ring, or not. Similarly, she must agree to be his wife, or not; if she is less than fully convinced about it, she cannot act accordingly by becoming less than fully a wife, for there is no such thing, and if there were he is not asking her for it.

Faith is like that. It involves a commitment, not only of belief but of life. There is no faith without repentance (Acts 17:30–31) or without works (Jas 2:14–26). There is no faith without following Jesus, who says, "If any man will come after me, let him deny himself, and take up his cross, and follow me" (Matt 16:24). This commitment is meant to be total; we do not get to keep 10% of our idols and 10% of our sins, and follow Jesus carrying 90% of a cross if a good study of apologetics leads us to assess the probability that Jesus is the Messiah at just 90%. The evidence is not binary, but the action is: We do it, or not.

Now, as it happens, I think the evidence is pretty good. (In fact, at the time of the initial composition of this paragraph, I was on Hong Kong Island to do my bit to teach part of a course on the evidences for Christianity for the Hong Kong Center for Christian Apologetics!) Still, I have to admit that the evidence is, technically, uncertain. My commitment to Christ must be 100% *precisely*. My decision to follow him when I was nine years old was between two choices—yes and no. But my evidence is not binary; it is only very good, but less than 100%. In other words, the evidence is best understood probabilistically. Let's look at this a bit more closely.

It is relevant that some arguments for God's existence are inductive; in other words, their premises are not designed to render their conclusions certain, but merely probable. Such, for example, would be a typical teleological argument, such as an argument from evidences for design in nature. Another typical kind of argument for God's existence is the cosmological, such as the *kalam* cosmological argument: Whatever begins to exist has a cause for its beginning; the universe began to exist; so there is a cause for the universe's beginning to exist, which is God. This is a deductive rather than an inductive argument; its premises are meant to guarantee the conclusion. But this argument, like the teleological arguments, works best after experience. There may, for example, be some good evidence from physics for the theory that the universe had a beginning. However, it is always possible that future physicists will find evidence to the contrary. The argument ultimately relies on probabilistic reasoning.[9]

Perhaps the infamous ontological argument establishes God's existence with certainty. Okay. But only if the argument works. I, like most, think that the original argument is not quite right.[10] Alvin Plantinga's analysis, if correct, shows that the argument works only given that the existence of God is a metaphysical possibility.[11] It might well depend on a probabilistic argument to prove *this*, however. Passing over other attempts to demonstrate God deductively,[12] let us note one limitation of such arguments. If they work, they demonstrate a higher power or even the greatest possible being Anselm wanted to prove—no small accomplishment. But they do not prove Christianity as such. The major religions have their specific doctrines; even those that teach a god, gods, or God (which Buddhism, for example, tends not to do) teach more than that he exists. The Abrahamic religions teach specific claims about historical events, miracles, and verbal revelation. The gospel is central to Christianity, and it consists of historical claims about the Messiah—about his birth, life, death, burial, and resurrection—and fulfilled prophecies (1 Cor 15:3–8). You can't prove this sort of thing with just an *a priori* argument—one not derived from experience. It also takes a historical argument, which is to say—an empirical and probabilistic one.

Even an *un*reasonable doubt ensures that the evidence for Christianity is only partial. As a Star Trek nerd, I can easily imagine an alternative account of the events surrounding the resurrection of Jesus the Messiah, without which (as Paul says in 1 Cor 15) my theology is so much fanciful error.

Stipulate that the best evidence from history, archaeology, and so on supports the resurrection.[13] It is still possible that things are not what they seem. Suppose dishonest but otherwise benevolent otherworldly

---

9. This is actually a bit of an oversimplification of the *kalam* argument; on the plausibility of *a priori* arguments that the universe had a beginning, see Loke, *God and Ultimate Origins*, chapter 2.

10. See Anselm, *Proslogion*, chapters 2–3. Roughly, the argument is: God is a perfect being, and non-existence is an imperfection; so if God does not exist then a perfect being has an imperfection, which is impossible; therefore God exists. But if God does *not* exist then there is no being that is perfect. If, using some Anselmian language, God only exists in our minds, then he is *not* a perfect being.

11. Plantinga, *Nature of Necessity*, chapter 10.

12. For example, arguments in Descartes's *Meditations on First Philosophy*, the Third and Fifth Meditations.

13. On this topic the interested reader might consult the likes of Bauckham, *Jesus and the Eyewitnesses*; Wright, *The Resurrection*; and Craig, *Assessing the New Testament Evidence*.

visitors came to Palestine at the time—perhaps extraterrestrials or even time-traveling humans from the future. Using holographic images, they rescued Jesus, faked his crucifixion, and had a good long talk with him aboard their cloaked spaceship. Meanwhile, Joseph of Arimathea mournfully buried a corpse the visitors had surgically altered and placed on the cross before switching off their holographic device. By Sunday morning, they had persuaded Jesus that it was necessary to fake his death and resurrection as an inspiration to his followers to teach his moral principles and spread them throughout the world. Bolstering the ruse with plastic surgery to give him the appearance of having been crucified, they returned Jesus to the tomb after rolling away the stone with a tractor beam and dazzling the guards with more holographic imagery. One or two stayed around long enough to impersonate some angels when some women arrived at the tomb. After Jesus had made enough appearances, the visitors drew him into the clouds before the apostles' eyes. After arranging his meetings with Paul a little bit later, they conveyed him to South America, where he later died at a ripe old age.

Is any of this likely? Not in the slightest. But is it *possible*? As far as I know. Thinking about it actually makes me uncomfortable: I am facing the possibility that my faith relies on such a ruse.

But this ruse is extremely improbable, so I follow the evidence as well as I can understand it: I remain a Christian, a believer in the historical events that constitute the gospel—that Jesus the Messiah died for our sins in accordance with the scriptures, was buried, and was raised miraculously to life on the third day. I commit to this my whole life, for the most part leaving such doubts behind. The evidence is good enough to convince me that I ought to go beyond the evidence, for my Lord Jesus Christ does not ask me for a 90-something-% commitment corresponding to my 90-something-% evidence.

KANT

We are considering two reasons faith may be said to transcend reason—that the teachings of faith are less than fully comprehensible to the human mind and that the commitment required by faith is a total commitment of one's entire life whereas reason cannot guarantee the truth of religious beliefs. Let's look at some great thinkers who concur.[14] First up is Kant. As Stephen

---

14. Much has been written on these matters. The interested reader might consult Evans, other sources cited below, or relevant articles in the Stanford and Internet Encyclopedias of Philosophy as paths into the secondary literature.

Evans summarizes Kant's perspective, "there are some truths that reason, in its theoretical employment, can say nothing about, but which can and should be accepted by faith."[15]

In Kant's view, some putative realities are beyond our ability to learn about. When reason tries to demonstrate the truth about them, it ends up confused and contradicting itself. Kant attempts to show that an attempt to uncover the truth about these matters will end up proving both sides of the question—we will have solid arguments both for and against the proposition concerned. These are Kant's (in)famous antinomies of reason,[16] the pairing of contrary arguments in order to show that reason and argument have certain limits. They must work within these limits, rather than try to demonstrate anything about matters beyond them. Such is God, outside the limits of reason. Trying to understand God using reason will end up in confusion. Considering the venerable strategy of using cosmological arguments to prove that God exists, Kant argues that we can actually prove both sides of the question of a supreme being—we can prove both that a first cause exists and that it does not. On the one hand, the changes we observe in the world must have a necessary first cause, or else there is no explanation for the fact that there are effects. On the other hand, the cause must be within time, for a cause always precedes its effect within time. Thus the first cause must be either the first link in the chain of causes, or else the chain must itself be a necessary being and the first cause. But everything within time, as we observe from experience, is subject to cause and not merely a cause in itself; so we cannot consider the first link in the chain to be a first cause. Nor can the whole chain itself be a necessary being, since it is made of all its parts, and nothing made of parts is a necessary being if none of its parts are necessary beings. In short, we have solid arguments both for and against the existence of God.[17] So there is no knowledge of God; to the contrary, Kant says, "Thus I had to deny knowledge in order to make room for faith . . . ."[18]

Now the point is not only to keep reason from straying out of its own proper sphere but also to free it to operate *within* that sphere. Something similar is the case with Kant's metaphysics and epistemology. We cannot prove that we exist in three-dimensional space, and do not need to. Kant

---

15. Evans, *Faith beyond Reason*, 65.

16. Or, as Kant himself refers to them, apparently considering them as a whole, the antinomy of reason. My gratitude to Stephen Palmquist for pointing this out.

17. To study the antinomy in more detail, see Kant, *Critique of Pure Reason*, Transcendental Doctrine of Elements, Second Part, Division Two, Book II, chapter II, section II. On the origins of Kant's idea of the antinomy and its influence on his philosophy, the interested reader might consult Al-Azm, *Origins of Kant's Arguments*.

18. Kant, *Critique of Pure Reason*, Preface to the Second Edition, 117.

does a bit of philosophical psychology and finds that this belief does not come from experience. The mind applies it to sensory experience in order to make sense of sensory experience. For example, take a few moments to search the internet for a picture of Victoria Falls and to think about what you're looking at when you look at that picture—perhaps some rocks or trees as well as the waterfall itself. What you're looking at is actually just a two-dimensional image; however, your mind knows how to apply the idea of three dimensions to it, so you can perceive that the rocks are behind the water, the trees are in the foreground, and so on.

But all you ever really see with the eyes (unaided by the mind) is, like this image, no more than an arrangement of shades and colors, which the eyes by themselves cannot tell you involve any three-dimensional objects. Depth-perception is not the gift of the eyes to the mind, but the mind's gift to what the eyes see in order to make sense of it.

So we do not need to prove that we exist in space. Rather, we should accept what we cannot help thinking—that the world as we know it is structured in three dimensions—and get on with the work that proceeds from that assumption, doing science to learn about that world. What is true of our concept of space is true of time and other matters, as Kant explains in the *Critique of Pure Reason*.[19]

Similarly, reason has no business proving God. However, moral reasoning requires us to believe in God.

Why is this? Well, Kant is a great ethicist, with a very influential and insightful analysis of the requirements of moral obligation. A proper analysis of this would make for a long digression.[20] For our purposes we need make only a few observations. Kant's view is that the requirements of morality can be known by pure reason; we do not need to learn them from experience or from an authority.[21] We can always be sure of following the requirements of morality if we test our actions by what Kant calls the "Categorical Imperative"—the test of whether our choices are consistent with moral law. Kant proposes three[22] formulations of the Categorical Imperative. But all this

---

19. Kant employs a similar analysis for other beliefs including the belief that we exist in time, the belief that there are substances underlying the properties of objects, and the belief in cause and effect. In fact, the concept of time also structures our perceptions of the waterfall. As Stephen Palmquist put it to me, "We *know* the water is moving, yet there's no actual movement in the pictures. When we think 'Victoria Falls,' the object is schematized insofar as we think the whole space-time body of water that runs over the rocks, down the cliff, and between the trees."

20. The interested reader might seek an introduction in Johnson, "Kant's Moral Philosophy."

21. On this topic I suggest Palmquist, *Comprehensive Commentary*, 8–9.

22. Or four. Kant presents the third one in two different ways, the second of which looks like a fourth to some readers.

is only enough to know what morality requires of us. Actually *living* by morality is another matter, for frail beings such as we are easily tempted by the flesh. Kant thinks we need religious hope to properly inspire us always to act morally. Specifically, he thinks we need to believe that God will eventually make circumstances line up with the requirements of morality. In our experience, moral goodness does not always correlate with happiness, but we understand that it *should*. God can make this happen, and a belief that he exists and will ultimately do so helps us live morally, looking with hope toward that end and sticking with morality even when things are tough, believing that it will be worth it.[23]

So, although faith is necessary, the defense of faith is not based on evidence for its truth but on evidence for its practicality.[24] Faith is a matter of reason, to be sure, but of reason knowing what moral law requires of us, not reason knowing that God exists. The putative facts about God and about life after death remain beyond our understanding. This is a permanent fixture of the human condition: We cannot have knowledge of God, and we must act, for the sake of morality and despite our lack of theological knowledge, as if God exists. Kant even claims that the moral theology he is developing is more reliable than speculative theology.[25] He goes on to explain what are the different modes of taking a proposition to be true: *Opinion*, where we are neither 100% committed to a theory nor persuaded by logical proof, is the weakest; *knowledge*, where both of these things are the case, is the strongest form of belief.[26] Between these is *belief*, in which state we are entirely committed but lack proof. Faith in God and in his final justice is found in this middle ground.

Note that what we have in Kant does not fit the transcendence model of the relationship between faith and reason quite so well as it fits a separation model. Although it is true, in Kant's view, that the content of faith is not known by reason and that a moral life requires action beyond what the evidence can justify, he is not in favor of all aspects of the account overviewed in the previous section of this chapter.[27]

23. Again, Palmquist is helpful; Palmquist, *Comprehensive Commentary*, 14–15, 21.

24. Note that Kant is not opposed to attempts to understand the truth about God. Systematic theology from a biblical perspective is okay by Kant's lights; see Palmquist, *Comprehensive Commentary*, 28–30.

25. Kant, *Critique of Pure Reason*, Doctrine of Method, chapter II, section II.

26. Kant, *Critique of Pure Reason*, Doctrine of Method, chapter II, section III. My gratitude to Stephen Palmquist for pointing me to this passage in connection with this topic.

27. In my analysis a necessary condition for X transcending Y is that Y have some relevance to X—not merely about what we should think about X. In Kant's analysis

AUGUSTINE

Augustine points to both reasons that faith may be said to transcend reason; in his way of thinking this is largely a temporary situation. In the future, sufficient mental and moral training may give us the ability to see God and know firsthand his existence and nature, and then of course this knowledge will be fully justified and will fully justify a total commitment to following Christ. (This is a perspective drawn largely the early writings; his later writings, in which I have spent less time, may be less optimistic about reason.)

Although these matters appear in many of his books, a brief look at three will suffice. In his first surviving writing, *Contra Academicos* or *Against the Academics*, we read:

> Moreover, no one doubts that we are urged on to learn by the twin weight of authority (*auctoritas*) and reason (*ratio*). Therefore, I am determined not to depart ever, in any way, from the authority of Christ. . . . But what should be pursued by a most subtle reason (*sublitissima ratio*)—for I am now of such a mind that I impatiently long to apprehend what is true not only through believing (from *credo*), but also through understanding (from *intelligo*)—I am confident that in the meantime I shall find among the Platonists, and that it won't be incompatible with our sacred [teachings].[28]

Closely related and written in the same year (386 A.D.) at the same place (Cassiciacum, near Milan), we read in *De Ordine, On Order*:

> Twofold is the path we follow when we are moved by the obscurity of things: either reason (*ratio*), or at least authority (*auctoritas*). Philosophy promises reason but it barely frees a very few. Nevertheless, it drives them not only not to disdain those mysteries, but to understand them alone, as they should be understood.[29]

Philosophy here means the Neoplatonic tradition's insights into non-physical reality. And, as he goes on to explain, it teaches that God exists, but authority teaches the Christian mysteries of the incarnation and the Trinity.

---

reason can tell us we should have faith, but does not give any evidence for the truth of the religious doctrines in question. So faith may only be said to transcend reason in a looser sense, such as that used by Evans, *Faith beyond Reason*, 66.

28. *Against the Academics*, 3.20.43. Foley notes that Augustine later regretted his overstatement concerning the overlap of Christianity and Neoplatonism.

29. Augustine, *On Order*, 2.5.16.

In a letter to his old friend Honoratus, whom he had formerly led into the Manichaean heresy and whom he now hopes to free from it, Augustine explains that to believe by trust is different from *intellegere*, to understand, or *discere*, to know.[30] However, both are important. We must seek the truth in both ways. First we must seek by faith in orthodox Christianity.[31] Later we seek by means of reason added to faith—a reason for which our minds have been trained by faith.[32] In his own words:

> when you do not have the ability to appreciate the arguments, it is very healthy to believe without knowing the reasons (*ratio*) and by that belief (*fides*) to cultivate the mind and allow the seeds of truth to be sown. Moreover, for minds that are ill this is absolutely essential, if they are to be restored to health.[33]

In short, according to Augustine's usual way of talking, faith and reason are not the same thing. Although faith is rational and useful, reason requires firsthand understanding, and faith necessarily involves trust. Trust must go beyond what reason alone can guarantee. This is the case with respect to action, for we must trust Christ, the Bible, and the church; trust involves obeying their commands and reordering our lives and our loves around them. It is also true with respect to evidence, for this trust is in truths that we find ourselves incapable of knowing for ourselves. Yet, hopefully, this is a temporary situation, not a permanent feature of the human condition. We may, in time, come to understand these truths by means of contemplating the nature of immaterial reality with minds trained by Neoplatonic insight.

JAMES

We will not look here at what James may have to say about some points of theology being beyond human ability fully to comprehend. We will only look at his very interesting analysis of action as that which must go beyond mere reason—and in other spheres of life as well as in religion. Like Augustine, he thinks of this as a temporary situation. Knowledge may come later, after—indeed as a result of—faith. One difference between the two is that James is more empirical than Augustine; that knowledge which he hopes to add to faith he hopes to gain from experience—not, as in Augustine, from

---

30. Augustine, *Advantage of Believing*, 11.25.
31. Augustine, *Advantage of Believing*, 8.20.
32. Augustine, *Advantage of Believing*, 17.35.
33. Augustine, *Advantage of Believing*, 14.31.

contemplation. For our purposes, a brief look at James's most famous work, his essay "The Will to Believe," should be sufficient.

In James's view, knowledge of God must come from experience. As an empiricist, James thinks knowledge comes "by systematically continuing to roll up experiences and think."[34] James is, moreover, a member of the tradition of American pragmatism in philosophy. In other words, he is an intellectual descendant but not a member of the tradition of British empiricism. These British empiricists (such as Hobbes, Locke, and Hume) held that knowledge comes from sensory experience alone. James's pragmatism considers experience in broader terms. Knowledge comes from experience, and *religious* experience counts. James's *The Varieties of Religious Experience* is a long and systematic look at the past data of religious experience in hopes of getting a feel for how strong might be the evidence for God or some other spiritual reality.

In "The Will to Believe," James is considering something different—the rationality of belief in God when that evidence from experience is, for the present at least, inconclusive. He thinks it is rational, and his arguments to that effect are practical ones. There are two.

First, we each face an unavoidable decision whether to be religious or not. We can avoid choosing between being Southern Baptist or Roman Catholic by opting to be Presbyterians, materialistic atheists, or Confucians. But we cannot avoid deciding whether to have either no religious beliefs or at least one; that decision is forced on us. Moreover, the decision has a big effect on our lives. Not only does it change how we live, but religion alleges that there are significant positive effects even in this life, promising that we will benefit from believing that the eternal things are the more valuable ones. Now, although some of us may not be able to be atheist even if we were to try—or others to be religious—some of us really could go either way. For such, the decision is what James calls *live, forced*, and *momentous*: We could go either way, we must go one way, and there are big consequences.

In the absence of convincing evidence, we have the right to make such decisions not based on evidence alone. People normally do make such decisions in this way, and no one has a problem with it—Do I marry? Whom? How many kids do we want to have? Shall I become a philosopher or a dentist? Anyway, what choice do we have but to *make the choice*? When the evidence is lacking and the decision is live, forced, and momentous, deciding not based on convincing evidence is all we can do. Moreover, James thinks we have a right to take into consideration the possible good consequences promised by religion. In deciding whether to have a religious

---

34. James, "Will to Believe."

belief, we decide between two risks. If we believe and are wrong, we will be in error. If we do not believe, we will avoid that error but also avoid any possible good results of believing any religious truths there may be. We have a right, James says, to decide for ourselves whether we prefer the risk of not believing a religious truth or the risk of believing a religious falsehood.

Second, James draws an analogy from human relationships to the divine:

> We feel, too, as if the appeal of religion to us were made to our own active good-will, as if evidence might be forever withheld from us unless we met the hypothesis half-way. To take a trivial illustration: just as a man who in a company of gentlemen made no advances, asked a warrant for every concession, and believed no one's word without proof, would cut himself off by such churlishness from all the social rewards that a more trusting spirit would earn,—so here, one who should shut himself up in snarling logicality and try to make the gods extort his recognition willy-nilly, or not get it at all, might cut himself off forever from his only opportunity of making the gods' acquaintance.

There is a decent chance that, if there is a God, our major religions are right in thinking that this God is a person (or three). It is also likely that the divine person is like human persons in that he will not provide proof of his existence and good intentions prior to any willingness on our part to trust him. In the kind of relationships with which we are most familiar—the human-human variety—evidence of goodwill frequently comes *after*, not *before*, trust. Perhaps God exists after all, but the evidence for God's existence may come about after—even *because of*—our faith.

In sum, James thinks religious knowledge based on experience is a possibility. Given this knowledge, religious faith would be simply a matter of reason. In the present, however, many of us face the decision whether to believe in God. It is like other decisions along life's way—decisions we all recognize as rational despite their being based on incomplete evidence. Moreover, if indeed God is personal, it is likely that his making himself known to us will depend on our willingness to believe, and in this respect faith in God is much like the faith we regularly place in human persons—prior to the evidence, and (when all goes well) leading to confirmation later that our faith was well-placed. Faith, thus, goes beyond reason. It is belief in religious propositions not currently proven. It is an activity of life, a practical commitment beyond what the currently available evidence warrants. Faith transcends reason in this way, but temporarily—until future experience hopefully brings about the right evidence.

KIERKEGAARD

C. Stephen Evans observes that "Søren Kierkegaard is often cited in textbooks as a prime example of irrational fideism."[35] Chapters 6 and 7 of Evans's *Faith beyond Reason* are very helpful in explaining that Kierkegaard is actually "a responsible fideist": he thinks faith is not contained within reason, but his views "do not imply any repudiation of reason."[36] Kierkegaard is adamant that Christian faith transcends reason and cannot be made to answer to its standards. This does not make faith *against* reason—just a little bit *beyond* it. We might say, rather, that reason goes against faith sometimes—when reason gets a little uppity and oversteps its bounds. Unlike Augustine and James, Kierkegaard thinks reason will never quite catch up to faith in this life. In what follows, I will consider Kierkegaard's analysis in *Fear and Trembling* of Christian faith as that which goes beyond full comprehension. Then I will consider his analysis in *Philosophical Fragments* of Christian faith as requiring a leap of total commitment.

Fear and Trembling is probably Kierkegaard's most intoxicating book. The reflections on Abraham's act of faith in Genesis 22 may leave us speechless, breathless, or in tears. Yet this book is easily misunderstood. We should not presume that it is simply written by Kierkegaard. We could just as easily say that it is a piece of fiction written by Johannes de Silentio (John the Silent), the fictional character Kierkegaard made up to write it! To be a bit more precise, *Fear and Trembling* is one of Kierkegaard's pseudonymous works, and it is not quite right to say that what de Silentio says is what Kierkegaard says. Rather, de Silentio must be understood as representing a position Kierkegaard wants us to understand and to take seriously.[37]

As I understand him, de Silentio is under the influence of Enlightenment and post-Enlightenment philosophical concepts of reason. His worldview is more-or-less Hegelian. Hegel is one of the great philosophers of the late modern era of philosophy—the next truly great German philosopher after Kant. He is an influential character in the history of process theology—theology based on the idea that God grows and develops. In Hegelian thought, it is not easy to say, "In the beginning God created the heavens and the earth," because God in his final form was not *there* in the beginning. God emerges over time through the experiences and growth of the human race. That growth is moral, but also rational. The human race increases in

---

35. Evans, *Faith beyond Reason*, 78.
36. Evans, *Faith beyond Reason*, 78.
37. For guidance on reading Kierkegaard's pseudonyms, see Evans, *Faith beyond Reason*, 78–79 as well as Evans's longer analysis in *Kierkegaard's "Fragments" and "Postscript"*, chapter 1.

knowledge and reason. The perfectly rational and moral consciousness to emerge at the end of history—*that* is God. So God does not on his own authority lay down for us commands we must follow or propositions we must believe. God himself (in his final form) is largely the product of human reason. God is not above reason. All theology must submit to the requirements of reason, and human reason itself must grow as the human race works together to increase in understanding until it encompasses all reality.

Now de Silentio frankly admits that he is *not* a man of faith and cannot understand Abraham's. Yet he can understand what it is *not*, and *it is not Hegelian*. His central claim is that faith is absurd. This claim is made from a Hegelian perspective; if we have a different perspective, we may reject it. Too much under the influence of Hegelianism, de Silentio has no choice but to view faith as absurd. Kierkegaard himself, who is actually Hegel's biggest critic, can and does think otherwise.

Why is faith absurd from a Hegelian perspective? Abraham's faith is exemplified by his willingness in Genesis 22 to obey God and sacrifice his son. Hegelian reason can understand sacrificing one's child for the good of the community—as Agamemnon and Jeptha do. The Hegelian conception of reason recognizes the superiority of the community to the individual, considers that even destructive actions may be justified by their higher ends, and judges actions by the standard of the universal community. For the good of the many, the one may be sacrificed, as Spock says in *Star Trek II: The Wrath of Khan*.

But Isaac is Abraham's heir, the heart of the Hebrew community. There is no sacrificing *him* for the community; sacrificing him *is* sacrificing the community. Hegelian ethics can understand no higher end in Abraham's action. Abraham is the lone individual receiving instructions from God; there is no universal communal standard that can evaluate this.

Now Kierkegaard is writing in a time of confusion. Practically everyone in Denmark in the 1800s assumes that practically everyone in Denmark is a Christian. Yet the majority of Denmark's intellectuals are *Hegelians*! As a character in *Hamlet* observes, something is rotten here. Christianity and Hegelianism are not compatible, but most people do not realize that, and many fancy themselves to be *both*. Even those who are not intellectuals studying Hegelianism at the university typically have many of the same ideas—particularly that human reason can ultimately prove everything that is true and justify everything that is just.

If that is the case, what do we make of Abraham? Kierkegaard's goal in writing *Fear and Trembling* is to help people see that there is an inconsistency between Christian theology, based on Abrahamic faith, and these widespread Hegelian principles. The main lesson from *Fear and Trembling* is this argument: If Hegelianism is right, then Abraham has attempted murder and his actions are absurd. But Abraham has *not* attempted murder, and his actions are *not* absurd. So Hegelianism is wrong.

Having said that, the main thing is to understand the inconsistency—to understand the if-then premise. Kierkegaard would be delighted if people would follow through on the whole argument, renounce Hegelianism, and be faithful Christians. He would still be somewhat pleased with those who admit the if-then premise and proceed as honest Hegelians who admit that they are not Christians.

Johannes de Silentio is like that. He can see the first premise of the argument above, but he can't quite accept the second. In other words, he can see the conflict between Hegelian conceptions of reason and Christian faith, but he is not prepared to reject Hegel and accept Christian faith. More generally, de Silentio can see the tension between biblical faith and any standard of reason that insists that everything we believe submit to the full comprehension of the human intellect. He admires this faith but is not prepared to abandon his prejudice in favor of the ultimate authority of reason.

In short, faith is absurd when measured by the standards of comprehensive post-Enlightenment reason. It goes beyond full comprehension, and it requires trust in God's pronouncements and commands instead of perfect understanding.

Another pseudonymous character invented by Kierkegaard is Johannes Climacus, the author of *Philosophical Fragments* (or *Philosophical Crumbs*) and *Concluding Unscientific Postscript to the Philosophical Fragments* (*Crumbs*). The main point of Climacus's writing, as I understand it, is that the doctrine of the incarnation cannot be understood by those Enlightenment standards of reason culminating in Hegelianism. The incarnation goes beyond the limits of human reason. It is, in Climacus's recurring words, an "absolute paradox." It is the paradox that God became man, or, in Climacus's words, "The eternal truth has come into existence in time. That is the paradox."[38] This can be believed, but not understood. The result of making it understandable can only be that the doctrine loses its significance for life.

The only way to make the incarnation understandable is to abolish it, as Hegelian philosophical theology has done. It has not always done so explicitly or even knowingly. The typical Hegelian distances himself from the "modern mythical allegorizing trend" of denying the truth of Christianity, swearing his friendliness to the doctrine of the incarnation. Climacus's reply is biting: The allegorizers are at least "forthright" in their rejection of

---

38. Kierkegaard, *Concluding Unscientific Postscript*, 209.

Christian doctrine, but "The friendship of speculative thought" is different: "Speculative thought . . . accepts the paradox, but it does not stop with it."[39] With friends like speculative thought, who needs enemies? It goes on to explain the incarnation, thus disarming its paradoxical nature. Ultimately, the explanation is just an audacious correction.[40] The correction goes something like this: According to the carnal understanding of Christians from an earlier era, there was a paradox, but now that theology and speculative philosophy have come of age, we can look at the incarnation from a better perspective, that of speculation. From this vantage point, there is no paradox—only the truth that God and man are ultimately one. We can even imagine that, when everyone learns to be more speculative, "Christianity will have ceased to be a paradox."[41]

But the doctrine that God became a human like us does not admit of explanation. Christianity never ceases to be a paradox. The amended doctrine of the incarnation is without significance, but the historical doctrine has *enormous* significance for my life and yours. God became a human like you and me and lived a life like yours and mine; the significance of the doctrine is for everyday life. The claim of speculative thought removes the incarnation from human existence, establishing it as the ideal unity of God and man, a doctrine far removed from the real world where the incarnation has its significance. Climacus says this "is an explanation not for existing individuals but for the absentminded."[42] These Hegelians explain the doctrine only by denying its significance. These are the consequences of insisting that the true meaning of the incarnation is accessible to human understanding.

From God's perspective, the incarnation is no contradiction. In fact, Kierkegaard regularly lambasts Hegelian thought for giving up the principle of noncontradiction.[43] Speculative thought's mistake is, rather, that it claims to be able to view the incarnation from God's perspective. We do not have any access to this perspective. One would have to become God to have the intellectual capacity for understanding the incarnation.[44] Modern intellect has gotten big-headed. Moreover, speculation removes itself from the context in which the doctrine is significant. The incarnation presents itself to us as a momentous change in the meaning of our own lives. It does not call any

---

39. Kierkegaard, *Concluding Unscientific Postscript*, 218.
40. Kierkegaard, *Concluding Unscientific Postscript*, 219.
41. Kierkegaard, *Concluding Unscientific Postscript*, 221.
42. Kierkegaard, *Concluding Unscientific Postscript*, 221.
43. See, for instance, *Postscript*, 304–5. I am indebted to a comment from Dan Johnson for the insight that Kierkegaard's defense of noncontradiction is significant for his view of the incarnation.
44. Kierkegaard, *Concluding Unscientific Postscript*, 217–18.

person to become God so as to understand theology—only to do what God did as a man and to become a different kind of person.

What must we do with this doctrine, according to Climacus? The correct response to the incarnation is not primarily intellectual: We approach the truth of the incarnation with passion rather than speculation.[45] We must take a leap of faith, a decision of total commitment.

The truth of Christianity would preclude that everyone has access to the truth; only those in right relation to Christ have access to the truth. The incarnation spurs us more to live our lives in response to it, less to speculate in hopes of understanding it. The doctrine takes its stand in everyday human existence. God became a person and lived a human life; it is in the context of our own lives that we must respond to this fact. We realize the significance of the incarnation by living. It begins with a decision. As Climacus says at the beginning of *Postscript*, the issue of Christianity is not whether speculation can make sense of the incarnation, but "the issue is rooted specifically in decision."[46] The decision cannot be delayed indefinitely. The worst one can do is spend all his time speculating about the paradox and so never come to a decision.[47] Even rejecting Christ outright is better than thinking he does not demand decisive action.

The decision *is* decisive—and absolute. A good analogy is the decision required by erotic love. Listen to Climacus: "Much that is strange has been said about erotic love, much that is lamentable, much that is outrageous, but the most obtuse thing of all said about it is that it is to a certain degree."[48] Imagine our young man from earlier telling his girlfriend that he has great affection for her, estimates the odds that she is the girl for him at 95%, and is prepared to offer her 95% of the rest of his life, keeping the last 5% for whatever else may come up later. If a self-respecting girl prefers 100%, how much more so Jesus Christ, who says "any one of you who does not renounce all that he has cannot be my disciple" (Luke 14:33)? Climacus observes: "What does it mean to assert that a decision is to a certain degree? It means to deny decision. Decision is designed specifically to put an end to that perpetual prattle about 'to a certain degree.'"[49]

The absolute decision for Christ brings one into relationship with God. In this relationship one knows the truth. Ethics and religion are for practice.

---

45. As J. I. Packer said, "We shall be wise . . . to shun speculation and contentedly to adore." See Packer, *Knowing God*, 58.

46. Kierkegaard, *Concluding Unscientific Postscript*, 21.

47. Kierkegaard, *Concluding Unscientific Postscript*, Part I.

48. Kierkegaard, *Concluding Unscientific Postscript*, 229.

49. Kierkegaard, *Concluding Unscientific Postscript*, 221.

A person becomes ethical by striving to bring her life into concordance with the demands of ethics; so also for the demands of religion. This very striving is what Climacus calls knowledge: "all ethical and all ethical-religious knowing is essentially a relating to the existing of the knower."[50] We know the requirements of ethics and religion by expressing them in our lives. Christ requires that we follow him; we know him by relating this requirement to our lives. Expressing the truth of the incarnation in our lives is holistic. No part of our lives can escape it. It is at least as passionate as it is intellectual.[51] The truth must fill up every corner of a person's life.

CONCLUSION

What does the Christian worldview say about faith and reason? Quite a lot. Faith is beyond reason, at least according to the terms of Christian theology, and philosophers of religion help us to understand how and why this is the case. There are two ways in which we can say that faith transcends reason. Faith requires belief in that which reason has not first comprehended perfectly. Faith also involves *action* reason has not completely proven to be correct. Kant, Augustine, James, and Kierkegaard concur on these matters although they differ on the permanence of this arrangement this side of the grave—Kant and Kierkegaard being for it, Augustine and James being against. They differ in how we might add reason to faith if we can—James being more empirical than Augustine. They even differ in their Christianity—Kant and James, by my understanding, lacking Christian theology altogether! Yet they help to give us a clear picture of how faith may be beyond reason—in more ways than one—yet still be rational and necessary. "Of making many books there is no end," including books about faith and reason. But one of the points of these books is well made: We are justified in having faith; with or without reason, it's only reasonable.

WORKS CITED

Al-Azm, Sadiq J. *The Origins of Kant's Arguments in the Antinomies*. Oxford: Oxford University Press, 1972.

Anselm. *Proslogion with the Replies of Gaunilo and Anselm*. Translated by Thomas Williams. Indianapolis: Hackett, 1995.

Augustine. *The Advantage of Believing*. Translated by Ray Kearney, notes by Michael Fiedrowicz. The Works of Saint Augustine: A Translation for the 21st Century, Part

---

50. Kierkegaard, *Concluding Unscientific Postscript*, 198.
51. Kierkegaard, *Concluding Unscientific Postscript*, section II, chapter 2.

I-Books, Vol. 8: *On Christian Belief*, edited by Boniface Ramsey, Introductions by Michael Fiedrowicz. Hyde Park, NY: New City, 2005.

———. *Against the Academics: St. Augustine's Cassiciacum Dialogues, Volume I*. Translated by Michael P. Foley. New Haven, CT: Yale University Press, 2019.

———. *On Order: St. Augustine's Cassiciacum Dialogues, Volume III*. Translated by Michael P. Foley. New Haven, CT: Yale University Press, 2020.

Bauckham, Richard. *Jesus and the Eyewitnesses: The Gospel as Eyewitness Testimony*. Grand Rapids: Eerdmans, 2006.

Boone, Mark J. "Augustine and William James on the Rationality of Faith." *Heythrop Journal* (online edition 2018) 1–12. https://onlinelibrary.wiley.com/doi/10.1111/heyj.13123.

Craig, William Lane. *Assessing the New Testament Evidence for the Historicity of the Resurrection of Jesus*. Lewiston, NY: Edwin Mellen, 1989.

DeGraaf, David. "Some Doubts about Doubt: The New Testament Use of ΔIAKPINΩ." *Journal of the Evangelical Theological Society* 48.4 (2005) 733–55.

Descartes, René. *Meditations on First Philosophy*. Translated by Donald Cress. 3rd ed. Indianapolis: Hackett, 1993.

Evans, C. Stephen. *Faith beyond Reason: A Kierkegaardian Account*. Grand Rapids: Eerdmans, 1998.

———. *Kierkegaard's "Fragments" and "Postscript": The Religious Philosophy of Johannes Climacus*. Amherst, NY: Prometheus, 1983.

James, William. *The Varieties of Religious Experience*. New York: Longmans, Green, and Co., 1902.

———. "The Will To Believe." In *The Will to Believe and Other Essays in Popular Philosophy*. Available at https://gutenberg.org/files/26659/26659-h/26659-h.htm.

Howard-Snyder, Daniel. "Propositional Faith: What It Is and What It Is Not." *American Philosophical Quarterly* 50.4 (2013) 357–72.

Johnson, Robert. "Kant's Moral Philosophy." *Stanford Encyclopedia of Philosophy* (published February 23, 2004; revised July 7, 2016). https://plato.stanford.edu/entries/kant-moral/ (accessed November 27, 2018).

Kierkegaard, Søren. *Concluding Unscientific Postscript* to Philosophical Fragments. Translated and edited by Howard V. Hong and Edna H. Hong. *Kierkegaard's Writings*, Vol. XII. Princeton: Princeton University Press, 1992.

———. *Fear and Trembling*. Translated and edited by Howard V. Hong and Edna H. Hong. Kierkegaard's Writings, Vol. VI. Princeton: Princeton University Press, 1983.

Kant, Immanuel. *The Critique of Pure Reason*. Translated by Paul Guyer and Allen W. Wood. Cambridge: Cambridge University Press, 1998.

Loke, Andrew Ter Ern. *God and Ultimate Origins: A Novel Cosmological Argument*. London: Palgrave Macmillan, 2017.

Packer, J. I. *Knowing God*. Downers Grove, IL: InterVarsity, 1973.

Palmquist, Stephen R. *Comprehensive Commentary on Kant's* Religion within the Bounds of Bare Reason. Malden, MA: Wiley Blackwell, 2016.

Plantinga, Alvin. *The Nature of Necessity*. New York: Oxford University Press, 1974.

Wright, N. T. *The Resurrection of the Son of God*. Minneapolis: Fortress, 2003.

11

Dialogue on Faith and Reason

SOPHY: Hey, Phil!

PHIL: Hey, Sophy! Something about faith and reason, was it?

SOPHY: Yeah, it just sort of came up in history of philosophy class. We were talking about Kant, and we went off on a tangent about faith and reason.

PHIL: You Kant always avoid those tangents.

SOPHY: Ha!

PHIL: Yeah, old joke.

SOPHY: Old and dumb.

PHIL: Fair enough. So, anyway, . . .

SOPHY: Anyway, Thomas said something about how belief in God is supported by reason. But apparently Kant doesn't think so.

PHIL: He thinks belief that God exists is warranted—but not the proposition that "God exists"!

SOPHY: Yeah, yeah, that sounds right. No, wait—

PHIL: It's complicated. Kant doesn't think we can prove God exists. But he can prove that *belief* in God is necessary for . . . well, for . . . complicated moral reasons. We don't have to get into his ethics right now. Back to Thomas?

SOPHY: Okay, so Thomas said belief in God is justified by reason.

PHIL: Your Catholic classmate, right?

SOPHY: Yeah, him. But Kant is different.

PHIL: Right.

SOPHY: And then this other guy, David, said there's no reason to faith. Otherwise, it wouldn't be faith, he said. And a lot of the other students agreed with him.

PHIL: They usually do.

SOPHY: But for *totally* different reasons!

PHIL: Yeah?

SOPHY: One guy said faith is absurd, and said Kierkegaard was on his side.

PHIL: Not exactly!

SOPHY: And one student was saying that faith is just totally separate from reason and knowledge.

PHIL: Yeah, that's more like Kant—limiting knowledge to make room for faith.

SOPHY: But still giving us reasons to believe, right?

PHIL: Right—not reasons to think religious claims are *true*, but reasons to *believe* them.

SOPHY: Okay. And then this other student, Alfred, was saying that religious claims are just totally meaningless.

PHIL: Alfred—yeah, I know him. He says religious claims are meaningless because they cannot be . . .

SOPHY: . . . verified!

PHIL: Right!

SOPHY: So our professor didn't want to get too sidetracked from Kant, and we were running out of time anyway. But one interesting thing happened before we moved on.

PHIL: Yeah?

SOPHY: We took a poll. Turns out most of my classmates agree with David, for whatever reason. They think faith and reason can never overlap.

PHIL: And?

SOPHY: And I remembered what you said about it all a few weeks ago.

PHIL: Right. That thing I said about faith?

SOPHY: Yep.

PHIL: Plus, I'm the only one around here who reads Augustine, Plantinga, *and* William James. So . . .

SOPHY: So . . .

PHIL: So let's talk, I guess . . . . Well, the first thing to do is dispense with the verifiability criterion.

SOPHY: Meaning what?

PHIL: Well, there was this tradition in early 1900s philosophy called logical positivism.

SOPHY: Oh, I've heard of that.

PHIL: Logical positivism is all about the verifiability criterion of meaning. They got that from Hume and developed it a bit. According to the verifiability criterion, a statement is meaningless unless it can be verified in sensory experience. But they were missing something from Hume. Did you cover Hume in this class?

SOPHY: Yeah, we did.

PHIL: Do you remember what Hume said about causality?

SOPHY: That everything we learn from science depends on the proposition that cause and effect exist.

PHIL: Right. What else?

SOPHY: And that we don't know *that* the way we know the truths of mathematics or anything like that. We know it from *experience*.

PHIL: But there's a catch.

SOPHY: Yeah. We don't *really* know causality *just* from experience. We infer it from experience using inductive reasoning.

PHIL: Which is what?

SOPHY: It's how we make conclusions about what we have *not* experienced from what we *have* experienced.

PHIL: But it only works if we really *can*.

SOPHY: Right.

PHIL: And the principle that says we really can is . . .

SOPHY: . . . is the principle of induction.

PHIL: Right. But we don't really know that principle either, do we?

SOPHY: Not according to Hume. We infer the principle of induction from the uniformity of nature.

PHIL: Meaning . . . ?

SOPHY: The principle that things always work the same way in nature, or according to the same laws of physics.

PHIL: But we haven't experienced all of nature, have we?

SOPHY: No. And Hume also explains that we can't argue that induction has worked in the past or that nature has always been uniform in the past, and that therefore those principles will work in the future.

PHIL: Right! That would be circular reasoning.

SOPHY: So, he says, the only reason we do believe in induction, uniformity of nature, and causality is—well, I forget the word.

PHIL: *Custom*, or *habit*. But I think the word *instinct* is just as good.

SOPHY: Right, *custom*. And that's why we don't really know anything about the world. And why Hume is a skeptic.

PHIL: But what kind of skeptic?

SOPHY: Well, we should *believe* in these things, he says. But we should admit that we don't have any good evidence for them. We haven't learned them from experience, and all knowledge about the world outside the mind has to come from experience.

PHIL: Right. So *what kind of skeptic* is Hume?

SOPHY: Not the kind of skeptic who doesn't believe in an orderly world, but the kind of skeptic who thinks we don't have *knowledge* of it.

PHIL: Very well summarized! Okay, that's the right background information. And *that's* why the logical positivists were wrong about the verifiability criterion of meaning.

SOPHY: Sorry, you lost me.

PHIL: It's like this. Hume is an extreme empiricist. He thinks knowledge of the world outside the mind comes from experience and experience alone.

SOPHY: Okay.

PHIL: But he also understands that there are principles by which we learn about the world from experience, like induction and the uniformity of nature.

SOPHY: Okay.

PHIL: We don't learn them from experience, because we have to already know them if we're going to learn anything from experience.

SOPHY: Got it.

PHIL: So Hume understands that his extreme empiricism leads to skepticism: There can't be any actual knowledge of the world outside the mind.

SOPHY: Okay, I get it.

PHIL: So the logical positivists had their verifiability criterion of meaning, saying that every meaningful statement can be verified by sensory experience.

SOPHY: Yeah.

PHIL: They were following Hume in being extreme empiricists.

SOPHY: Right. I see that.

PHIL: But they didn't follow through on what Hume noticed—that if all knowledge of the world comes from experience and experience only, then there is no knowledge of the world.

SOPHY: Because knowledge from experience needs things like induction and the uniformity of nature?

PHIL: Right.

SOPHY: Because if we're going to learn anything about the world from experience, there are some things we have to know *first*.

PHIL: If there is even one such thing—it doesn't even matter which one—then not all knowledge of the world outside the mind can come from experience. That one thing must be known in some other way. Or, basically, we can't know anything about the world—anything at all.

SOPHY: Is this the same thing as the problem of induction?

PHIL: More or less. It's what people sometimes call the problem of induction, but that's probably not a good name for it.

SOPHY: Why?

PHIL: Because it's easy to explain induction. Do it Hume's way: We base induction on uniformity of nature.

SOPHY: But then you have the problem of the uniformity of nature instead.

PHIL: Right.

SOPHY: Is that really such a problem?

PHIL: Not necessarily. It's only a problem if you insist knowledge can only come from experience.

SOPHY: So that's why the verifiability criterion is wrong?

PHIL: That's why.

SOPHY: Is that why logical positivism died out?

PHIL: That's a complicated story. It *did* die out, very quickly. At one point it was all the rage in philosophy. Just a few decades later, nearly everyone in philosophy knew it was wrong!

SOPHY: Just because of that problem?

PHIL: I think that was a big part of it. Bertrand Russell ends his article on logical positivism by mentioning that this is the reason he's now convinced it's wrong.

SOPHY: Wow. That's a big deal.

PHIL: It is.

SOPHY: Anything else?

PHIL: You might want to ask a better historian of analytic philosophy. But I have a few pointers.

SOPHY: Let's hear them.

PHIL: Quine, Wittgenstein, Popper, and Kuhn.

SOPHY: Wait. I thought Wittgenstein had something to do with logical positivism.

PHIL: You're thinking of *early* Wittgenstein. In his later writings his philosophy of language starts to be a problem for logical positivism. Similar with Quine, in his "Two Dogmas of Empiricism."

SOPHY: Wait. You mean that article I couldn't understand?

PHIL: Yeah. That one. Don't worry. Everyone has that problem.

SOPHY: Oh, good!

PHIL: But I do understand that Quine helped to kill empirical reductionism.

SOPHY: What's that?

PHIL: A topic for another time. Let's just say it's an idea in the philosophy of perception and it was part of logical positivism.

SOPHY: Okay, fine.

PHIL: And Quine rejected empirical reductionism in the "Two Dogmas."

SOPHY: Is that why the "Two Dogmas" was so important?

PHIL: Well, that's part of why, anyway. It's actually pretty similar to what later Wittgenstein's philosophy of language said that was bad for logical positivism.

SOPHY: Okay, what about those other guys? You mentioned Karl Popper, right? The falsifiability guy?

PHIL: Yep. He gives the famous falsifiability answer to the question of what makes a theory scientific.

SOPHY: And what's that got to do with logical positivism?

PHIL: More than you'd think. So we were talking about the problem of how we can learn anything from experience without relying on a principle we did *not* learn from experience.

SOPHY: Right.

PHIL: And sometimes they call that the problem of induction.

SOPHY: Right.

PHIL: Well, Popper doesn't think the problem of induction can be solved.

SOPHY: And that's a big problem for logical positivism.

PHIL: Yep. It means science can't verify anything.

SOPHY: Okay, I think I get it.

PHIL: But there's another, simpler way of looking at it.

SOPHY: Shoot.

PHIL: Popper thinks the essential aspect of science is falsifiability. But the positivists think it's *verifiability*.

SOPHY: Those aren't the same things?

PHIL: Not quite: Verification is finding evidence consistent with a theory. Falsification is finding evidence *not* consistent with a theory. Think of white swans a long time ago.

SOPHY: Okay, so that theory that all swans are white was apparently verified for a while.

PHIL: Yes.

SOPHY: But then it was falsified.

PHIL: Yep. It's also a logic thing. Verification involves an *inductive* inference from some observed things to a universal claim about all things.

SOPHY: Like, we've seen a lot of white swans and never any black ones. So all swans are white.

PHIL: Just like that.

SOPHY: Okay

PHIL: And falsification is a *deductive* inference.

SOPHY: Like we found this black swan in Australia or wherever, so it's not true that all swans are white.

PHIL: Precisely.

SOPHY: Traditional Square of Opposition stuff from logic class!

PHIL: Yes!

SOPHY: And since science does that deduction thing, the logical positivists are wrong about science.

PHIL: I *think* so—well, maybe not. The real point is that *Popper* thinks so, and that he thinks they're also wrong because science doesn't need verifiability, and he thinks verifiability can't be done at all.

SOPHY: Okay, and that helped kill logical positivism? Okay, what about Kuhn?

PHIL: Okay, what do you know about Kuhn?

SOPHY: Isn't he the guy who says science is subjective?

PHIL: That's a totally different guy. Name starts with an F, I think. I'm not even sure how to pronounce it! Kuhn just says that science is *not totally objective*. Scientists interpret data through paradigms, or ways of looking at the world.

SOPHY: Oh, right, and the paradigms shift sometimes.

PHIL: Yes. A paradigm shift is a scientific revolution. Usually science just presumes a paradigm—like Newtonian physics, then Einsteinian, then later quantum mechanics—and they work with that, trying to solve puzzles using the paradigm.

SOPHY: Okay.

PHIL: Sometimes, unsolvable puzzles pile up, and new, younger scientists start thinking outside the box—meaning that they try thinking with a new paradigm. When that paradigm becomes dominant, a revolution has happened.

SOPHY: And what's that got to do with logical positivism?

PHIL: Well, the positivists thought that science was totally objective, and Kuhn sort of undermined that.

SOPHY: Oh, okay.

PHIL: But there's a bit more.

SOPHY: Like what?

PHIL: Kuhn's idea of science, as puzzle-solving within a paradigm punctuated by revolutionary paradigm shifts, is a totally different idea of science from the logical positivists' idea. It's not just the lack of complete objectivity. It's also abandoning verifiability as the criterion of science.

SOPHY: Oh, so Kuhn is like Popper on that one?

PHIL: Right—they both disagree with logical positivism on that one! But Kuhn is different from Popper in thinking science isn't totally objective. Actually, Kuhn believes in something like verification and *also* something like falsification.

SOPHY: So . . .

PHIL: So philosophy of science is *complicated*.

SOPHY: And what do *you* think?

PHIL: Nothing if I can avoid it! Not without another shot of caffeine, a pen, and a clean piece of paper. Then I might think *something*. Right now, I'm just sure I think this is part of the story of how logical positivism died.

SOPHY: Okay, but do we have to be skeptics?

PHIL: Well, *I'm* not. Why do you ask?

SOPHY: Well, what's the solution to the problem of induction, or the problem of those principles you were talking about?

PHIL: The ones that we need to accept if we're going to learn anything from experience that can't be learned from experience themselves?

SOPHY: Yeah, those.

PHIL: As far as I can tell, there's only one alternative.

SOPHY: What's that.

PHIL: Reject extreme empiricism. We don't have to think that knowledge can come from experience and experience *only*.

SOPHY: Okay, but how? Why? What sort of epistemology would that be?

PHIL: Honestly, I don't know for sure, and I'm not even sure I *care*. I need more time to figure this out. I don't have my own definition of knowledge. But there's this YouTube philosopher I know who might have an opinion.

SOPHY: Oh, that guy. Right.

PHIL: The important thing is that there are alternative epistemologies, like from Kant and Thomas Reid.

SOPHY: Okay, so where does that leave us?

PHIL: You tell me.

SOPHY: Okay, fine. I'll try to summarize. One of the reasons people think faith and reason are separate is that faith can't be verified, and everything reasonable can.

PHIL: And what do we call that?

SOPHY: The verifiability criterion.

PHIL: Is that really the verifiability criterion?

SOPHY: Well, I guess not. The logical positivists had a verifiability criterion for *meaning*.

PHIL: Right. And they were wrong. Otherwise, induction and the uniformity of nature would be meaningless. And there goes science.

SOPHY: Right. Because at least one of those principles has to be known independently of experience for us to be able to learn anything about the world from experience.

PHIL: And so that principle, whichever it is, can't be learned from experience.

SOPHY: But which is it?

PHIL: I don't know. I think that logically it has to be one or the other. I don't care which. Maybe it's both.

SOPHY: And so that's what's wrong with logical positivism.

PHIL: Right.

SOPHY: And Bertrand Russell said so too?

PHIL: Right.

SOPHY: But other people have other problems with logical positivism?

PHIL: Right.

SOPHY: Okay. But why are we talking about logical positivism and a verifiability criterion of meaning? So what if it's wrong?

PHIL: I don't follow.

SOPHY: Wasn't the point of the thing people say about faith and reason that reason has to be verifiable or whatever? Not *meaning*, but *reason*?

PHIL: Well, the point is that science has a foundation.

SOPHY: You mean induction, or the uniformity of nature. *That's* the foundation?

PHIL: Right. Now, if we say that that foundation is meaningless, then there goes science.

SOPHY: Right.

PHIL: So what if we say that that foundation is *meaningful,* but not *reasonable,* or *meaningful* but not *known*?

SOPHY: Oh, I get it. *That* kills science, too. If the foundations of science are unreasonable, or unknown, then nothing we learn from science is reasonable, or nothing is known.

PHIL: You got it.

SOPHY: Okay, so verifiability doesn't make a good criterion for knowledge, or for rationality, *or* for meaning. Okay, but so what? What does that have to do with faith? I mean—if this is all correct, then it shows that we need at least one truth to be meaningful, reasonable, and knowable without verifiability.

PHIL: Right.

SOPHY: But *just one*. Maybe faith is different.

PHIL: You mean maybe induction or the uniformity of nature is the *only* thing that doesn't need to be verifiable.

SOPHY: Right!

PHIL: Well, sometimes people object to faith because they say it isn't verifiable. My point is that that doesn't *matter*. The objection is that everything true, or meaningful, or knowable, or reasonable has to be verifiable—but that objection has a false premise! *Not* everything needs to be verifiable.

SOPHY: But so what? The objection can still work. You just have to modify it a little. Other than these one or two foundational truths, maybe everything *else* needs to be verifiable.

PHIL: Well, yeah. That objection *might* work. At least you and I haven't found any evidence against it. But . . . but three things.

SOPHY: Bring 'em on.

PHIL: One: Hardly anyone makes *that* objection.

SOPHY: But they *could*.

PHIL: Fair enough—they *could*. Two: If Popper or Kuhn are right, it's not verifiability as such that matters. What matters is testing in experience. By verification, falsification, good puzzle-solving, or whatever *exactly* science does to test things.

SOPHY: Okay.

PHIL: And three: Maybe there's a way to know God in the same way.

SOPHY: You mean the same way we know *induction*? You mean *without evidence*?

PHIL: I mean that. Well, *I* don't necessarily mean that. But I know of a philosopher who does—Alvin Plantinga.

SOPHY: Okay, let's hear it.

PHIL: Not yet. I gotta figure out where we go from here.

SOPHY: Okay. Are we at least done with all this philosophy of science?

PHIL: I think so. For the moment at least.

SOPHY: That seems like a big detour.

PHIL: It was. Maybe it's good practice for thinking through epistemology. But I guess there's another reason.

SOPHY: What's that?

PHIL: Logical positivism is pretty much dead in philosophy. It went from being dominant all over philosophy departments in American and Britain to being maybe the biggest flop in the history of philosophy ever.

SOPHY: Impressive.

PHIL: But outside of philosophy it's still very influential. Especially the idea that meaning or reason or knowledge always—*always*—requires verifiability. And some of the things that followed from that. Like emotivism.

SOPHY: What's that?

PHIL: A topic for another day.

SOPHY: Okay, fine. But what was your point?

PHIL: The point was that maybe it was important to get a good picture of what logical positivism was and what it would mean for faith if it were true, but also why it's wrong.

SOPHY: And what would it mean for faith if it were true?

PHIL: That faith is meaningless. And now that I think of it—one *more* thing.

SOPHY: Okay, fine.

PHIL: If logical positivism is right, then religious claims are meaningless. So the claim that God exists is meaningless.

SOPHY: Right.

PHIL: And the denial of a meaningless claim is meaningless. The positivists pointed this out too.

SOPHY: Okay.

PHIL: So religion is meaningless. And so is *atheism*.

SOPHY: What? Why. Oh, wait—okay, I see that.

PHIL: According to logical positivism anyway. But here's something Plantinga mentions in passing, in his talk, "Advice to Christian Philosophers." If logical positivism is right then people who think they believe in God are wrong.

SOPHY: Obviously.

PHIL: But not wrong about *God*. They couldn't be, because there's no religious claim to be wrong about.

SOPHY: Okay.

PHIL: They're wrong when they think they *believe* in God.

SOPHY: Right.

PHIL: So the Pope isn't really Catholic, if logical positivism is right.

SOPHY: Ha! That's funny.

PHIL: People who believe in God don't exist. No Christian, no Muslim, no one at all believes in God, if logical positivism is right. So normal atheists deny the existence of God. *Logical positivists deny the existence of Christians!*

SOPHY: And of actual atheists too!

PHIL: Yep.

SOPHY: Yeah, that *can't* be right.

PHIL: So back to faith and reason?

SOPHY: Yep.

PHIL: What's interesting is the different definitions of faith people use.

SOPHY: Yeah. Like one person thinks faith is justified by reason. Another thinks faith is just separate from reason.

PHIL: And another one thinks that faith is downright *un*reasonable.

SOPHY: Yeah. That's not the same thing as *separate*, is it?

PHIL: It's not. If faith and reason are separate and have nothing to do with each other, then faith can't be unreasonable.

SOPHY: Right. How can faith be unreasonable if it doesn't even answer to reason?

PHIL: Yeah. If faith doesn't answer to reason, then it's not reasonable *or* unreasonable. It's neither.

SOPHY: So something can be reasonable, or unreasonable, or neither.

PHIL: That's what I think. And if it's *neither*, then there's still a question about it.

SOPHY: What's that?

PHIL: Is reason even *relevant* to it?

SOPHY: But if reason is relevant to it, then isn't it reasonable?

PHIL: Not necessarily. It depends on what reason means. I guess we should talk about that.

SOPHY: Do we have to define *reason* now? Aren't we talking about the definition of *faith*?

PHIL: I think we'd better do both.

SOPHY: Sure, whatever.

PHIL: Okay, let's start again. I think the first question we should ask about something like faith is whether it answers to reason.

SOPHY: Okay.

PHIL: And if it does, we ask how it measures up.

SOPHY: Right. If it measures up well, it's reasonable. If it doesn't, then it's unreasonable.

PHIL: Right. But if it doesn't answer to reason, then we ask whether it has anything at all do with reason.

SOPHY: I still don't understand how reason can be relevant to something that doesn't answer to reason.

PHIL: If reason points the way. In one thing I read somewhere—I think it was in Kierkegaard—I picked up this analogy from romance.

SOPHY: Okay.

PHIL: Say, maybe a few years from now, I'm in love with some girl. I'm thinking about marrying her, and it seems reasonable to do that. But I can't be completely certain.

SOPHY: Why not?

PHIL: Well, maybe it won't turn out well for some reason.

SOPHY: Maybe she's secretly a vampire.

PHIL: Yeah, or a robot.

SOPHY: For you? I picture a vampire.

PHIL: Maybe so. Either way, I have to make a decision, and she wants 100% of a ring, and I'm just old-fashioned enough to believe in marriage as a total commitment.

SOPHY: Yeah. I always suspected you were secretly very romantic.

PHIL: Well, don't tell anyone my secret.

SOPHY: My lips are sealed.

PHIL: So reason might be able to tell me that it's likely that I should give her a ring.

SOPHY: But it can't give 100% proof that it's the best thing.

PHIL: Right. I have to take a leap beyond what reason can fully justify.

SOPHY: Okay, so reason tells you that you should *probably* do this, but it can't give it 100% proof. Reason is *relevant* to love, but love doesn't *answer* to reason.

PHIL: More or less.

SOPHY: So that's what you mean when you say that reason could be relevant to something that doesn't answer to it.

PHIL: Yeah, that's what I mean. I think the best word is *transcend*. If faith is not reasonable it might have nothing to do with reason at all. Or it might transcend reason.

SOPHY: So we have four options.

PHIL: Right. Faith might be reasonable, unreasonable, or have nothing to do with reason. Or it might *transcend* reason.

SOPHY: But what is *reason*?

PHIL: And what is *faith*?

SOPHY: Okay, let's try some definitions.

PHIL: I think reason can mean a few things. Sometimes reason just means the things our minds do when they're working properly.

SOPHY: Okay.

PHIL: Sometimes reason means believing based on good evidence. And sometimes reason means perfect knowledge or total understanding, or complete comprehension.

SOPHY: Reason at its best?

PHIL: Yeah. So sometimes when people say that faith isn't the same thing as reason, I think they mean that theology involves doctrines we can't fully understand.

SOPHY: Like the Christian doctrine of the incarnation, or the doctrine of the Trinity.

PHIL: Right!

SOPHY: But sometimes people say faith isn't reason, and they mean something different. Like my classmates who think faith involves belief without evidence, or belief *against* the evidence.

PHIL: Right. Like the quote William James attributes to a schoolboy. Faith is believing something when you know it ain't true.

SOPHY: So which is the best definition of faith? What actually *is* faith?

PHIL: Check a dictionary. You'll probably find at least two definitions.

SOPHY: Which two?

PHIL: Well, belief without good evidence is one that gets used often enough when people talk about faith.

SOPHY: Okay, is *that* the right definition of faith?

PHIL: Well, it's not *wrong*. It's one definition. But it's not the only one. There's another one.

SOPHY: What's that?

PHIL: Faith means trust.

SOPHY: Just that?

PHIL: That's the idea. There are Greek and Latin words too that mean the same thing. *Pistis* and *fides*. They mean *trust*.

SOPHY: And that's what faith is?

PHIL: It's another definition. It's not a bad definition. It's also much closer to the idea of faith in the books I've been reading.

SOPHY: Okay, so what about trust and reason? How do they connect, or disconnect, or whatever?

PHIL: That depends. The Kool-Aid people trusted . . . that guy.

SOPHY: Jim Jones?

PHIL: Yeah, *that* guy. And was that trust rational?

SOPHY: Not at all.

PHIL: And every day millions of people trust people who aren't trustworthy.

SOPHY: Like politicians

PHIL: Like politicians. Well, lots of them. Maybe not all of them.

SOPHY: Most of them

PHIL: Yeah, probably. *Nearly* all.

SOPHY: And salespeople.

PHIL: Them too sometimes. *Lots* of people *lots* of the time.

SOPHY: Trust is dangerous.

PHIL: It is. But it's perfectly rational. One of Augustine's points.

SOPHY: Explain.

PHIL: Whose face is on the dollar bill in my pocket?

SOPHY: How do I know there's a dollar bill in your pocket?

PHIL: Trust me.

SOPHY: Okay.

PHIL: And whose face is on it?

SOPHY: George Washington.

PHIL: And who's he?

SOPHY: The first president of the United States.

PHIL: How do you know that?

SOPHY: *Everyone* knows that.

PHIL: Have you met him? Did you see him take the oath of office?

SOPHY: Obviously not.

PHIL: So how do you know? Everyone knows, but *how* do they know?

SOPHY: Maybe everyone knows because everyone knows.

PHIL: Maybe *you* know because everyone knows. But not *everyone* can know that way. The knowledge had to start *somewhere*. Evidence has to *come from* somewhere.

SOPHY: Okay, fine. I guess it comes . . . from historians.

PHIL: And where do *they* get it from?

SOPHY: From history.

PHIL: That just means what happened. But how do they *know* what happened?

SOPHY: Okay, I get it. They know it from testimony from other historians, from written records, from old newspapers, old letters, all the boring old documents historians have to work with.

PHIL: Yeah, that's how we know history. Socrates, now—we know about him from Xenophon and Aristotle and Plato.

SOPHY: So your point is we know by trust.

PHIL: Yeah. History gets a little help from archaeology sometimes, but mostly we know history by trusting reliable testimony.

SOPHY: Okay, so that kind of trust is rational. What does that have to do with religious faith?

PHIL: Maybe a lot. But that's not the point.

SOPHY: So what *is* the point?

PHIL: Well, I guess there are *lots* of points. The first point is Augustine's point that faith, or trust, is rational and necessary.

SOPHY: Okay, it is in *history*, but so what? We don't have to rely on trust for anything else. In fact, it's a fallacy, right? Appeal to authority is one of the fallacies in the logic textbooks.

PHIL: Nope. Not in the best ones anyway.

SOPHY: Come again?

PHIL: A good logic textbook will tell you that an appeal to an *unqualified* authority is a fallacy. Appeals to authority are not necessarily fallacious.

SOPHY: Example?

PHIL: If you're not sure how to spell chartreuse, what do you do?

SOPHY: So guys do know about tertiary colors?

PHIL: Not *this* guy. I think it's some kind of red. But I do know how to *spell* it.

SOPHY: Well, I don't. But I'm pretty sure of the first few letters, so I could probably find it in the dictionary.

PHIL: And *I* could check it to learn what it *means*.

SOPHY: It doesn't mean red.

PHIL: I trust you. You and the dictionary are both reliable authorities on that sort of thing.

SOPHY: Okay, fine. Anything else?

PHIL: Augustine emphasizes geography. You know Tokyo exists, but you've never been there. You trust people who have, and people who make maps and so on.

SOPHY: Fair enough.

PHIL: And Augustine's best example is your parents. You know who they are by trusting them. In fact, your father only knows he's your father by trusting your mother, and even *she* can't know she's your mother without trusting the hospital nurse not to switch the babies.

SOPHY: Ouch. Okay, fine. Well, fine for Augustine. But not fine now. Now we can do DNA tests.

PHIL: Do most people need that to know who their parents are?

SOPHY: No, but the point is that now we don't have *only* trust. Now we can do a DNA test without relying on trust.

PHIL: Okay, but are you doing the test yourself?

SOPHY: I see your point. But I could *learn* how to do it.

PHIL: How would you learn without a teacher?

SOPHY: You're right—I would have to trust my teacher! Unless I became a genetic scientist myself.

PHIL: But, even *then*, you'd have to confirm all the science *yourself*. If you want to learn who your parents are without trusting anyone, you have to learn how to do a DNA test *and* do a DNA test, *but also* become a genetic scientist and do *all the experiments* that support genetic science.

SOPHY: It's worse than that.

PHIL: How so?

SOPHY: Science relies on repeatable experiments.

PHIL: You're right.

SOPHY: So I would have to do the experiments *twice*.

PHIL: It looks like it. So you'll have to waste your whole life reinventing genetic science, and then it really will be a waste unless other people trust *you*.

SOPHY: But scientists do test things.

PHIL: Yes, that's true.

SOPHY: Scientists verify.

PHIL: They verify, but they also build on each other's work. They trust, and verify. There's no escaping trust.

SOPHY: Okay, I'm convinced that trust is okay.

PHIL: More than okay. It's rational, practical, necessary. It's a big part of how we get most of our knowledge. I like how James puts it. He says knowledge is for the most part a credit system. The whole thing works because we can cash in, by checking for error and verifying things. And everyone has to verify *some* things, and probably everything *should* be verified by *someone*. But most of us most of the time just pass knowledge around by trust. That's normal—even in science.

SOPHY: Okay, sure. But verifying matters, and you can do that in science. But you can't do that in religion.

PHIL: Why not?

SOPHY: Because religion isn't a science. It's not empirical.

PHIL: Yeah, people say that.

SOPHY: What do you mean, people say that? It's the truth, isn't it?

PHIL: Maybe, maybe not.

SOPHY: Let me guess. You have philosophers up your sleeve who say otherwise.

PHIL: More or less. I try to keep them in my head.

SOPHY: Okay, bring it on.

PHIL: Well, for one thing, there are people who write books about religious experience and knowledge. Richard Swinburne, William Alston, Kai-man Kwan. In earlier days there were William James and John Dewey, who wanted an entirely empirical religion.

SOPHY: Okay, that's interesting.

PHIL: What really impresses me is these five guys I recently noticed.

SOPHY: We're talking about philosophy, right? Not food.

PHIL: Yes, philosophy—not French fries. You've heard of at least two of them. And they all say that their religions are empirical. And we're not talking little religions here no one's ever heard of.

SOPHY: Really? I haven't heard any of this.

PHIL: But you've heard of the Dalai Lama.

SOPHY: Seriously?

PHIL: Oh yeah. And C. S. Lewis.

SOPHY: Really?

PHIL: Oh yeah. A Christian philosopher and a Buddhist philosopher. Representing their religions and explaining their relationship to modern empiricism. And they say their religions are *empirical*.

SOPHY: No way.

PHIL: Oh yeah. It's been right there in *Mere Christianity* all this time—Book 4, chapter 2.

SOPHY: And where does the Dalai Lama say this?

PHIL: In a speech to neuroscientists.

SOPHY: Really?

PHIL: Yeah, I read it on the internet.

SOPHY: And who else you got?

PHIL: Whom.

SOPHY: Oh, just answer the question!

PHIL: Fine. Allama Iqbal, an Indian Islamic philosopher. I looked him up online too. He has a rare distinction: He has an international airport named after him, in Pakistan.

SOPHY: Awesome. And he says Islam is empirical too, huh?

PHIL: Yep. In his book *The Reconstruction of Religious Thought in Islam*.

SOPHY: Okay, keep going.

PHIL: Sarvepalli Radhakrishnan, once the president of India.

SOPHY: A philosopher-king?

PHIL: Right on. And he represents Hinduism. In his book *The Hindu View of Life*. And then we have a Jewish philosopher, Eliezer Berkovits. In his book *God, Man, and History*.

SOPHY: And if you're sticking to the same pattern you're about to tell me that they say their religions are empirical too.

PHIL: That they do.

SOPHY: Okay, so Option 1: They're just wrong.

PHIL: Maybe. But then C. S. Lewis doesn't understand Christianity. And the Dalai Lama doesn't understand Buddhism, and so on.

SOPHY: So we go to Option 2: Maybe they're right.

PHIL: Maybe.

SOPHY: But what does that mean? How can religion be empirical?

PHIL: Well, empiricism can mean several things.

SOPHY: Right. Empiricism is the tradition in European enlightenment philosophy with Hobbes, Locke, and Hume.

PHIL: Right. That's *British* empiricism. Empiricism can also mean the theory they were interested in—that all our ideas come from sensory experience.

SOPHY: Okay, so it can mean a tradition in philosophy, or that tradition's main idea.

PHIL: Or several ideas. That's just the main idea of British empiricism. Then there's the idea we talked about earlier from Hume—the idea that all knowledge comes from experience and experience only.

SOPHY: Right.

PHIL: And then there's just the more general idea that we get knowledge from experience.

SOPHY: Okay.

PHIL: And one more thing.

Sophy: What's that?

Phil: It doesn't have to be sensory experience. That was the idea of the *British* empiricists. But some people who count as empiricists think not all experience has to be sensory. Like William James and John Dewey. That's how they try to be better empiricists than the classical British empiricists.

Sophy: What else is there in experience?

Phil: Mental experience, religious experience. Everything, really. History and literature even. All life is experience. But who says all life is just the experience of the five senses?

Sophy: The *empiricists* say that.

Phil: The original *British* empiricists.

Sophy: But not *all* empiricists. Okay. And so these religious philosophers of yours think religious experience counts, like James and Dewey?

Phil: You got it.

Sophy: Okay, so tell me about these five religious empiricist philosophers of yours.

Phil: Okay, here's the short version. The Dalai Lama says Buddhism gets its ideas from reason, tradition, and experience, but mostly experience, and experience overrules the others.

Sophy: Okay.

Phil: Radhakrishnan says Hinduism gets its ideas from religious experience. The Hindu Vedas, their most ancient scriptures, don't have any authoritative teachings as such. They're just the data of religious experience. Like the data a scientist records in the laboratory.

Sophy: Interesting. So the theories don't matter as much as the data?

Phil: Not exactly. We get theories from interpreting the data. And the data by themselves aren't much. We need both.

Sophy: The data *aren't* much? Oh, right—you think the word *data* is plural.

Phil: It's better Latin. That makes better English.

Sophy: Whatever.

Phil: And he says the teachings of Hinduism can be revised. Every teaching should be tested in two steps.

Sophy: Yeah?

Phil: First, logic. Second, send that theory back to experience for more testing.

Sophy: Interesting.

PHIL: And Iqbal is similar.

SOPHY: The Islamic philosopher?

PHIL: Yes, him. He says knowledge comes from interpreting experience.

SOPHY: Okay.

PHIL: There's sensory experience, and interpretations of it. That's where we get science.

SOPHY: Okay.

PHIL: But there's also religious experience. I think he actually cites James on this one.

SOPHY: So it's also a source of knowledge?

PHIL: Or at least it *can* be. And Lewis is weirdly similar.

SOPHY: Weird, huh?

PHIL: Weird, awesome—or something. Well, actually, maybe Berkovits first.

SOPHY: Fine.

PHIL: He talks about the experience at Mount Sinai, about the exodus and the giving of the Torah and the founding of the Jewish people.

SOPHY: Okay.

PHIL: The facts of Judaism—and they're real facts. They are facts of religious experience, and historical facts.

SOPHY: But even if I believed that, it was all a long time ago.

PHIL: Berkovits also says God can *still* be experienced. He says it's an important insight from Judaism, that God is the living God, a God we can still experience.

SOPHY: Hmm.

PHIL: And that's also like Lewis.

SOPHY: Your favorite.

PHIL: Well, he's one of them.

SOPHY: So what does he say?

PHIL: C. S. Lewis says that Christianity has its origins in experience. Specifically, in the historical events of the gospel.

SOPHY: So, yeah. That's like Berkovits.

PHIL: Right on. And like Iqbal.

SOPHY: How so?

PHIL: Iqbal says knowledge comes from experience plus interpretation.

SOPHY: Yeah, I remember.

PHIL: Lewis says the early Christians got knowledge of the Trinity pretty much the same way, from their experiences of God and then working out what it meant.

SOPHY: Cool.

PHIL: And something else where Lewis is also like Radhakrishnan and, again, like Berkovits.

SOPHY: Bring it on.

PHIL: The living God can still be experienced. We can take our theories from old religious experience and, to some extent at least, try them out now.

SOPHY: How does that work?

PHIL: In church, basically. Experience of God requires good character, and it's also a communal thing. Lewis says theology is an experimental science, and the laboratory instrument for seeing God is the human community loving and living properly.

SOPHY: Okay, something's bothering me with all this. What if religious experience turned up evidence against the old theology?

PHIL: What if it does? We can revise our theology, can't we?

SOPHY: But religion is dogmatic.

PHIL: Okay, let's talk about that. And I guess I left out one thing.

SOPHY: Okay.

PHIL: I forgot to go over the standards of empiricism.

SOPHY: What do you mean?

PHIL: If we get knowledge from experience, we should act accordingly.

SOPHY: Oh, you're talking about epistemology again—the rules for rational belief.

PHIL: Yeah, that. The empirical rules you find when you study these five guys are three.

SOPHY: Five guys, three rules.

PHIL: Rule One: Get your beliefs from experience.

SOPHY: Okay.

PHIL: They all have that rule, and they say their religions get their knowledge that way.

SOPHY: So far, so good.

PHIL: Rule Two: Try to test your beliefs in future experience.

SOPHY: Okay, no problem.

PHIL: Rule Three: Be willing to change your beliefs if future experience turns up evidence against them.

SOPHY: Yeah, *there's* my problem. Religion isn't like science. Religion is about dogmatic belief.

PHIL: Is it?

SOPHY: Isn't it?

PHIL: The Dalai Lama and Radhakrishnan say no. Not to mention James and Dewey. Then there's Unitarianism. Maybe Confucianism?

SOPHY: Okay, so *some* religions don't have dogma.

PHIL: Not just some. If those guys are right, Hinduism and Buddhism don't have dogmas. That's a big deal.

SOPHY: Yeah, but the Abrahamic religions all have dogmas. Isn't that a bigger deal?

PHIL: Fair enough. *They're* dogmatic. Well, usually.

SOPHY: So they can't have Rule Three.

PHIL: Why not?

SOPHY: I shouldn't have to explain this. Rule Three and dogmatism are just direct contradictions.

PHIL: Check the dictionary.

SOPHY: Say what?

PHIL: Dogma can mean different things. *Sometimes* it means what you're talking about—unquestioning belief or absolute commitment or whatever. Yeah, *that* sort of dogma has a problem with Rule Three.

SOPHY: And Rule Two.

PHIL: Why is that?

SOPHY: If you can't change your beliefs, why test them?

PHIL: You already know that.

SOPHY: Do I?

PHIL: You said I was a romantic.

SOPHY: Yeah, so?

PHIL: So, there's your answer. I can learn from experience that I should marry some girl.

SOPHY: She needs a name!

PHIL: Arwen.

SOPHY: That's perfect!

PHIL: And maybe I think it should be an absolute commitment to . . . Arwen—till death parts us. But it's the nature of the belief that it ought to be *tested*.

SOPHY: Okay, that's beautiful.

PHIL: But there's another kind of dogmatism: official or established or settled belief. That can actually be tentative.

SOPHY: So Rule Three is okay for that kind of dogmatism?

PHIL: Rule Three is okay.

SOPHY: Okay, so maybe if a Christian is dogmatic only in that way, he can have all three of your empirical rules.

PHIL: They're not *mine*.

SOPHY: Okay, those five guys' rules.

PHIL: And if they're *right*, the *right* rules.

SOPHY: Okay, fine. Maybe even the *right* empirical rules. But how are you supposed to *test* religious beliefs? You can't put God in a laboratory.

PHIL: You can't put a herd of elephants in there either, but we still study them.

SOPHY: True.

PHIL: But you're right about God. This is one of the points of James and Lewis.

SOPHY: So an American pragmatist and a British Anglican agree about something.

PHIL: Lots of things. This one is a really neat insight.

SOPHY: Bring it on.

PHIL: Knowing God is not like knowing *rocks*. You can just study a rock. It's totally passive.

SOPHY: Yes.

PHIL: A plant is like that, but maybe easier to damage.

SOPHY: Okay.

PHIL: And an animal might actually run away from you while you're trying to learn about it.

SOPHY: Okay.

PHIL: But can you really know *a person* without some cooperation on his part?

SOPHY: No, you really can't.

PHIL: Well, God is like that. Anyway, that's how Lewis puts it. And he goes on to explain that God cooperates with us in letting us know him only under the right conditions.

SOPHY: What conditions?

PHIL: We have to be *good*. And we have to be *together*. The church living in love and holiness is the laboratory instrument for seeing God.

SOPHY: But why doesn't God just show himself to all of us?

PHIL: I think Lewis's idea is that it just doesn't work that way, and we shouldn't expect it to. That's not how knowing works. We can only know a thing in the right way. We see colors with our eyes, we hear sounds with our ears. That's how knowing colors or sounds works. And if we want to know *God* in the right way, then all this morality and love and church stuff is the right way.

SOPHY: Interesting.

PHIL: And James's point, I think, would be that God is a person and might require a little faith before we can know him. Some willingness to trust.

SOPHY: Why is that?

PHIL: Would you expect that to work with regular people?

SOPHY: I'm not sure what you mean.

PHIL: Let me see if I can remember how James puts it. Imagine I go through life not trusting anyone about anything. I expect proof of everyone's goodwill beforehand. No willingness to meet anyone halfway; they have to prove themselves to me before I trust them at all.

SOPHY: You make yourself sound like . . . kind of a jerk.

PHIL: Yeah, I probably would be.

SOPHY: Okay, so we should be willing to trust people.

PHIL: Yeah, that's it. We should at least be *willing*. What if I'm at a new job and my coworker so-and-so is a decent guy I can work with, but I don't believe that until he proves it?

SOPHY: Yeah, you still sound like a bit of a jerk.

PHIL: But if I'm less of a jerk, then I'll meet him halfway. I believe it, or I believe it's possible at least. But I show some *willingness* to believe.

SOPHY: Hang on. I think you're really on to something. If you believe it, it's more likely to actually be true. I think I see what you mean.

PHIL: Not me. James.

SOPHY: Okay, *James* is on to something. So, if you believe he's a good guy and a good coworker, how will that affect the way you act around him?

PHIL: Right on. I'll probably treat him better.

SOPHY: Yeah. So how will he respond?

PHIL: He'll probably treat me better in return.

SOPHY: So maybe he'll become more decent, because you *thought* he was decent.

PHIL: Maybe.

SOPHY: And even if he was decent to begin with he'll be an easier guy to work with.

PHIL: Yep. That's how I know about his character—by being willing to believe. That's James's point. He actually says faith in a fact can sometimes *create the fact*.

SOPHY: But even if it was always true, you'll still know it better because you believed it.

PHIL: Yes! That's why James also says that faith in a fact can *create its own verification*.

SOPHY: Okay, so I'm convinced that this makes sense for *some* of our beliefs. But our beliefs don't create God.

PHIL: No. Well, maybe in some extreme version of process theology. But not for any form of Christianity or anything like that.

SOPHY: Okay, so I'm not sure I see James's point then.

PHIL: Say God exists and is benevolent.

SOPHY: Okay.

PHIL: And suppose God is personal, like our religions say.

SOPHY: Okay.

PHIL: Is God that much more accommodating than any person we know, or can we expect to act like antisocial jerks when it comes to God without any negative consequences?

SOPHY: How should I know? I haven't met him.

PHIL: Well, I have. But . . . but just suppose he's *not* more accommodating, and there *would* be consequences.

SOPHY: Consider it supposed.

PHIL: Then—well, then you tell me.

SOPHY: Then—then I guess we ought to be willing to meet God halfway.

PHIL: And faith in God, or at least some willingness to have faith before all the evidence comes in, might create its own verification.

SOPHY: Okay, I think I see James's point.

PHIL: But not his next point.

SOPHY: What's that?

PHIL: The faith-deniers want belief to follow evidence—always. They think it's a rule of logic.

SOPHY: Okay. And I guess you'll tell me it isn't.

PHIL: *James* will. Actually, *he* says the *logic* itself tells us that.

SOPHY: Why?

PHIL: Because of what we just talked about. With some truths, some of their evidence follows belief. That's just how reality works—when reality is *personal.*

SOPHY: And since God, if there is one, is a personal reality—

PHIL: —faith without waiting for all the evidence to come in is logical.

SOPHY: Interesting. But that's just about why it's *okay* to believe, right? Is there any reason I *should* believe? And *what* should I believe *if* I should believe?

PHIL: It's permissible. But is it required?

SOPHY: Exactly.

PHIL: Well, James only gets us as far as permissibility of whatever belief we're interested in. People like Lewis go farther.

SOPHY: Okay, so why should we believe according to people like that?

PHIL: The first thing is to note that history is a source of knowledge.

SOPHY: Haven't we been over this with Augustine?

PHIL: Yep. Just a reminder.

SOPHY: Okay.

PHIL: And the next thing is that the Abrahamic religions rely on historical claims.

SOPHY: I think I see where you're going with this, but I think I have an objection.

PHIL: Bring it.

SOPHY: It's not a historical claim that God exists, or that there's three of them.

PHIL: *One* of them—three *persons.*

SOPHY: Right. Or *one* person. Or whatever. The different religions say different things.

PHIL: Okay, fair enough—some claims they rely on are not historical. But some *are.*

SOPHY: Okay, like . . . the death and resurrection of Jesus.

PHIL: Yes, for Christianity.

SOPHY: And for Judaism, the exodus and the stuff at Mount Sinai.

PHIL: Which is also important to Christianity. The Bible starts with the Torah, you know.

SOPHY: Okay, there's some overlap with the historical claims.

PHIL: Yup.

SOPHY: And the story of Gabriel revealing the Qur'an in Islam.

PHIL: Yes.

SOPHY: Any other major ones?

PHIL: Maybe some stuff about King David, for example. And the exile to Babylon. If we're going to be thorough.

SOPHY: Some other time. What about the angel Moroni and the golden plates?

PHIL: Key historical claims for Mormonism.

SOPHY: Which you classify as separate from Christianity.

PHIL: Yes, the fourth major Abrahamic religion—that's how I tend to think of it.

SOPHY: I have my doubts, but maybe another time.

PHIL: Cool.

SOPHY: So what's the next point?

PHIL: So, history can be a source of knowledge, and there are historical claims these religions rely on.

SOPHY: Okay.

PHIL: Is historical knowledge *a priori*?

SOPHY: You mean independent of experience? No, it couldn't be.

PHIL: So it's empirical?

SOPHY: Yeah, I guess it is.

PHIL: *A posteriori*.

SOPHY: But not the best kind. It's hard to test without a time machine.

PHIL: Fair enough. But that doesn't mean it's not empirical, since it comes from experience.

SOPHY: Fair enough.

PHIL: And it doesn't mean it can't be tested at all.

SOPHY: How so?

PHIL: Well, there's archaeology for a start.

SOPHY: Okay, that's fair. You can verify some history with archaeology.

PHIL: And I think falsification with historical claims is a possibility.

SOPHY: Okay, like how?

Phil: Well, Augustine says he spent some time at a place called Cassiciacum, near Milan, in 386 AD.

Sophy: Okay.

Phil: Say we find an inscription on a stone at the modern-day site of Cassiciacum, and it says "Augustine was here, at the villa of Verecundus, year of our Lord 386."

Sophy: If anything, that's verification, not falsification.

Phil: Right. But say we find the same inscription at the remains of a villa near Rome, not near Milan.

Sophy: Okay, but that's not exactly perfect proof that Augustine was there instead of the other place.

Phil: I don't think that matters.

Sophy: Sure it does! It's not exactly a black swan.

Phil: But what *is* a black swan? Very little falsification is all that cut and dry. The point is that it's data inconsistent with a theory. If the probability that that data is legitimate and that we aren't somehow misunderstanding its significance is high, then that's good enough in science, and it's good enough in history.

Sophy: Okay, sure.

Phil: Okay, maybe an easier example.

Sophy: Okay.

Phil: How about the theory that Confucius built the pyramids?

Sophy: That's silly. No one thinks that.

Phil: But it's a possible theory about history, isn't it?

Sophy: Okay, it's *possible*.

Phil: And why don't we accept it?

Sophy: Because there's no evidence for it.

Phil: And?

Sophy: Okay, and there's a bunch of evidence *against* it.

Phil: Yeah. We can *disprove* it.

Sophy: So it's falsifiable.

Phil: As far as I can tell, more or less.

Sophy: And that means . . .

Phil: Well, I think it means that some religious claims can be verified or falsified, at least in principle.

SOPHY: But *how many*? I mean, that's not about the existence of God, or about the Golden Rule, or . . .

PHIL: Thousands of them.

SOPHY: Come again?

PHIL: How many historical claims are there in those books? Like claims about where Paul went, or where Jesus went, or who the kings of Judah were, or about the Nephites.

SOPHY: Okay. Lots.

PHIL: And those are claims that are part of the religion.

SOPHY: But some people don't believe all of them.

PHIL: But some historical claims are essential to some religions.

SOPHY: Yeah, but not that many.

PHIL: And how many of those historical claims do some people believe just because they're in those books?

SOPHY: Okay, there's a lot of *that*.

PHIL: How many?

SOPHY: All of them. By *some* believers. Not all believers.

PHIL: Fair enough.

SOPHY: But just because some historical things can be tested doesn't mean we should believe all historical claims.

PHIL: Definitely not. We should believe a few, if we have good evidence for them.

SOPHY: What sort of evidence?

PHIL: Historical. What else?

SOPHY: But we're talking about *religious* claims, right? Like the resurrection?

PHIL: Yeah.

SOPHY: But belief in the resurrection is not based on evidence, is it?

PHIL: Who says?

SOPHY: I don't know—lots of people!

PHIL: Okay, so maybe people *say* that. But so what? *I* believe in the resurrection because of the evidence. People do give evidence, too. There are books on the evidence by people like Andrew Loke, William Lane Craig, N. T. Wright, and Richard Bauckham.

SOPHY: Okay, so at least *some* people who believe in the resurrection . . .

PHIL: . . . believe because of evidence.

SOPHY: Okay, but how much can you prove with historical evidence? I mean, we're talking about *God* here. Can you prove God with history?

PHIL: Not directly, but good enough evidence for a miracle would show that it happened. That's not the whole story of any religion. But a miracle like the resurrection is a big part of a religion like Christianity, and indicates a real God of some sort.

SOPHY: Okay, but what do you say about people who say science disproves miracles and stuff like that?

PHIL: I think we should handle this question empirically.

SOPHY: Yeah, but you're a Christian.

PHIL: So?

SOPHY: So atheists say *they're* empirical and religious people *aren't*.

PHIL: Okay, but we're not talking about that.

SOPHY: What *are* we talking about?

PHIL: Whether we should handle the question of miracles empirically.

SOPHY: The atheists say *they* do.

PHIL: But they *don't*. At least not the ones you're talking about.

SOPHY: You mean the ones who say science disproves miracles?

PHIL: Yeah, them.

SOPHY: Why isn't that empirical?

PHIL: Here's what I think we should do *empirically*. I think a miracle is a suspension of the laws of physics, caused by God.

SOPHY: Okay.

PHIL: And I think we can let experience tell us what the laws of physics are. I also think we're not supposed to just assume that the laws of physics are absolute. We should let experience tell us whether those laws are ever suspended.

SOPHY: Okay, but that's what those atheists say they're doing.

PHIL: When do they say that? What do they say that about?

SOPHY: About miracles, like the resurrection.

PHIL: What do they say?

SOPHY: They say we don't have good evidence for those miracles.

PHIL: Why don't we?

SOPHY: Because a miracle needs evidence *so good* that . . . so good that evidence like that . . . would take a miracle!

PHIL: Then they're arguing against the historical evidence for a miracle on the grounds that no evidence is ever good enough?

SOPHY: Yeah, yeah I think so.

PHIL: So the evidence isn't good enough because . . . it isn't good enough?

SOPHY: Um . . . yeah.

PHIL: Then it's circular reasoning.

SOPHY: Hmm.

PHIL: And why does the evidence need to be so good anyway?

SOPHY: Because miracles are so unlikely.

PHIL: So unlikely that we can know *in advance* that the evidence for them is bad?

SOPHY: Yeah. At least . . . I *think* that's what they say.

PHIL: Then they're evaluating the evidence before they even look at the evidence. That's not empirical.

SOPHY: Interesting. I'm not convinced, but I'll try to give it some thought and get back to you.

PHIL: Look, I think it's fine to use it *as a conclusion*.

SOPHY: Explain, please.

PHIL: Well, I think we could argue that we have no experience of events which violate the laws of physics, and we have lots of experience of events which do *not*. And therefore the laws of physics can never be violated.

SOPHY: Yeah, what's wrong with that argument?

PHIL: Nothing that I know of. I just don't accept the premise. I think there *is* experience of miracles.

SOPHY: Oh, okay. Again, I'll have to think about that try to get back to you. But what about Hume?

PHIL: What?

SOPHY: This has something to do with Hume, right?

PHIL: Yeah, Hume doesn't believe in miracles, and I think his argument is not actually very empirical. He's categorizing the evidence for a miracle as not good enough before he even examines it. I think Robert Larmer's book on miracles is more to the point. We evaluate miracles empirically. If we have good historical or scientific evidence for them, we should believe in them.

SOPHY: Okay, so if all of this is right, what do you do with your buddy Plantinga?

PHIL: I only *wish* I knew him *that* well.

SOPHY: He says faith doesn't use evidence, right?

PHIL: More like it doesn't *need* any.

SOPHY: So it *can* use evidence?

PHIL: I think Plantinga's okay with that. He actually talks about maybe two dozen arguments for the existence of God that he thinks are pretty good.

SOPHY: So his point is that evidence for faith is good but not necessary.

PHIL: Right! He describes how we can have knowledge without evidence.

SOPHY: Wait. I thought he was going to say that faith doesn't *need* knowledge. Isn't that the point of saying that faith doesn't need *evidence*?

PHIL: Not even close.

SOPHY: Seriously?

PHIL: Seriously! His point is that *knowledge* does not need *evidence*. We've already seen this before.

SOPHY: We have?

PHIL: Yeah, we just talked about it.

SOPHY: We did? Oh, right—that *other* Hume thing! We know some things without evidence! We have to, or else we wouldn't be able to *have* any evidence.

PHIL: Right. Because evidence . . .

SOPHY: . . . has to come from somewhere! Okay, that's fine. But how does that get us to faith?

PHIL: It helps to know Chisholm.

SOPHY: Who?

PHIL: Roderick Chisholm, the epistemologist.

SOPHY: Oh, I think I know a YouTube channel that can help with that.

PHIL: Chisholm is good at explaining the idea of an epistemic criterion. Like what is the criterion for saying that a belief is knowledge?

SOPHY: Okay.

PHIL: Long story short, he thinks the best strategy is to start with examples of things we know we know, and look at them to figure out what they have in common.

SOPHY: And that's how we know what knowledge is?

PHIL: Yep. The rest of Plantinga is Thomas Reid.

SOPHY: Yeah?

PHIL: He looks at Reid's commonsense beliefs as examples of knowledge, and uses Chisholm's strategy on them.

SOPHY: Okay.

PHIL: And he looks at faith and concludes that it looks like people believe God exists in the same way we believe that a world outside the mind exists, that other minds exist, that the past exists, and so on.

SOPHY: And since those commonsense beliefs are knowledge...

PHIL: So is my belief that God exists—probably. Well, *if it's true*. There's a complication, but... I don't know that we have time for it.

SOPHY: Okay, that doesn't tell us how we actually know anything. What's the criterion if it's not *evidence*?

PHIL: Right. That's just the general strategy. The criterion for knowledge is that it comes from properly functioning faculties that are aimed at true belief. They also have to be reliable and working in the right environment—like not in the Matrix.

SOPHY: Okay, so we have faculties for knowing commonsense beliefs, and ...

PHIL: ... and a faculty for knowing God.

SOPHY: Do we all have this faculty?

PHIL: Yes, but it's not functioning properly in all of us. Because of sin.

SOPHY: Convenient.

PHIL: Look, there's a lot more there. This takes him more than a thousand pages, and it's a lot more than we have time for now!

SOPHY: Okay, fair enough. So the point of Plantinga is that we can know without evidence.

PHIL: Precisely. He gives us a model for how we might know God exists without evidence.

SOPHY: And that doesn't mean there *is* no evidence.

PHIL: No. It doesn't mean there aren't any good arguments, or that arguments would not be useful.

SOPHY: Yeah, what about those arguments?

PHIL: Which ones?

SOPHY: The classics!

PHIL: Like the ontological argument and the teleological arguments?

SOPHY: And the cosmological argument.

PHIL: Cosmological argu*ments*. There's several of them.

DIALOGUE ON FAITH AND REASON 243

SOPHY: Okay, yeah, what about them? What do you make of all these arguments?

PHIL: What do *you* make of them?

SOPHY: Well, I think William Paley's watchmaker argument is probably not that good. Outdated and all that.

PHIL: Seems fair. But I haven't thought about it in a while.

SOPHY: Now those arguments about the universe being set up perfectly for life as we know it, or the similar arguments about the *earth* being set up . . .

PHIL: Anthropic teleological arguments.

SOPHY: So those are teleological arguments too?

PHIL: Yeah. So are arguments involving intelligent design. One of Aquinas's famous Five Ways was a teleological argument. There are a lot of them.

SOPHY: Okay, so I don't know what to make of the anthropic-thingy arguments.

PHIL: Why not?

SOPHY: Well, lightning isn't likely to hit any particular place.

PHIL: Right.

SOPHY: But if lightning does hit a place it wasn't *likely* to hit, that doesn't mean anything. It was going to hit *somewhere*, right?

PHIL: Right.

SOPHY: But I don't think that's the right analogy for these arguments because they talk about *lots* of things that could easily have been different all converging to make this universe able to support life.

PHIL: Right.

SOPHY: So it's more like lightning striking the same place lots of times.

PHIL: And that's no coincidence!

SOPHY: Yeah.

PHIL: That's exactly why I like *that* teleological argument.

SOPHY: But what about the multiverse?

PHIL: What about it? If there are other universes, then probably most of them are pretty boring, and the ones that could support life are nothing special.

SOPHY: Right. If you roll the dice enough times you'll get any number.

PHIL: Yep.

SOPHY: So why do you like these arguments?

PHIL: Because I'm not convinced there are other universes. They make good sci-fi sometimes, but I don't understand the physics. It's not like I have any big objection to them. It's more like . . . if there are good reasons to believe in them *I* don't know what they are.

SOPHY: Okay.

PHIL: And I think there's more than one way to interpret the quantum physics stuff that goes into parallel universe theory.

SOPHY: Oh, really?

PHIL: Yep. So I doubt there are other universes, but if other universes are likely then that would really kill this particular argument.

SOPHY: What about the Aquinas one?

PHIL: The Aquinas argument? The teleological one from the Five Ways? I'd need some more caffeine, and a chance to review my notes. I think it might still work.

SOPHY: And all the others?

PHIL: Much the same. I like the *kalam* cosmological argument, and I think Aquinas's arguments are probably better than we think.

SOPHY: Right. Cause people don't understand Aquinas properly, like you always say.

PHIL: Right—including me, probably! And I think some moral arguments are good, like Lewis'. And I think it's right that there's no moral law without a moral lawgiver.

SOPHY: Okay.

PHIL: There's a great article that's partially about that by Elizabeth Anscombe.

SOPHY: I'll look it up at this YouTube channel I know.

PHIL: I don't think it's true that there can't be any moral truth without God. Some of those arguments are overstated.

SOPHY: Yeah?

PHIL: Aristotle's ethics is about proper function and happiness, and I think it works well enough, and I don't think it requires God. It's *moral law* that requires God, not the basics of Aristotle's ethics. As far as *I* can tell!

SOPHY: Interesting. And the ontological argument?

PHIL: Not *nearly* as confusing as some people think, but not *convincing*. If there's no God then there actually is not a perfect being who has an imperfection, so no problem.

SOPHY: Okay. I'll try to keep that in mind next time I tackle Anselm.

PHIL: But Plantinga's approach is interesting.

SOPHY: What's he say?

PHIL: He goes along with just about everyone else in thinking Anselm's argument isn't quite right. But he develops the argument with modal logic.

SOPHY: You mean possible worlds stuff?

PHIL: Right! And he thinks the argument shows that God has to exist if it's even *possible*. So God is either a *necessary and real* being, or *not even possible*.

SOPHY: Okay.

PHIL: So my working understanding is that a lot of the classic arguments for God are pretty good, but not all of them. I think they do provide some relevant evidence for the existence of a God. But I'm not an expert in any of them, and the logic can get pretty technical, and we don't have much time.

SOPHY: Okay, supposing all that, how do we weigh the arguments for God against the problem of evil?

PHIL: Yeah, that's the big one! The problem of evil . . .

SOPHY: Can it even be solved?

PHIL: That depends. Can biology be solved?

SOPHY: I don't know what you're asking.

PHIL: I mean, can we ever *finish* biology? Will scientists ever finish the job of learning about life?

SOPHY: No, probably not.

PHIL: But they can get closer and closer, and understand it better and better.

SOPHY: Right.

PHIL: I think that's what we're doing with the problem of evil. Philosophers and theologians are always writing new books on this stuff.

SOPHY: Right. More than an ordinary person can even keep track of.

PHIL: And most of it is probably pretty good. Insightful. But I think Augustine was right about free will.

SOPHY: They had the right answer way back then, huh?

PHIL: No—they just had a big piece of it.

SOPHY: But there was more.

PHIL: Lots more. Boethius was right to talk about it like a hydra.

SOPHY: What now?

PHIL: He said that when you answer one question about the problem of evil, two more spring up in its place.

Sophy: Awesome!

Phil: But he still gave three or four answers himself! I just think you have to give a lot of answers if you're going to be thorough. Augustine, Boethius, Aquinas, Lewis, Plantinga, Swinburne, Marilyn Adams, Trent Dougherty, and so many others.

Sophy: We need them all?

Phil: If we want to know as much as we can, yes. And we need to study the Bible too to see what it says. Not just Genesis either. Psalm 2, Daniel, Second Peter 3, Romans 7 and 8, Revelation, and more.

Sophy: What about where the different philosophers and theologians disagree?

Phil: We piece them together the best we can, prioritizing the better and more orthodox answers.

Sophy: Like free will.

Phil: Yeah, I think that one's a keeper! But I think they don't conflict with their different answers so much as help to fill in more details.

Sophy: And so where does that leave us?

Phil: Not knowing for sure *everything* there is to know about evil. Especially since some answers from Augustine and Boethius point to God's knowledge being better than ours!

Sophy: Interesting.

Phil: And I think that leaves religion in a good place as far as evidence is concerned.

Sophy: Why, if we can't even have all the evidence?

Phil: We probably can't do that in physics either, and if we *could* then most of us wouldn't be able to understand much of it. But we have some pretty good arguments for God's existence, and one big question about evil. And we have some very good answers to that question. I think the overall result is strongly in favor of religious belief.

Sophy: Okay, that's based on *your* understanding of the arguments. But what if *I* don't think so?

Phil: Like, what if you evaluate the arguments more harshly?

Sophy: Yeah. Or what if I can't understand them? Or think less of the free will answer to the problem of evil? Or if I just haven't had time to sort it all out yet? And what if I'm also just not believing in God the same way Plantinga thinks we do?

Phil: Good question. But there might be reasons to believe in the absence of evidence.

SOPHY: You're not going to go all Pascal on me, are you?

PHIL: Why not? It's one thing to give evidence that God exists, but another thing to give evidence that we should believe in it. Kant did one, but not the other. Pascal gives his argument that we should believe in the absence of evidence. James argues that we don't have to, but we can.

SOPHY: Yeah, the same James who refuted Pascal.

PHIL: In "The Will to Believe." Yes, but not the way you might think.

SOPHY: Explain.

PHIL: James basically thinks Pascal's logic is great. Well, almost. He doesn't argue that we have to believe, but he uses very similar logic arguing that we *can* believe.

SOPHY: We can believe based on the benefits. Okay.

PHIL: Yes.

SOPHY: So how does he refute Pascal?

PHIL: His logic is good, but one of the premises is wrong. Pascal is only giving us two choices, atheism and Catholicism.

SOPHY: Oh, right.

PHIL: Those were the options that were available in polite society in France in his day.

SOPHY: Oh, okay—but there are more options available to us *now*?

PHIL: Yes.

SOPHY: So is James a cultural relativist or what?

PHIL: Not that I know of. The point is just that the options that are open to us are shaped partly by culture, among other things.

SOPHY: Okay.

PHIL: Anyway, the reason isn't that important. The point is that most of us have a different set of live options. But the kind of logic Pascal uses is okay when it comes to the options that *are* live for us.

SOPHY: Okay, good to know.

PHIL: If you wanna get technical, there's probably more. Like James is looking at benefits in this life, but Pascal is looking at the afterlife.

SOPHY: And the long and short of it is that there are interesting arguments that it's okay to believe even without evidence.

PHIL: Yep.

SOPHY: And you think these are good arguments.

PHIL: Probably! Maybe it would be better to say that I just don't happen to know of anything much wrong with them.

SOPHY: Okay, but even if those arguments were good, if we don't have any convincing evidence, then that is itself an argument against God, right? Like, if there were a God he'd make himself obvious, right?

PHIL: Right on! The problem of divine hiddenness. People talk about that.

SOPHY: So my logic teacher was explaining this last semester.

PHIL: Right. She was good at that topic!

SOPHY: So she said there is a premise that makes arguments like this work. That is, they work if the premise works for that kind of argument!

PHIL: You mean the premise that if a thing were real then there would be evidence for it?

SOPHY: Right. So it's a bad argument that there are no spiders in this room just because I can't see any.

PHIL: And a *good* argument that there are no *elephants* because I can't see them.

SOPHY: Yes.

PHIL: So the question is . . .

SOPHY: . . . if there is a real God, would there be evidence for him?

PHIL: Right. And *would* there?

SOPHY: I think so. Why not?

PHIL: Why would there be?

SOPHY: Okay, so your point is . . .

PHIL: It's not all that obvious that God would make himself all that obvious. At least it's not obvious *to me*.

SOPHY: But you also don't care because you think there *is* evidence.

PHIL: You got me. Well, almost—I don't care *as much*. I might care a little. It's kind of an interesting topic.

SOPHY: Okay, but take it as a challenge. If your God is real and if there's no evidence, then . . .

PHIL: —hypothetically—

SOPHY: Then, hypothetically, why doesn't he *show* himself? Or show himself *more*, or more plainly?

PHIL: I don't know.

SOPHY: That's it?

PHIL: No.

SOPHY: So you don't know, but . . .

PHIL: ... but I have some ideas. Not mine, as usual. Borrowed from some of my usual people.

SOPHY: Augustine, for example?

PHIL: For a start. He says that our ability to know God is limited by our own sin and our inability to understand immaterial reality.

SOPHY: Go on.

PHIL: We have to be trained in order to know God.

SOPHY: Let me guess. Platonic contemplation and stuff. Like learning to see the Forms, only it's more like learning to see *God*?

PHIL: Very well put. That's *exactly* right. But there's more.

SOPHY: Yeah?

PHIL: It's also about religious trust. It's also very pious, very traditional Christianity. You have to trust Christ, church, and Scripture, and believe what they teach. That trust—that *fides* in Latin—comes before knowledge, but it also prepares us for knowledge.

SOPHY: Okay, cool. So the idea is that knowledge ...

PHIL: Knowledge works *best* after we've had some faith first!

SOPHY: Okay, is this about that famous line you like?

PHIL: "I believe in order to understand."

SOPHY: By the way, is that like Anselm's "faith seeking understanding"?

PHIL: Yes, but no—Anselm is like Augustine!

SOPHY: Right—Augustine came first!

PHIL: And one more thing comes to mind.

SOPHY: What's that?

PHIL: Back to Lewis and James.

SOPHY: Okay.

PHIL: They both make one really important point.

SOPHY: Yeah?

PHIL: If God is a person, we aren't going to know him the same way we know rocks.

SOPHY: Oh, right? Weren't we just talking about this?

PHIL: Probably. But I don't think we went over this aspect of it exactly.

SOPHY: Okay.

PHIL: We know people when they *let themselves* be known. Not just when *we* want to know them. There's an initiative on *their* side.

SOPHY: Okay.

PHIL: And people don't prove themselves and their goodwill before anyone is willing to believe in it. It's usually the reverse.

SOPHY: Go on.

PHIL: We usually have to at least be willing to trust someone. Then that trust builds the relationship where we really get to know them.

SOPHY: Like Beatrice and Benedick in Shakespeare!

PHIL: Perfect!

SOPHY: Maybe they already loved each other. I don't know. But they only learn that it's *true* because they *believed* it!

PHIL: Right.

SOPHY: So the idea is that God is like that?

PHIL: The idea is that if God is a person, or three people, as we have been told, then we shouldn't expect him, or *them*, to act totally unlike people we know.

SOPHY: Maybe God won't show all the evidence in advance.

PHIL: Right.

SOPHY: So if there is any divine hiddenness, the lesson we can get from James and Lewis is that it has . . . a *purpose*. It keeps back those who are unwilling to believe.

PHIL: Something like that. Maybe. But I wonder if it would be better to say that something *else* does *not* serve a purpose.

SOPHY: What something else would that be?

PHIL: The kind of evidence that shows up in all its glory before we have a chance to decide whether we are even willing to believe. I just don't know why God should make it all obvious in advance.

SOPHY: Hmm.

PHIL: And that brings us back to maybe the most important point.

SOPHY: What's that?

PHIL: Faith transcends reason!

SOPHY: Right! You talk about these arguments and these reasons to believe, but you don't *really* think faith is the same thing as reason!

PHIL: It depends on how we define reason.

SOPHY: So you said.

PHIL: If reason means full comprehension, being able to wrap our brains around something, then it's best to say that faith transcends reason.

SOPHY: Okay, I agree.

PHIL: One reason for this is that doctrines like the Trinity and the incarnation are not fully comprehensible.

SOPHY: Right.

PHIL: Other reasons come from some of the same people we've been talking about.

SOPHY: Okay.

PHIL: So we were just talking about James, and that made me think of it.

SOPHY: Think of what?

PHIL: James says that faith is a trust, a willingness to act.

SOPHY: Okay.

PHIL: And faith comes before knowledge, but it might also lead to knowledge later.

SOPHY: So faith transcends reason.

PHIL: Yeah. That's James's version. Now Augustine—he thinks faith is trust in Christ, Scripture, church. It's a reasonable and justified sort of trust.

SOPHY: Okay.

PHIL: It's trust rather than the sort of rational comprehension of God that can be called knowledge. But it leads to knowledge.

SOPHY: So, again, faith transcends reason.

PHIL: Yeah, that's Augustine's version. Now back to where we started, with a bit of Kant. Kant says we Kant know whether God exists.

SOPHY: Still a dumb joke.

PHIL: And still awesome! But we have good reason to believe God exists. Maybe we'll know more in the afterlife.

SOPHY: The difference between an argument that God exists and an argument that we should believe.

PHIL: Right.

SOPHY: So once again faith transcends reason.

PHIL: Yeah. That's Kant's version. Now for the best, Kierkegaard.

SOPHY: *He's* the best?

PHIL: Sometimes I feel that way. So you know how in *Fear and Trembling* he says faith is absurd?

SOPHY: Yeah.

PHIL: No, you don't.

SOPHY: What?

PHIL: He doesn't say that.

SOPHY: Yes, he does.

PHIL: No, he doesn't.

SOPHY: You just said he does.

PHIL: Irony to make a point.

SOPHY: What point?

PHIL: That he doesn't say that.

SOPHY: What?

PHIL: Johannes de Silentio says that.

SOPHY: Oh, you mean his pseudonym!

PHIL: Right. Kierkegaard is using Johanne, who thinks faith is absurd, to make a point.

SOPHY: What point?

PHIL: That faith looks absurd if you're too much of a Hegelian, like Johanne is.

SOPHY: Okay.

PHIL: So faith isn't absurd. It just *looks* that way if you make too much of reason.

SOPHY: Okay, cool.

PHIL: And in the works by Johannes Climacus, another pseudonym Kierkegaard uses, we have more.

SOPHY: Yeah?

PHIL: The decision to follow Jesus has to be 100%. You either *do* it or you *don't*.

SOPHY: Okay.

PHIL: But the *evidence* will never be 100%. It's like what James says.

SOPHY: Back to him again, huh?

PHIL: It happens. You have to decide without having all the evidence you'd like to. That's just life.

SOPHY: Fair enough. Anything else from Kierkegaard?

PHIL: Not that we have time for now.

SOPHY: Never enough time to figure everything out! But what have you been able to do with the time you did have, Phil?

PHIL: Haven't I been saying that all this time? The whole point is to make a decision, Sophy. You know mine. What's yours?

Index

Aristotle, 152, 170–72, 224, 244
Anselm of Canterbury, 108, 192, 46–246, 249
Aquinas, Saint Thomas, 8, 16, 9n36, 108, 116, 189, 243, 244, 246
Augustine, Saint, xi, xii, xiii, xiv, 23, 45–63, 86, 91–93, 94, 99n49, 104, 108–9, 116–17, 119, 130n16, 135, 149, 156, 157, 165–66, 175, 177–82, 186, 189, 197–98, 201, 206, 209, 223–25, 235, 237, 245–46, 249, 251
Ayer, A. J., 95n41

Bell, William E., 151, 152–55, 156n62, 158, 160
Berkovits, Eliezer, xiv, 84, 88, 90–91, 93, 94, 99, 104, 105, 227, 229, 230
Boethius, 245, 246
BonJour, Laurence, 25–26, 30, 31–37, 143n6

Chicago Statement on Biblical Inerrancy, xiii, 100, 140, 147, 149, 155–56, 159, 169–73, 176, 177n43, 178, 181n64
Chisholm, Roderick, 1–24, 25, 29, 241–42
Confucius/Confucianism, 172, 199, 231, 237
Craig, William Lane, 94n40, 190, 192n13, 238

Dalai Lama, 84, 87–88, 90, 104 105, 226–28, 231

demarcation of science, 95–96, 118n20, 209–18, 237
Descartes, René, 6n25, 8, 25, 38, 85n5, 143, 146, 147, 148, 150, 192n12
Dewey, John, 85n5, 88, 226, 228, 231

falsification/falsifiability, xiv, 22, 84, 95, 96, 99–101, 105, 118, 213–14, 218, 236–38

Geisler, Norm, 172, 181n64
Gettier, Edmund, xi, 24n1, 26, 32, 33, 37–39, 119n23, 129n14

Haack, Susan, 41, 104, 143–44, 145n17, 146, 154, 159
Heidegger, Martin, xv, 166, 167–68
Hume, David, 6–7, 65, 85n5, 104, 144, 199, 209–18, 227, 240, 241

induction, problem of, 7, 144, 209–18
Iqbal, Allama, xii, xiv, 64–83, 84, 88–90, 93–94, 95, 104–5, 118, 227, 229

James, William, xi, xii–xiii, xiv, 23, 45–63, 64–83, 84–86, 88, 91, 96–97, 104, 108–9, 111, 113, 117–18, 186, 198–200, 201, 206, 210, 222, 225, 226, 228, 229, 231, 232–35, 247, 249–50, 251
Johnson, Dru, 86n7, 91n31, 108n1, 114n10, 121, 129n15, 130, 134

Kant, Immanuel, xi, xiv, 64, 85n5, 111, 112, 186, 193–96, 201, 206, 208–9, 216, 247, 251
Kantzer, Kenneth, 151, 152, 155, 156, 157, 160, 174, 175, 177
Kierkegaard, Søren, xi, xiii 103, 186–87, 201–6, 209, 220–21, 251–52
Kuhn, Thomas, 92n35, 95n41, 96, 108n1, 116, 213, 214–15, 218

Lewis, C. S., xiv, 61, 84, 85, 93–94, 96–99, 104–5, 118, 149, 189, 226–27, 229–30, 232–33, 235, 244, 246, 249, 250
Logical Positivism, 12, 66, 85n5, 95n41, 112, 118n20, 209–19
Loke, Andrew Ter Ern, 6n25, 94n40, 192n9, 238
Lyotard, Jean-Francois, 166–67

Marion, Jean-Luc, xii, xiii, xv, 108, 166, 168–69, 174, 175, 176
McGrew, Timothy, 6n25, 144–45, 159n80, 161–62

Nietzsche, Friedrich, 64

Packer, J. I., 151, 152, 155, 156, 157 158, 160, 205n45
Plantinga, Alvin, xi, xii, xiv, 1–24, 25–44, 85n4, 104, 126, 127, 128n11, 131, 136, 139, 140, 141, 142, 143–44, 151, 154, 156, 157, 160, 161–62, 172, 189, 192, 209, 218, 219, 240–42, 244–45, 246

Plato/Platonism, xii, 5, 37, 46–49, 59, 60, 61, 129n15, 141, 170, 197–98, 224, 49
Popper, Karl, 95n41, 118n20, 213–14, 215, 218

Quine, Willard Van Orman, 13, 85n4, 213

Radhakrishnan, Sarvepalli, xiv, 84, 86–88, 90, 93n39, 95, 104, 105, 227–28, 230–31
Reid, Thomas, xii, 1–24, 29–31, 35, 104, 172, 216, 241–42
Russell, Bertrand, 213, 217

Shakespeare, William, 55, 97, 250
Socrates, 37, 38, 92, 141, 224

Vanhoozer, Kevin J., 108, 149n32, 150, 165, 169, 172–74, 178, 181, 183
verification/verifiability, xiv, 12, 22, 51, 55, 61, 67, 84, 91, 95–96, 96–99, 101, 105, 117–18, 209–18, 225, 234, 236–38

Westphal, Merold, 166–67, 174, 175n34, 176–77
Wittgenstein, Ludwig, 108n1, 213
Wright, N. T., 191n13, 238

Zagzebski, Linda, xi, xiv, 25n1, 26, 37–39, 130n15
Zeis, John, 27, 42, 104, 143–44, 145n17, 154

www.ingramcontent.com/pod-product-compliance
Lightning Source LLC
Chambersburg PA
CBHW071934240426
43668CB00038B/1641